Also available...

Canada and the Theatre of War
Volume I

Selected and edited by
Donna Coates and Sherrill Grace

Part I – WORLD WAR I
The Lost Boys by R.H. Thomson
Soldier's Heart by David French
Mary's Wedding by Stephen Massicotte
Dancock's Dance by Guy Vanderhaeghe
Vimy by Vern Thiessen

Part II – WORLD WAR II
Ever Loving by Margaret Hollingsworth
None is Too Many by Jason Sherman
Burning Vision by Marie Clements

Canada
and the
Theatre
of War

Volume II – Contemporary Wars

Canada and the Theatre of War
Volume II

CONTEMPORARY WARS
Game of Patience by Abla Farhoud, translated by Jill Mac Dougall
A Line in the Sand by Guillermo Verdecchia and Marcus Youssef
The Monument by Colleen Wagner
Palace of the End by Judith Thompson
Scorched by Wajdi Mouawad, translated by Linda Gaboriau
Man Out of Joint by Sharon Pollock

Selected and edited by
Donna Coates and Sherrill Grace

Playwrights Canada Press
Toronto • Canada

Canada and the Theatre of War, Volume II © Copyright 2009 Donna Coates and Sherrill Grace

PLAYWRIGHTS CANADA PRESS
The Canadian Drama Publisher
215 Spadina Ave., Suite 230, Toronto, ON Canada M5T 2C7
phone 416.703.0013   fax 416.408.3402
orders@playwrightscanada.com • www.playwrightscanada.com

For professional or amateur production rights, please see the following page,
or contact the publisher for more information.

The publisher acknowledges the support of the Canadian taxpayers through
the Government of Canada Book Publishing Industry Development Program,
the Canada Council for the Arts, the Ontario Arts Council,
and the Ontario Media Development Corporation.

Cover image: *The Centurion Tank* by Claude Dumont (1972). Copper enamelling.
With permission from the Canadian War Museum.
Production Editor/Cover Design: JLArt

Library and Archives Canada Cataloguing in Publication

Canada and the theatre of war / selected and edited by Donna Coates and Sherrill Grace.

Includes bibliographical references.
ISBN 978-0-88754-834-5 (v. 1).--ISBN 978-0-88754-841-3 (v. 2)

1. World War, 1914-1918--Canada--Drama. 2. World War,
1939-1945--Canada--Drama. 3. Canadian drama (English)--20th century.
I. Coates, Donna, 1944- II. Grace, Sherrill E., 1944-

PS8309.W3C35 2008   C812'.54080358   C2008-902995-X

First Edition: February 2010
Printed and bound in Canada by Gauvin Press, Gatineau

Dedicated to Angela Rebeiro,
whose belief in Canadian theatre has made so much possible.

Table of Contents

Between Remembering and Forgetting: Contemporary Wars and Canadian Theatre

by Sherrill Grace

> The only way writing after Auschwitz… could proceed was by becoming
> memory and preventing the past from coming to an end.
> —Günter Grass

In his 1999 Nobel Prize lecture, Günter Grass claimed that writing after Auschwitz was only possible by balancing forgetting with remembering. Without doubt, he was remembering his own past as well as Theodor Adorno's famous pronouncement that "*nach Auschwitz ein Gedicht zu schreiben, ist barbarisch*" ("To write poetry after Auschwitz is barbaric").[1] But just as similar unthinkable, unwritable barbarisms continue to stalk the post–World War II world, so too does the need to write and create art about atrocity, suffering, terror, guilt, and the obvious persistence of war. Despite the flagrant failure of human beings to learn from the past, from the horror of the Great War to end all wars or the Holocaust that followed, we keep trying to understand our capacity for violence on the one hand and our longing for peace and compassion on the other. This desire to understand by refusing to let the past come to an end has been apparent in many countries over the past two decades. I see it take form in literature, film, music, painting, and art photography, in exhibitions and memorials; the Canadian War Museum's 2009 touring exhibition called *A Brush with War: Military Art from Korea to Afghanistan* is just one example.[2] This cultural memory work, mounting almost to obsession, raises many important questions such as why now, why through the arts, and to what conceivable purpose? No poem or novel, painting or play, ever stopped bombs from falling, as a character in *Game of Patience* in this volume laments, so what do artists hope to achieve?

While this second volume of *Canada and the Theatre of War* focuses on Canadian plays that respond to recent conflicts, it is worth noting that a much wider, global context exists for these acts of remembering, and it is equally important to recognize that live theatre plays a strategic role—perhaps one that no other art form and certainly no scholarly study can—in "preventing the past from coming to an end."[3] In our first volume, we selected eight works to represent what contemporary Canadian playwrights have said about the two world wars. The six plays chosen for this volume all address contemporary wars, including ones in which Canada has not played an official military role; however, there are some fascinating through lines connecting the two volumes, as well as some crucial differences. In teaching, reading, watching, and reflecting upon all fourteen plays, I have been struck, not only by the craft and theatrical power of these works, but also by the steady, clear-eyed shift from *finding* meaning, reconciliation, and identity (notably a Canadian identity) in the World

War I plays to an increasingly guilt-laden confrontation with Canada's past failures and complicities in the World War II plays. To put this simply, it is still possible to see Canadians as the good guys, or as the suffering victims, in World War I, but that innocence and nostalgia are not possible for the next world war. In plays about the Second World War, Canadians are among the bad, if not the most evil, guys, and in the plays for Volume Two that perspective becomes increasingly disturbing. While plays like Vern Thiessen's *Vimy*, R.H. Thomson's *The Lost Boys*, or Stephen Massicotte's *Mary's Wedding* describe the horror of war, they are, first and foremost, about celebrating the birth of the nation (at Vimy Ridge), commemorating family and community (in Thomson's vigil for his past), and the assuaging of regret and of ghosts (when Charlie, in *Mary's Wedding*, releases Mary—a symbol of the young country, Canada—into her new future). Even Esau Mercer in David French's *A Soldier's Heart* achieves a degree of forgiveness and reconciliation with his past, his son, and his pain, by remembering and telling his story. Such release, never mind forgiveness, is much more hard won in the plays about Canada's role in World War II. In Margaret Hollingsworth's *Ever Loving*, the post-war lives of the brides and their veteran husbands are plagued by broken promises and blasted hopes; the dreams of a bright future fade in the face of harsh, Cold War realities. But it is in works like Marie Clements's *Burning Vision* and Jason Sherman's *None Is Too Many* that I find the closest, most unnerving connection with the plays collected here in this second volume.

These two plays, like John Murrell's *Waiting for the Parade* (which we could not include in Volume One but which presents a bitterly ironic picture of the home front), are anti-war to a degree not found in the World War I plays.[4] They are also accusatory and intended to remind Canadians of things they prefer to forget or pretend they never knew; these plays refuse to let the past end. *Burning Vision* obliges audiences and readers to contemplate the aftermath of uranium mining in the shape of bombs dropped on Japan, in the nuclear threat that hovered over the Cold War era and in the cancer killing Dene miners and their families in the Northwest Territories to this day. The play also reminds all Canadians of the need for atonement and of our fundamental connection with other people in other parts of the world. *None Is Too Many* has a similar purpose and creates a comparable impact. Closely based on Irving Abella and Harold Troper's important 1982 study *None Is Too Many: Canada and the Jews of Europe, 1933–1948*, Sherman's play asks us to acknowledge and believe that before and during World War II Canada closed its doors first to Jews attempting to escape Nazi terror and the death camps, and later to the refugees who survived. Such blows to Canadian pride and feelings of moral superiority turn our image of ourselves—as romantic, idealistic heroes or colonial, peace-loving victims—inside out to expose our complicity with prejudice and barbarism and to remind us that we are part of a larger world for which we share responsibility and to which we are accountable. This combined purpose of reminding/informing and holding accountable connects these plays unequivocally with the ones in this volume. Another powerful link between both volumes is their emphasis upon the home front. While remembered scenes of battle, torture, ethnic hatred (here at home and in other lands), and persecution contribute to the plots and characters' lives in these plays, they are not *war* plays in the strict sense that R.C. Sherriff's *Journey's End* can be called a war play because they do not focus exclusively on soldiers in battle, or even on veterans. Instead they privilege the families, descendants, ordinary citizens, and survivors caught up in war; they foreground the lasting scars of trauma and the ghosts that embody a past that refuses to go away. They break the silence to reveal terrible truths. They open windows on where Canadians have come from—whether we have been here for generations or arrived a decade ago—to help us understand where and who we are today, as a nation among nations in a globally interconnected world.

· · ·

In a recent article called "Where's Our War On Our Stages?" J. Kelly Nestruck, a reviewer for *The Globe and Mail*, complained that Toronto theatres were full of plays about Americans and the Iraq war (including Judith Thompson's *Palace of the End*), but that the only Canadian play about Afghanistan was *The Adventures of Ali & Ali and the aXes of Evil*, which is more about ugly Americans than it is about Canada's role in the war on terror. But the plays in this volume, as well as many others we could not include, show that Canadian theatre about Canadians in, or as survivors of, recent wars are there if we know where to look for them. And that is the challenge: if we search for dramatizations of violent combat or of soldiers behaving heroically or despicably, we will not see what is there. Every play in this volume, even *A Line in the Sand*, which features a Canadian peacekeeping soldier, explores the effects of war—its causes, costs, and casualties (beginning with the truth)—the suffering inflicted, the trauma faced by survivors—women or men, civilians or soldiers—in the struggle to go on living responsibly in the face of paralyzing terror, propaganda, guilt and grief, and the urgent need to sweep away the lies and rhetoric that promote hatred and revenge.

Between 1994 and 2009, as this volume goes to press, a number of plays have been written about the war experiences of Canadians.[5] *Game of Patience* (*Jeux de patience*), which premiered in French in 1994, is set in Montreal against the background of the civil war in Lebanon (1975–1990) and the 1982 siege of Beirut. Its characters, like the characters in several of these plays, are recent immigrants to Canada and they are held in a form of emotional and psychological suspension between the life they knew in the land of their birth and their new home. Many things make adjusting to Canada difficult for them, but chief among these are the ghosts from the past that they cannot leave behind. In *Game of Patience* the most powerful ghost is a young daughter called Samira, and the relatives who struggle with their grief and loss are her mother and her aunt. In addition to addressing the trauma of war, this play, like several of the others, and like those in Volume One, interrogates what it means to be Canadian: What language does one speak? Which country is truly *yours*? How do you remember what you have left behind and, at the same time, forget enough to be able to accept the safety you enjoy here and now? In *Game of Patience*, playwright Abla Farhoud also takes up the challenge faced by Adorno and Grass: the need to write about barbarism after Auschwitz when acts of unintelligible violence and destruction continue to occur. This play, like *The Monument, Scorched,* and *Palace of the End,* is very much a women's play because it is the women (mothers, sisters, aunts, daughters) who are left to pick up the pieces of their shattered lives and make sense of the past. In this respect, these plays differ markedly from several in the first volume that emphasize the roles of men. *Game of Patience,* moreover, places the challenge to any writer who wishes to create art out of these extreme experiences at the centre of the play so that the very creation of the script is a sign of art's victory, the victory of creativity over destruction, of love over hatred, and of remembrance over forgetting.

The *Monument* and *A Line in the Sand* premiered in 1995, and they both explore the confusion faced by a young male soldier who is completely unprepared for the realities of war and peacekeeping in alien landscapes and under extreme conditions. In both plays, the young man fails to behave with honour; in both he rapes and/or kills to preserve what he has been taught to think of as his superiority over others—women, Arabs, people of colour, *others.* And in both he is left to face the ghosts of his victims who, the plays suggest, will haunt him to his grave. In *The Monument,* the country and the war are left unspecified and there is no particular reason to identify the mother or the soldier as Canadians. *A Line in the Sand* is more explicit and more rooted in document and history. The history behind this play is the tragedy of Canadian peacekeeping in Somalia and the brutal killing of Shidane Arone in 1993, but in Guillermo Verdecchia and Marcus Youssef's retelling of this story, the young victim, called Sadiq, emigrates to Canada as a ghost to remind the Canadian soldier, Mercer, about what Canadians are capable of. In the playwrights' hands, this is less the story of one confused soldier than the tale of a national failure to understand the humanity of other people in other countries. The system, as much as any personal flaw, fails Mercer, just as the system failed and denied the Jews or the Dene during World War II.

Wajdi Mouawad's *Scorched* premiered in French in 2003, and in some ways it stands out from the others in its extreme depiction of horror and grief. It is also remarkable for its mobilization of silence, surely the least theatrical of human expressions. But silence about the past lies at the heart of this extraordinary play, and the breaking of that silence is its central theme. So horrifying is the truth of violence, torture, and trauma revealed in this play that one might be justified in asking how any immigrant with such a past could possibly find peace here, but that is what Mouawad's characters seek. His point, I feel, is that one can never leave the past behind, that it is not and never can be finished, and that part of becoming Canadian, of creating a new life here, involves bringing that past into this present. Like those potential Canadian citizens in Sherman's *None Is Too Many,* the refugee, once here, adds his or her experience to the growing life of the imagined nation. *Man Out of Joint* and *Palace of the End* move in the opposite direction—from inside Canada out towards world crises—and are less concerned with being or becoming Canadian. They are the most recent plays chosen for this volume and each responds to the so-called war on terror that enveloped the equally *so-called* free world after 9/11 and the American invasion of Iraq. These are very tough plays, harder to stage and watch even than *Scorched* or *The Monument.* But they also address our relationship to the wider issues of terrorism, the rhetoric of terror, torture in the name of truth, the erosion of democratic rights in what Giorgio Agamben calls states of exception, and the bearing of witness that can, perhaps, end such violence.

Man Out of Joint is deeply informed by Sharon Pollock's interest in the reports of detainee abuse at Guantanamo Bay that were released by the American Centre for Constitutional Rights. The play stages some aspects of this abuse as a background for the main story of the Toronto lawyer, Joel Gianelli, who chooses to defend these detainees. His decision to take on this challenging and potentially dangerous work is motivated by several factors, including his compassion for fifteen-year-old Omar Khadr, whom he believes was unjustly picked up and incarcerated. But the key factor driving Gianelli lies closer to home in his own family story, and in the ghostly presence of his father who reminds him that paranoia and persecution have occurred before in Canada when, during World War II, Gianelli senior was torn from his home in the middle of the night and dragged away to be interned as an "enemy alien." In 1940 these violent arrests were legitimized by the Defence of Canada Regulations, and today in a post-9/11 world dominated by the rhetoric of anti-terrorism and by racial profiling, innocent people will once more lose their rights and worse—be tortured in prisons like Guantanamo Bay and Guantanamo North right here in Toronto. The vocal ghost of Dominic Gianelli, the Italian-Canadian father, is reminiscent of the many other ghosts in these plays about war, but his specific function in *Man Out of Joint* is to keep the *Canadian* past from ending and to remind his son—and us—that by forgetting the past we risk repeating it.

Judith Thompson's *Palace of the End* begins from a very different place and is a Canadian play only insofar as it addresses the news items that we have all been battered by since 9/11 and the second war in Iraq in which Canada played no official military role. Thompson selects three very different characters and stories, each of which is inspired by actual people and their suffering, to construct the three parallel monologues for her play. Her characters are Private Lynndie England, the young US Army reservist photographed while abusing prisoners in Abu Ghraib; Dr. David Kelly, the English weapons expert and scientist who was found dead in July 2003 in a park near his home shortly after he went to the British media to insist that, in his view, Saddam Hussein had no weapons of mass destruction; and Nehrjas Al Saffarh, an Iraqi mother come back from the dead to tell us all what life under Saddam Hussein was like. England, pregnant, disgraced, and scapegoated by the US military, plans to hide in Quebec, where she can bear her child and assume another identity, but judging from her confusion, rage, and sense of betrayal, she will never make a success of her new life and never be able to escape her past.[6] Kelly pronounces what is perhaps the central message of this excoriating play when he tells us that "the greatest sin of our time" is "knowing, and pretending that we don't know, so we won't be inconvenienced." His suicide—or was it murder?—his *death*, however, does not silence him because Thompson has brought him to life to hold us all to account. But the witness to the heart of darkness at the centre of this play is Nehrjas who, with her husband, belonged to the Iraqi Communist Party and was arrested and tortured by Saddam Hussein's secret police in the 1970s.[7] It is her story of inconceivable torture, rape, and murder that leaves audiences and readers stunned by what can no longer be avoided and not known. The ghosts in *Palace of the End* certainly recall the ghosts in *Dancock's Dance, Vimy, A Line in the Sand,* or *Scorched,* but they are much more harrowing because they speak of events that are so immediate and because they tell their stories directly to us.

• • •

The plays in Volume One, even plays like *Burning Vision* and *None Is Too Many,* will seem gentle by comparison with several of the plays in this volume. However, the warnings, the writing on the wall as it were, are there in those attempts to write the stories of the Great War and of World War II. Where World War I still inspires our writers to imagine and celebrate the founding of the nation despite the enormous costs, the stories about World War II and recent wars keep returning to questions about nation and identity, except that they ask very difficult questions about who gets to call themselves Canadian and at what price of exclusion and about how, in a multicultural Canada, new immigrants can find peace here and establish new lives unless they too preserve the inconvenient truths of their pasts. Above all, these plays, like those about World War II, insist that Canadians remember, not simply the reassuring stories about war and forgiveness and family, but also the terrible ones in which we failed to act or speak or in which we were complicit through our willed forgetting or were directly responsible for war crimes. The power, artistic skill, and creative experimentation with which these playwrights present these stories and enact the dilemma of remembering and forgetting are never merely theatre, never an aestheticization of violence and cruelty. Their purpose is always, and successfully, more serious and responsible—responsible to the characters, to their personal and our shared public history, and to the work that art does in this world.[8] As the writer Monique/Kaokab in *Game of Patience* confesses, she has written to forget and has "lived between the heartbreak of remembering and the heartbreak of forgetting," until, that is, she writes the play we watch or read where she achieves that miraculous balance we call theatre.

Notes

¹ Theodor Adorno's statement, quoted in Helms and Egan (32), was originally made in 1951 and published with his collected works in 1977.

² This exhibition opened at the McMichael Canadian Art Collection in 2009 and it will tour to Ottawa, Hamilton, Victoria, and Calgary through 2010 to 2012. Recent artistic treatments of war are too numerous to list here, but a few examples, in addition to *A Brush with War*, will suggest the range of current attention to this subject. *The Armed Man: A Mass for Peace*, the stunning oratorio by Welsh composer Karl Jenkins (premiered and first recorded by the London Philharmonic Orchestra in 2000), has earned high praise in England; films like *The Reader* (2008) and *The Lives of Others* (2006) have achieved great popular success, and Paul Gross's *Passchendaele* (2008), if less successful at the box office, challenges the near mythic power of Vimy Ridge as Canada's defining moment. Canadian war art by Gertrude Kearns portrays Canadian soldiers in Afghanistan and her depiction of Canadian peacekeepers torturing Shidane Arone (*Somalia 2, Without Conscience*, 1996) provoked protest when it was exhibited at the Canadian War Museum. Some of Kearns's work is reproduced in *A Brush with War*.

³ In addition to the catalogue for the exhibition *A Brush with War*, London's Imperial War Museum has recently held a special exhibition on the Holocaust, and Berlin has established major open-air exhibitions about World War II, the Berlin Wall, and the Cold War years. A number of special conferences on recent wars have been held in the United States, where the impact of 9/11 continues to be debated and commemorated.

⁴ *Waiting for the Parade* is an interesting example of a popular play about World War II that on close inspection delivers a very sombre and complex message about propaganda, prejudice on the home front that led Canadian authorities to intern citizens as "enemy aliens," and the role that music plays in whipping up racist sentiment. The German-Canadian woman, Marta, who is chastised and ostracized for her love of Richard Tauber's singing, is a subtle reminder for anyone who knows that Tauber was a Jew forced to flee the Nazis and that the song he sings is a love song, of what ignorance and prejudice can and did lead to.

⁵ Among other plays I might mention are Hannah Moscovitch's *East of Berlin*, Jason Sherman's *Reading Hebron*, and Sharon Pollock's *Sweet Land of Liberty*. Stephen Massicotte is writing a stage adaptation of the German opera *The Emperor of Atlantis* and Christopher Moore is gathering stories from Canadians, Afghanis, and Pakistanis for a play about the conflict in Afghanistan; see Bradshaw. See also Redhill and Sanger.

⁶ The real England was sentenced to three years in a military prison for her participation, under orders, in the abuse. News and Internet headlines about her (easily accessed on Google) continue to spew venom and disgust over this "ugly she-man." David Kelly's death continues to be debated because the conclusion that he committed suicide leaves many questions unanswered. By claiming that Saddam

Hussein had no weapons of mass destruction, Kelly cast serious doubt on Tony Blair's reasons for joining the United States in the invasion of Iraq.

[7] Nehrjas Al Saffarh lost most of her family under Saddam's regime, and she herself died when Americans bombed her home during the first Gulf War.

[8] We would like to thank the Canadian War Museum for permission to reproduce Claude Dumont's *The Centurion Tank* (c. 1972) on the cover of this volume. The painting, with its brilliant colours (produced by copper enamelling), depicts two British-made tanks that were used by Canadians at Lahr, Germany, during the Cold War. We chose this painting, in part, for its sharp contrast with the intimate, personal imagery of remembrance in Bruno Bobak's *Still Life, Army Kit* (1943), the cover image for Volume I, and, in part, for its paradoxical combination of colours representative of life with lethal machines of war. Moreover, Dumont's image seems to gesture towards a militarized future and the constant threat of conflict that is a fact of contemporary reality.

Game of Patience

Jeux de patience
Translated by Jill Mac Dougall

by Abla Farhoud

Abla Farhoud

Abla Farhoud, Montreal playwright and novelist, was born in 1945 in Ain-Hirche, a small village in the mountains of southeast Lebanon. In 1952, her family immigrated to Quebec, a traumatic experience which would later influence her writing. Fortunately, a theatre program at school helped her shape a sense of identity and belonging in the new land. Farhoud began appearing on Radio-Canada television when she was seventeen. She returned to Lebanon in 1965, where she acted on stage, radio, and television, and then moved to Paris to study at the Université de Vincennes in 1969. She came back to Quebec in 1973 and began her writing career in the early 1980s. She has written short stories, radio scripts, eight plays, which have been performed nationally and internationally, and three novels.

Farhoud wrote her first play, *Quand j'étais grande* (*When I Was Grown Up*, translated by Jill Mac Dougall), as part of the master's program at the Université du Québec à Montréal. A strongly feminist work that tells the story of a woman's stoning channelled through the voice of a young girl living in Montreal, it was first performed in 1983 at the Théâtre Expérimental des Femmes in Montreal. Her next work, *Les Filles du 5–10–15¢* (*The Girls from the Five and Ten*, translated by Jill Mac Dougall), which tells of two adolescent sisters forced to work in their father's store, to which they eventually set fire, was presented at the Festival des francophonies de Limoges (France) in 1992, remounted at the Théâtre international de langue française in Paris in 1993, and performed off-Avignon that same year. Her next play, *Quand le vautour danse*, which combines dance and dialogue, weaving the daily life of a choreographer coping with a schizophrenic brother and her ballet based on an ancient tale of love, violence, and death, was initially performed by Théâtre d'Aujourd'hui in 1997. Farhoud reworked the story and retitled it *La possession du prince*, which in 1993 won the Prix Théâtre de la liberté de la SACD. The same year, Farhoud also won the 1993 Prix Arletty de l'universalité de la langue française.

Farhoud has also published three novels. The first, *Le bonheur à la queue glissante* (1998), which received the 1999 France-Québec prize, tells the story of a successful Montreal writer who asks her mother, who can only speak Arabic and has never learned to read or write, to recount the story of her life so that she may recreate it in a book. The mother of six reveals a rich and deeply troubled life, marked by her isolation as an illiterate immigrant, but also by the joys she finds in her family and daily life. Farhoud's second novel, *Splendide solitude* (2001), focuses on a middle-aged woman who struggles to find meaning in her life since her children and husband have left the nest. Farhoud's third novel, *Le fou d'Omar* (2005), which received the 2006 Prix du roman francophone, revolves around the death of Omar and a Lebanese immigrant family's story told through four male voices: a bipolar son, a successful son, a sympathetic neighbour, and the deceased Omar.

Jeux de patience (*Game of Patience*, translated by Jill Mac Dougall), the first Farhoud play to be published in Quebec and the first to earn critical acclaim, underscores the ways women—those who suffer history, not make it—are decimated by war and exile. Although Farhoud refers directly to the war in Lebanon in the work, like Wajdi Mouawad and Colleen Wagner, she has also stated that it could be set in any of the many places where wars are occurring.

The play tells of two cousins, one a successful writer who immigrated to Quebec from Lebanon four decades earlier, and the other a few weeks ago. The latter has fled the violence of the war but not the memory of her dead daughter, a lively teenager who dreamt of becoming a filmmaker before she was shot on her way to school. Only visible to the audience, the daughter appears throughout the play, wielding an imaginary camera. The grief-stricken mother is unable to find solace or envision a new life for herself in Montreal because no one in the secure and comfortable environment can understand her suffering. Farhoud's writer figure, despite having profited as an author, also feels alienated. Even though she has never known the violence of war first-hand, she must now bear witness to her family's personal loss and the collective tragedy of civil war, and must help her cousin find peace.

Jeux de patience had a dramatic reading on April 14, 1992 during CEAD's Semaine de la dramaturgie, directed by Abla Farhoud, with Micheline Lanctôt as Monique/Kaokab, Kim Yarochevskaya as the Mother, and Maude Guérin as Samira. It premiered in Montreal by the Théâtre de la Manufacture at the Théâtre de la Licorne in March 1994 and was reprised in April 1995 with the following company:

MONIQUE/KAOKAB	Pol Pelletier (First week of 1994 production), then Christiane Proulx
MOTHER	Hélène Mercier
SAMIRA	Maude Guérin (1994), Catherine Lachance (1995)

Directed by Daniel Simard
Music by Pierre Moreau
Sound by Hélène Gagnon
Lighting by Benoît Fauteux
Set designed by Marc-Antoine Choquette

• • •

Jeux de patience was nominated in 1995 by the Académie québécoise de théâtre for a Masque for best new play.

A dramatic reading took place at the Festival de Trois on August 12, 1996, directed by Lise Vaillancourt, with Danielle Proulx, Lise Roy, and Isabelle Leblanc.

A dramatic version of *Game of Patience* took place at the UBU Repertory Theater in New York on May 9, 1994 and at the InterAct Theater Company of Philadelphia on June 19, 1994, translated and directed by Jill Mac Dougall, with Basha Raboy, Jean Korey, and Ana Ortiz. Mac Dougall's translation was granted the 1994 National Theater Translation Fund award. The North American premiere production of the English version was held at the Zebra Crossing Theatre in Chicago in November 1995, directed by Lynn Ann Bernatowicz, with Jane de Laubenfels, Pamela Feldman, and Michele Di Maso.

Characters

MONIQUE/KAOKAB, between forty and fifty, novelist and playwright, immigrated
to North America when she was nine.
THE MOTHER/MARIAM, her cousin, also between forty and fifty, a recent
immigrant.
SAMIRA, the MOTHER's daughter, around fifteen or sixteen years old.

Space

A panel representing a map of the world covers the back wall of the stage. A dozen or
so drawers are placed at "hot spots" on the map, where wars are today occurring. The
drawers, which are accessible from behind the panel, pop open and shut throughout
the play.

The *mappa mundi* blends into a large bookcase, the author's library.

Monique/Kaokab's studio occupies most of the stage: a large desk, plants, an
ornate chest, and a kitchenette.

The Mother's space, at the extreme upper-right corner of the stage, is described
by a single overhead spot. At the opening she is sitting in a rocking chair with her back
to the audience. She rocks incessantly, holding a rolled prayer rug that she cradles like
a baby. She is wearing a red dress.

Samira darts around the entire theatre, penetrating the protagonists' space,
scaling the catwalks, or moving through the audience. Her head or hands appear
periodically in one or another of the drawers in the backdrop map. She may speak into
a microphone that sometimes deforms her voice.

Pronunciation Aid

The following key should be used as an initial aid to pronunciation and not a
substitution for oral coaching. The transliteration is based on the French script and
the author's pronunciation of popular Lebanese Arabic. Any Arabic dialect may be
used since the play is not geographically specific.

Kaokab: roughly *cow-cob*
ey, eh (bayey, waladey, tabouleh): as in "pay"
i (bi): as in "to be"
min rhymes with "pin"; *bint* rhymes with "mint"
ou (noushkor, boukra): as in "soup" or "pool"
aa (baaref) or *'a (ya 'ayouni):* Arabic *'ain* sound
aiy (laiyla): as in "eye"
kh (khwata): as in German "*ach*"

Translator's Note

patience, n. 1. the bearing of provocation, annoyance, misinformation, pain, etc., without complaint, loss of temper, irritation or the like. 2. an ability or willingness to suppress restlessness or annoyance in waiting... 3. quiet perseverance; even-tempered care; diligence... 4. cards, solitaire... [1]

Author's Note

I offer this play to all who have lost their child, their country, their dreams, their taste for life.

I offer these words to all those forgotten and all who are trying to forget...

to everyone who, every day, every moment, confronts the silence of death.

I would have liked to offer them a glass of water, at least a glass of water.... [2]

---

[1] From *Webster's Encyclopedic Unabridged Dictionary of the English Language.* New York: Gramercy Books, 1989.

[2] Read/recorded in the author's voice at the beginning of the performance.

GAME OF PATIENCE

Scene One

The entire theatre is dark.

The panting and footsteps of someone running emerge from the darkness at the back of the audience.

Gradually a light comes up on SAMIRA. She is running without moving forward. Arms and legs are attached to her limbs. Shards of flesh stick to her skin. She tries to rip them off. A baby dangles from a rope around her neck.

Music, mixed with the sounds of war, swells.

With all her might, SAMIRA breaks away and runs down the aisle. The baby falls to the ground. She rushes back, picks it up, sticks her fingers in its mouth. The child breathes again. She takes it in her arms and continues to run.

On stage MONIQUE/KAOKAB remains riveted to her chair, apparently intent on a game of solitaire set out on her desk. She seems winded, gasping for breath.

Suddenly she jumps up and sweeps the cards to the floor. She paces the room like a caged lion.

MONIQUE/KAOKAB   Solitair… ry confinement. Come on, Kaokab, get with it, make your move. I am losing my patience. "In the face of death, any risk is petty." [1] Write, just write, Kaokab.

SAMIRA continues to run. She crosses the stage to the bookcase. She climbs in and out of the drawers.

A spot comes up on the MOTHER. With her back to the audience, she is sitting in a rocking chair, clutching a rolled prayer rug, cradling it like a baby.

MONIQUE/KAOKAB paces back and forth, muttering to herself in search of an inspiration. Her gaze falls on the chest. She approaches, hesitates, and then opens it. She takes out objects and clothing, some photographs that she stares at with emotion. Last, she removes a large Oriental rug. She unrolls the rug. She lies down. She wraps herself in the rug and rolls back and forth as she speaks.

(invoking her family, one by one) Bayey, Mounir, Samir, Boulos, Kaokab Amira, Immey. [2]

---

[1]   From a Spanish proverb.
[2]   Monique/Kaokab invokes her family, beginning with *bayey* [papa], listing the proper names of her brothers and sisters, and ending with *immey* [mama].

(with the father's voice) Nemo ya wled, nemo, Allah kbir.[3]

(with the mother's voice) Allah ma bi sakerha min kil el mayl. Bieyfreyja Allah.[4]

(with her natural voice) We could have been sleeping in the street. We have a roof over our heads. God never closes all doors at once. In winter we could have died of cold. Thank God, it's summer, *noushkor Allah.*[5]

(with her voice as a child) Immey, I thought it always snowed here. I love snow because I can roll in it… make snowballs. And I can get warm, warm again when I come home. But I love summer better, because it reminds me of…. What's it called, Immey? Yeah, Bir Barra, that's it. In Bir Barra we'd eat grapes right off the vine. Are you going to plant some grapes, Bayey? I could pick them like in Bir Barra and eat as many as I want. It would be as good as being there. Same thing.

(with the father's voice) It will never be the same, even with a grape arbour. This will never be our country.

(child's voice) It'll be the same, with the grapes; it'll be like our country, huh, Bayey?

(mother's voice) No, Kaokab, never. It will never be our country.

> She closes her eyes and falls asleep.

> SAMIRA enters. Flesh and limbs are still hanging from her body, but she does not bother to try pulling them off. With the baby in her arms she walks slowly forward, her head high, fearless. Music and sounds of war grow louder.

> A volley of shots. SAMIRA's body stiffens and lifts before falling on MONIQUE/KAOKAB, sleeping.

> MONIQUE/KAOKAB wakes screaming. SAMIRA's eyes are riveted on her. Crawling as fast as possible to her desk, MONIQUE/KAOKAB writes feverishly.

MOTHER   *Ya waladey… ya waladey… ya waladey…*[6]

> SAMIRA has disappeared.

MONIQUE/KAOKAB   *(writing)* She runs. The bodies are piling up, half dead, half alive…. She knows where she's going… she steps over barricades of corpses. The music is calling her, she follows, she moves closer. The baby falls. She picks it up in her arms and breathes life into it again. She wants to die alive, she is no

---

[3]   *Nemo ya wled, nemo, Allah kbir.* [Sleep, children, sleep, God is great.]
[4]   *Allah ma bi sakerha min kil el mayl. Bieyfreyja Allah.* [God never closes all doors at once. God will deliver you.]
[5]   *Noushkor Allah.* [Thank God. Praise be to God.]
[6]   *Ya waladey.* [Oh, my child.]

longer running, she has stopped running, she walks toward the music. Drawers slam shut. Drawers fly open. She is walking straight ahead.... She is walking...

Blackout.

Scene Two

The lights come up on SAMIRA, sitting on a swing high above the stage. Dressed in jeans and a white T-shirt, she looks like any normal teenage girl.

MONIQUE/KAOKAB is writing. Frequently she rubs her stomach and her chest. Sometimes she gets up, paces, pours a glass of water, looks up at SAMIRA, before returning to her desk. Her facial expressions often resemble the girl's.

A song by Egyptian singer and musician Oum Kalsoum is playing.[7]

SAMIRA   *(swinging)* In my mother's belly I was already getting used to things. That's where I learned how to sing, too. *(She begins to hum a lullaby.)*

Salam ya Salam, ya, ya albey
Salam ya Salam, ya 'ayouni, ya rouhey
Salam ya Salam, ya waladey...[8]

I wasn't scared. The explosions don't scare you when your mother is talking and singing softly in your ear. And it's the best way to learn how to count. Even when she was singing, my mother never stopped counting. That's real important. 'Cause if you're not careful, if you forget to count while the bombers are on their business trips right over your head... tough luck. One hit is enough. Without your head you can't count or sing anymore. Maybe it's easier that way. My mother is still counting. She counts the days, the minutes, the hours, the months, the years, the centuries. I don't need to count anymore. I learned too early and I got sick of it.

Like I got sick of my name. Salam, Salam, Salam... I mean there were too many Salams around. All the mothers seemed to have the same idea the year I was born. Unfortunately Salam is the only name you can give to a boy or a girl. *(emphatically)* Salam! *(mimicking a "salaam" typical of "Hollywood Arabs")* *Salam alaykoum.* May peace be with you. *(a laugh)* In first grade there were dozens of Salamalaykoums in the class. What a tower of Babel! Course we were used to that. Babel, I mean. We lived right in the middle of it.

---

[7]   The famous Egyptian singer Oum Kalsoum was a living legend in the Middle East. Her recordings have remained popular throughout the Arab world.

[8]   *Salam ya albey/ ya 'ayouni/ ya rouhey/ ya waladey...* [Peace my soul, my eyes, my heart, my child...] Throughout her monologue Samira plays with the multiple meanings of *salam* as her given name, as peace and its ironic opposite, as a common greeting or an Orientalist projection of the Arab.

By second grade we'd all changed our names. No more Salam. It was the only thing we could change, so we did.

To relieve the tension, MONIQUE/KAOKAB slowly rotates her head, her shoulders, her hips. Her movements resemble a Middle Eastern dance.

Auntie Kaokab changed her name too. Not for the same reasons. In her school there weren't any Kaokabs at all. Nobody could pronounce her name. They'd say Cow-cab... Corn-cob... Ca... Cacao-bob... and everybody would burst out laughing. In school any silly thing makes you laugh. Somebody farts or a shell explodes and the whole class is rolling in the aisles. In school it doesn't take much to die laughing. So Kaokab decided to change to... Monique. Mo-ni-que. Sounds nothing like Kaokab, does it? Not even the same initials. Me, at least I kept part of my name. Salam Samira, *(with a goofy expression)* Samira salam.

My aunt Monique/Kaokab should have played with her name too. Maybe that's why she hardly ever laughs. No, that's not why. She doesn't laugh because you can't laugh all alone, by yourself. I know something about that. It's easy to cry alone, but just try laughing all by yourself.... It looks crazy. How many people have been put away because they laughed alone? But suppose they threw everybody who cries alone in an insane asylum? It would be like millions, I mean just forget it. The asylums could never hold them all. Where I come from there's no more asylum...

MONIQUE/KAOKAB pauses in her writing. SAMIRA observes her.

MONIQUE/KAOKAB   No more... A-S-Y... A-S-I? A-S-Y-L-UM.... The entire city has become a... an...

SAMIRA   The city has become an...

MONIQUE/KAOKAB   ...an open house.

SAMIRA   We have become one big open house, a gigantic party, one enormous outdoor asylum, a party big as the country, the continent, and *(radio newscaster's voice)* "the entire Third World." *(mocking tone)* The Third World. That's what they call us in the West. *(She looks at MONIQUE/KAOKAB.)* Does that mean we're one-third of the world's population or that each of us is one-third of
a person?

Abruptly, MONIQUE/KAOKAB stops writing. She picks up her cards scattered on the floor and rolls up her rug.

Uh, oh-h.... Looks like this solitaire game is over. Sometimes you need more than patience to play. My aunt's problem is she worries too much. She doesn't laugh enough. She doesn't even cry. So all that stuff stays stuck in her throat. She doesn't know that, from up here, laughing or crying sounds the same. It's just time goes faster when you laugh. Even here. I don't know why that is...

As for my mother, she simply gave up. On life. She cries because it's become a habit, like she used to laugh. Course I was the one who made her laugh…. My aunt Kaokab, that's another story. She's so proud. She's always trying to prove she can make it alone, I realized a while back that she really needs my mother.

MONIQUE/KAOKAB moves toward the MOTHER. Gently, she stops the rocking chair and turns it around to face the audience. Standing behind the chair, MONIQUE/KAOKAB puts her arms around the MOTHER's shoulders and holds her in a long, tender embrace. The MOTHER seems to expect this and does not react.

MOTHER   Kaokab, tell me, do you think my daughter would be dead if we had gotten out in time? If my arms had been long enough, if my belly had been big enough, would Samira be alive today?

MONIQUE/KAOKAB   *Ma baaref, ya oum Samira, ma baaref.*[9] I don't know…. Come…. Come with me.

The MOTHER stands. MONIQUE/KAOKAB pushes the rocking chair to centre stage. The MOTHER follows, clutching her rolled rug to her chest. SAMIRA, who has left her swing, accompanies them. She hovers behind or twirls in front of the two women. The MOTHER sits again on the rocking chair. MONIQUE/KAOKAB prepares Turkish coffee. SAMIRA flits around her.

MOTHER   Would you please… stop that music.

MONIQUE/KAOKAB turns off the music. She brings a tray with a Turkish coffee pot and two small cups, a glass of water, a bowl of sugared almonds. She serves and the two women sip in silence.

MONIQUE/KAOKAB   You'll… you'll be fine here, you'll see.

MOTHER   Sometimes I miss the music of the bombs.

MONIQUE/KAOKAB   My mother used to say, "A man can get used to anything; a dog needs to be trained."

MOTHER   No dog lived through what we did. We tied them up. Still, they managed to run away.

MONIQUE/KAOKAB   Animals… animals have a sense of survival… *(She is breathing with great difficulty.)* Humans get lost sometimes; they lose that second sense…. They lose…. I want to write… a story about that. I've wanted to write about that for a long time.

MOTHER   You write?

MONIQUE/KAOKAB   …Yes.

---

[9]   *Ma baaref, ya oum Samira, ma baaref.* [I don't know, oh mother of Samira, I don't know.]

MOTHER   You write books?

MONIQUE/KAOKAB   …Yes.

MOTHER   Many books?

MONIQUE/KAOKAB   *(meaning too many or never enough)* Well, yes…

MOTHER   Why didn't you ever come to see us? That would have made a great book for you.

MONIQUE/KAOKAB   You know there are plenty of subjects to write about.

MOTHER   Were you afraid?

MONIQUE/KAOKAB   *(having trouble breathing)* That's… an understatement.

MOTHER   Were you afraid you would be killed?

MONIQUE/KAOKAB   …Worse than that.

MOTHER   What's worse than dying?

MONIQUE/KAOKAB   I just didn't want to die before… before I had… *(in a gasp)* I wanted to choose my death.

MOTHER   Choose your death? What is this planet I have landed on? Choose your death! Did Samira choose her death? Tell me, you who write therefore you think, did Samira and millions like her choose to die?

MONIQUE/KAOKAB   I… don't know.

MOTHER   You speak madness and then you say I don't know. Your books must be highly entertaining.

> *A pause while they sip their coffee.*

I have been in this country exactly sixty-four days.

MONIQUE/KAOKAB   And me, forty years.

MOTHER   This is the first time I've ever gone out of the house.

MONIQUE/KAOKAB   The first fifteen years my mother didn't even know the colour of the sky here. She never went out to visit, never had coffee with anybody, just to talk. Not even a glass of water…. I don't know how she survived.

MOTHER   She became accustomed. You became accustomed to the worst… and then you miss it.

MONIQUE/KAOKAB   *(with a sad smile)* At least you can read and write. And you speak the language.

MOTHER   Knowing a language doesn't mean you can speak. I have said nothing. I don't even know the name of this country.

MONIQUE/KAOKAB   This country can't decide what its name is. [10]

MOTHER   Not to decide, not to have a name is better than to lose it in a blood bath. Samira will never answer to her name, my country lost its name. I have no country, no children.

MONIQUE/KAOKAB   *(trying to calm her)* You're here now; you're safe... far away…. You'll be fine here…. The problems are less bloody. They get buried in the snow. Here, patience... is still a virtue. You'll be fine here. If you're able to forget.

MOTHER   Never.

They sip in silence.

Why did you come to me?

MONIQUE/KAOKAB   Why? I... don't know... how... to write anymore. This is the first time I...

MOTHER   You write every single day?

MONIQUE/KAOKAB   Just like you feed your family.

MOTHER   Sometimes there was nothing to eat.

MONIQUE/KAOKAB   I haven't been able to write for sixty-four days.

MOTHER   Well, it won't kill you.

MONIQUE/KAOKAB   Are you sure?

MOTHER   Yes, I'm sure.

MONIQUE/KAOKAB   There are many ways to die.

MOTHER   Only one is final.

They sip in silence.

Samira died centuries ago. Four hundred and twenty-nine days ago. At four in the afternoon.

MONIQUE/KAOKAB   It's five to four.

MOTHER   I know. Without looking at the clock, I know... *(with a strange light in her eyes)* I feel her breath... her last breath. I tore my dress to make her a bandage, she was still breathing.

MONIQUE/KAOKAB   *(to herself)* I tore my dress to make her a bandage, she was still breathing... the warmth of her breath. *(pause)* Samira was fifteen when she...

---

[10]   The country that has not chosen its name is a reference to Quebec's ambiguous status.

MOTHER   She is sixteen years, two months, and three days old. I fought so hard to live… for my children… to live… so we would stay… alive. Alive.

MONIQUE/KAOKAB   *(suffocating)* You do have other children, *noushkor Allah,* you have other—

MOTHER   *(exploding)* Not you, too! Forty years away and you still say "*noushkor Allah*, praise God Almighty," just like those who see the blood pouring from the body next to them, even splashing on them. As long as they are still breathing, they say, "Thank God, *noushkor Allah*." They get used to the worst and the worst must come, because they have already accepted it. *Noushkor Allah, bieyfreyja Allah,* everything is written in the big book, we deserve this, we have so many sins to purge. What sins? To be born there rather than here? Who chooses their birthplace? You who pretend to choose your death, did you choose your birth? Now there's a subject for one of your books! You know nothing of your mother tongue, except these sugar-coated words. I never want to hear them again. Least of all from you.

MONIQUE/KAOKAB   I'm sorry. When… when you don't know what to say, that's what comes to mind… homilies, formulas…

MOTHER   Keep them for your books. An exotic word now and then, that sounds good.

> *MONIQUE/KAOKAB pours another coffee. They drink in silence.*

Maybe they are right. I am not alone. Here I have all I need. I have my children. Four healthy children left. But, Kaokab, can a mouth replace an eye? Can a heart do for an ear? Can a nose walk, laugh, dance? My children surround me, they keep me alive, yes, I will not fall to the other side. Yet if all had died, the hole would not be any bigger, the emptiness would not be greater. My soul went with her last breath.

MONIQUE/KAOKAB   You'll be fine, *ya oum Samira.*

MOTHER   Yes… yes… I don't hear the bombs anymore. Just the snow… the sound of the snow falling. I've always loved snow. I remember a postcard Uncle Walid sent when I was a little girl. I showed it to all my school friends, then I pasted it on the mirror behind the buffet. It was the most beautiful postcard of all. I don't know where it is now. *(with a disturbing light in her eyes)* I don't know where she is now. I don't know… in the flames, the bombs… under the ice, the snow…? Samira… Samira, are you warm, *ya albey*? Are you cold, *ya rouhey*? Are you hungry, *ya 'ayouni*?[11] We have a lot to eat now. Here, water flows from the pipes, hot or cold, you can take as many showers as you want, even a bath. You can turn on the light, all of the lights if you want. You can play your music all day. You can go to the movies, Samira, you can take classes in movies. We don't have to keep running, to change neighbourhoods, cities,

---

[11]   *Ya albey… ya rouhey… ya 'ayouni.* [My heart, my soul, my eyes.]

countries all the time. We are safe here. You can come and go at whatever hour. You can make movies here, as you wished. The danger has passed, the danger has passed, the danger has passed, there is only snow… snow.

> *They sip coffee in silence.*

MONIQUE/KAOKAB   How are your brothers and sisters?

MOTHER   Scattered. Leaves in the wind. Orphans. Everybody went where they could. My parents stayed behind. They were happy to know we were safe.

MONIQUE/KAOKAB   And the son of your uncle?

MOTHER   You are funny… the way you have kept these old expressions. No one says this "son of your uncle" now. You mean my husband? When Samira left us, so did my husband. He is now only the father of my children. A very good father. He is back there, in a neighbouring country. The heat is unbearable. He is like a prisoner, dying a slow death so that his children might survive. He telephones sometimes. Each of the children talks to him, not for too long. Then it's my turn. "How are you?" he asks. I say, "All right and you?" "Yes, all right," he says. I ask him, have you seen Samira, he says, "Yes, I have seen Samira." Too much to say or too little, it amounts to the same. He always closes with "*Noushkor Allah*, we are alive, that's what counts." I can say nothing. I hear the click. The last time I said praise to God, Samira was still breathing.

> *Slow fade-out.*

Scene Three

> *MONIQUE/KAOKAB is leaning on the bookcase. She is lost in her thoughts. She breathes with great difficulty.*
>
> *SAMIRA is somewhere in the audience.*

SAMIRA   One day, you don't know why, you just can't take it anymore. You can't, that's all. You can't breathe. I wanted to breathe.

MONIQUE/KAOKAB & SAMIRA   You can't be free and imprisoned, young and old, dead and alive at the same time.

MONIQUE/KAOKAB   At the same time.

SAMIRA   I wasn't asking for the moon, just some peace and quiet. No more orders. I wanted to sleep in my room when I needed to sleep, go out when I felt like it, and visit my friends, Amal and the others, whenever I wanted. That's not a lot to ask, is it? I didn't expect to get a car on my sixteenth birthday or a camcorder until I got my 16mm. I didn't. I just wanted to take a bath or go see a movie when I felt like it, without waiting for a ceasefire. Those days we didn't know where to start. We were like crazy people released for a day. Or prisoners on the lam. I didn't want anybody telling me what to do and certainly not when to do it. I wanted to be free.

On one raid we ran into a shelter. That was a big change from being outside, right? Most of it was pretty funny. We agreed not to listen to our radios all at the same time. Everybody was assigned a quarter of an hour. When it was my turn, I tuned in a Bob Dylan song I liked a lot. *(speaking then singing)* "How many years must a man live through before they call him a man?" It was like I was hearing it for the first time. And I saw all of our lives through a zoom lens. "How many stairs must a man climb up…" *(humming through to the end of the line)*

I felt like throwing up or shitting or dying and I couldn't breathe. At the same time I managed to make everybody laugh. All that at once. My mother held up a sheet to hide me, so I could do all that stuff alone in a big basin that was already full. She was laughing so much that the curtain slipped and everybody saw my behind. One more naked behind is no big deal. It doesn't change a thing, I know that now.

That time she laughed so much she couldn't help it, but otherwise my mother did everything she could to protect me. I guess that's what mothers are for. She'd put her hands in front of my eyes so I wouldn't see. She couldn't cover my ears at the same time. It became like a game. A weird sort of parlour game. We were all huddled there together, counting the strikes. It was kind of fun. I thought people everywhere lived like that. But when I got older, I began to realize that… un-unh… nay, nay… this couldn't be what life was about. I saw movies, which helped me understand, which showed me the difference.

My parents wanted to emigrate, go into exile, I mean just get out! But they couldn't and it's not just because they didn't have enough money. *Bieyfreyja Allah… bieyfreyja Allah* they kept saying. Wanting to believe. After each raid, they thought that was the last time the sky would dump bombs on our heads. Yeah. My parents grew up in a mountain village, poor things. They still think that day breaks after night, that fruit falls when it is ripe, that the sun shines after the rain, that spring follows winter. Maybe it was like that when they were kids. I saw a lot of my friends go, not die, but leave. Die, I've seen that too, a lot.

We never made it out. Money helps, it sure does. If we could at least have gone on a trip like the rich, until things got better. *(imitating an affected bourgeoise)* Farewell, my dahlings. I simply can't bear it anymore. All that noise has been hell. And all those corpses, it's so, so depressing. *Au revoir*, dear hearts. You're so quaint. Dead or alive, you don't know the difference do you, poor things? *Ciao mes chéris…* *(She blows kisses right and left.)*

My friend Amal didn't have enough money to leave either. Her parents were suckers like mine. Full of hope. So we stayed together longer. I don't know if Amal did it on purpose… I still don't know. You always think someday you'll find the answer…

MONIQUE/KAOKAB   ...You always think someday you'll find the answer. *(She is staring at the MOTHER.)*

MOTHER   You look as if you wanted to eat me alive.

MONIQUE/KAOKAB   *(taking a deep breath)* That little rug.... That look, like someone from another planet, from inner space.... Your eyes...

MOTHER   What are you talking about? What's wrong with my eyes?

MONIQUE/KAOKAB   Ever since I saw you at the airport with your four kids and that little rug you held so tightly.... Ever since.... I can't get rid of it.

MOTHER   Why get rid? What do you mean?

MONIQUE/KAOKAB   Nothing... just an expression.... I've wanted... *(with a gesture of pulling something from the inside)* For fifteen years I've wanted to write about that.

MOTHER   About my eyes and my rug? That will be a great contribution to literature.

MONIQUE/KAOKAB   I don't know why I keep talking about that, you're not interested anyway.

MOTHER   You're right. I'm not. *(pause)* But if you could somehow bring Samira's eyes back, just for an instant, yes, I would be interested, but otherwise...

MONIQUE/KAOKAB   I am not a magician, nor *aafrita* nor *djinia.* [12]

MOTHER   *Aafrita, djinia*.... You know some rare words. I thought you only remembered "*noushkor Allah.*"

MONIQUE/KAOKAB   I've been reading *Arabian Nights*. There are some words they can't translate.

MOTHER   *(laughing)* If I could still laugh, I would laugh very hard. You learn our language from a translation of *A Thousand and One Nights*. You are so funny.... You are a "riot," as my children say. They are learning quickly. Every day they come home with some new expression.... While I sit and watch the snow fall, you are reading *Alf laiyla wa laiyla* [13] in a foreign language and my children are absorbing a foreign culture that will become their own culture. It will not be mine or their father's or their grandparents'. They will forget everything.

MONIQUE/KAOKAB   Childhood leaves indelible marks.

---

[12] *Aafrita* [she-devil], *djinia* [genie]. Monique/Kaokab pronounces the words in a hesitant rendition of classical Arabic. The Mother pronounces the words in popular spoken Arabic.

[13] *Alf laiyla wa laiyla* translates literally as "a thousand and one nights."

MOTHER   Still, they will forget. "Blood does not change to water," they say. No, it doesn't. It dries up and dies. What stayed with you, beside tabbouleh? The memory of the stomach resists, but the rest?

MONIQUE/KAOKAB   *(after a pause)* I remember a song my mother used to sing. And I know a few words: *sharaf, haram, maalesh, boukra, noushkor Allah, leysh, ma baaref, bledna, badi ekol, badi nem, badi mayi, badi mout....* [14] I remember the smell of the earth and the scent of my mother.... I remember her solitude. Nothing else. Nothing.

I learned everything here. I learned winter just like arithmetic, with frozen fingers. I learned to blend in, to disappear, to forget. I earn my living in a borrowed language, a language that won't let me cry out. The cries ring false. Even the moans.... Pain does not have the same sound. What makes them laugh makes me weep, what makes them weep makes me laugh. I've adapted, I've succeeded as a writer. I write what they like; the royalties from just one of my books would feed three entire villages in Africa or Asia.

I've written the surface of things. To please, to rock people to sleep. I've written to put myself to sleep, to forget. I have written pushing my memory back inside, deep in my stomach. I borrowed a language and I lent my soul. I have lived between the heartbreak of remembering and the heartbreak of forgetting.

MOTHER   I am cold, Kaokab, I'm so cold.

MONIQUE/KAOKAB gets a blanket and tenderly covers the MOTHER. The MOTHER closes her eyes.

Slow fade-out.

Scene Four

MONIQUE/KAOKAB is writing. The MOTHER is sleeping fitfully. She is muttering inaudible words in her sleep.

Music. Sounds of war. The music grows louder.

Drawers pop open. Arms, heads, legs are visible. The drawers snap shut. Other drawers open, revealing eyes, hearts, intestines.

A drawer opens revealing SAMIRA, her head hanging over the edge. It closes and she appears at another drawer.

Blood is streaming over the map.

---

[14] The list of words Monique/Kaokab remembers is: *sharaf* [honour], *haram* [forbidden], *maalesh* [no matter], *boukra* [tomorrow], *noushkor Allah* [thank God], *leysh* [why], *ma baaref* [I don't know], *bledna* [our country], *badi ekol* [I want to eat], *badi nem* [I want to sleep], *badi mayi* [I want some water], *badi mout* [I want to die].

MONIQUE/KAOKAB stops writing. Breathing heavily, she gets up and goes to her rolled rug. She begins kicking it over and over.

MONIQUE/KAOKAB   Why? Why? Why? I'll ask why until the end of time, until my tongue dries up in my mouth. Why her? Why him? Why Beirut? Why them? Why this baby, why Bethlehem? Why that child, why Bir Barra, why our village, our neighbourhood, our city, why Babylon, why our country, why our planet? I'll ask why why why until my lungs burst and nobody answers me, nobody will ever answer me.

And I want to write! *(between clenched teeth)* I want to write, goddamn it all, I want to stupid fucking write.

(She takes a few deep breaths, moves to the MOTHER, and wakes her. The MOTHER jumps.) Don't be afraid, it's just me. Mariam... Mariam, do you remember the last meal we ate together?

MOTHER   When you came to visit us? That was over twenty years ago.

MONIQUE/KAOKAB   Where did we go? I can't remember where we were...

MOTHER   It was a restaurant on the beach, in Bir Baroud. There were about twenty of us. There was a slight breeze, a moon, the water at our feet. A hundred little dishes, each one lovelier than the others. Do you remember? You wanted to taste everything. You said: "We are in heaven, eat, eat... before it's all lost. We mustn't waste a bit."

MONIQUE/KAOKAB   *(sadly)* Yes... yes.

MOTHER   And you closed your eyes at each bite. You looked at the sea, you looked at the mountains, and you closed your eyes.... Your eyes were wide open or they were shut tight.

MONIQUE/KAOKAB   It was nineteen years ago.

MOTHER   When the old people in the village saw you, they said, *"Kaokab bint Abou Mounir*[15] left us a young girl and she comes back still a young girl. This must be some American invention, to get younger rather than older. We could use their secrets for our old bones, couldn't we?"

MONIQUE/KAOKAB   I was a little girl when I left. I went back thirteen years later. And now I can't be like the salmon who swim back to die where they were born. The country of my childhood died before me. A wall of fire has cut me off... *(to herself)* And if I can't write about it, I'll die with it.

MOTHER   "Another eccentric American," they said. "They're all the same, they leave, they come back to visit a few years later. Tourists, foreigners! Didn't they grow up here with the goats and the sheep? Didn't they learn to walk barefoot here on our soil? They act as if they've forgotten everything, our language, even

[15]   *Kaokab bint Abou Mounir.* [Kaokab, daughter of the father of Mounir.]

our names. We remember each one of them, but they don't remember a thing." It's true, you'd forgotten everything, your manners, the polite forms. You wore shorts and you muttered phrases nobody could understand. You know very well villagers don't speak any languages but our own. And you would laugh…. Were you making fun of us?

MONIQUE/KAOKAB   Of course not! I'd forgotten my own language. I could have cried, but instead I laughed. Here, when I was little, it was different. I cried because I couldn't understand. I didn't understand the word "where" until I was six years old.

    She begins setting the table.

MOTHER   We enjoyed watching you anyway. You would sniff the ground, climb trees, walk around barefoot like a child. Drink water from the village well rather than use our new faucets…. And to see you stuff yourself silly with figs and grapes!

MONIQUE/KAOKAB   I knew my childhood was over… I could never go back. It was like making love for the last time. I wanted…

MOTHER   You wanted to see everything, hear everything, do everything. You remember, you made us take you all over. You wore us out playing tourists. And you would shout with pleasure. Our country is beautiful, but shouting like that…. It's overdoing things. *(pause)* We could travel anyplace then. We could still move around freely.

MONIQUE/KAOKAB   Really? You had to have an ID card. I remember that struck me…. I'd never seen that here.

MOTHER   But we didn't have to show it! Just carry it around. Just a formality. Fear hadn't set in yet. You saw. You were a foreigner, my cousin perhaps, but still a foreigner, and you saw everything we couldn't.

    They sit at the table and eat in silence. SAMIRA is perched on the bookcase. MONIQUE/KAOKAB looks up at her from time to time and smiles.

SAMIRA   *(as if peering through the eye of a camera)* Seen from this distance human beings are really hilarious. They take themselves so-o-o serious. Ever since Aunt Kaokab's decided to use me as a character and to look at the world through my eyes, things are going much better. Now, zooming in on human beings… *(She makes a face.)* Sometimes I'd rather just look at ants or bees. Even flies. Before I thought life was pretty funny, too. Course, I forced things a little. Just to make life livable. I was always clowning. I liked to do it because people love to laugh. They love you when you make them laugh. Here I don't have to work at that anymore. I see the best bits from the best movies of Charlie Chaplin all the time. On any street, in any house, in any building. In any corner of the world where people are beating each other's brains out over nothing. In every church, every synagogue, every mosque.

Hilarious, I swear, you'd croak laughing. Just take religion for example. Humans always have to find a reason for everything and they always have to be right. Sometimes they fight so long they forget the reason, so they look for another one. But while they're finding the new reason, the other guys are diving headfirst into the flames, because they still believe in the old reason. *(clicking her tongue to say "no, not pity")* You should see them wandering around here in a daze. They don't even remember why they died. Not to know why you're alive is one thing. But not to know why you died… that's really sad.

My friend Amal… I don't even know if she was Catholic, Maronite, Druze, Shiite, Sunnite, Coptic, Greek Orthodox, or Jewish Orthodox. I don't remember and I couldn't care less. What I remember is everything we used to do together and everything we couldn't do. I remember her voice, her eyes that were always full of fear. Her dreams, the poems she wrote, her giggling when I made her laugh so she'd stop crying. I thought she would choke to death, crying and laughing at the same time like that…. But that's not how she died. I know. It's all recorded on film, here in the eye of my heart.

> *MONIQUE/KAOKAB and the MOTHER continue to eat in silence. The author is lost in her thoughts. The MOTHER gazes at the bookcase.*

MOTHER   So many books…. To think I spent hours cleaning off the dust…. Four years, three times a week.

MONIQUE/KAOKAB   …What?

MOTHER   That was my job, cleaning the library. Soon after your visit, I went to work in the city… for a rich family. They always spoke in French.[16] They didn't call me Mariam. It was "Marie! Marie!" all the time. How do you think I learned the language? I had to.

MONIQUE/KAOKAB   So did I.

MOTHER   It's not the same. You left your country. I was in my own country and I had to speak another language to survive. I kept thinking this can't go on. One day the whole thing will…

MONIQUE/KAOKAB   So you too…. You knew it would all blow up.

MOTHER   All I needed was to see their library. Not only were many of the books false, just cardboard, beautiful leather bindings with nothing inside, but all of the real books were in foreign languages. I worked there four years and not once did anyone take a book from the shelf. Not to leaf through it, read it, touch it, not just to say hello to the book. Not once. I would rather read books in my own language, so I searched and searched the shelves. I did not find a single one. Not one. You would have thought we had disappeared without leaving

---

[16] The use of French or English by the local bourgeoisie is a common fact throughout the post-colonial world.

a trace. There was nothing from us, not even a folk tale…. I get the same feeling looking at your books. Not one is in our language.

MONIQUE/KAOKAB   But I can't read our language.

MOTHER   Why didn't you learn? It didn't seem important? You were seduced like the others, conquered?

MONIQUE/KAOKAB   I was just pushed on a bandwagon that was already rolling. I didn't choose to emigrate. Nobody asked me what I wanted.

MOTHER   Fate never asks what we want. That's the rule. But you keep trying to convince me choice is possible. Who is the one who talked about choosing her own death?

MONIQUE/KAOKAB   Nothing is ever black or white in life.

MOTHER   One thing is irreversible.

MONIQUE/KAOKAB   You're always talking about death. There's not just death. Death is really simple, it's life that—

MOTHER   *(as if stabbed in the stomach)* Death is simple! When you feel it in your flesh, then we'll talk about it. Not before.

MONIQUE/KAOKAB   But I do feel it. Every time someone is killed, torn from life, I die a little. Every time someone is hungry, so am I. Every time someone is humiliated, so am I.

MOTHER   You're lying. That's just a speech by the famous author. When you're hungry, you open your refrigerator and you eat! You only see people die on television. You just get up and turn it on or off. You can still get up. You can move your hand. They can't. For them it's finished. You change channels and you're someplace else and you go on living.

MONIQUE/KAOKAB   You can't expect me to die for real!

MOTHER   That's exactly what I'm saying. It's all in your head.

MONIQUE/KAOKAB   But my head is me. I can't cut it off.

MOTHER   Compassion starts when you get out of your head, when you make a move to help someone.

MONIQUE/KAOKAB   What kind of move? There are so many we could make.

MOTHER   You could have come to see us, but you were afraid of being killed, of dying for real.

MONIQUE/KAOKAB   But you don't understand that grabbing a gun is no solution. It's impossible to take sides.

MOTHER   There were many things to do besides fighting. You preferred to do nothing.

MONIQUE/KAOKAB   Doing nothing is the hardest.

MOTHER   That's not true. The proof is you are still alive and they are dead. No one gave them a glass of water before they died. No one. They are dead and you are still breathing.

MONIQUE/KAOKAB   *(gasping, as if she were struggling not to drown)* No, no, no! You're wrong. I can't breathe. It was my country, too. It was my childhood, too. My feet still run there on the red earth. I have to cut them off and screw them back on my body if I want to live. Don't you get it? I protect myself so I won't die entirely. But the more I protect myself, the further I move from the bloody mess and the deeper I sink into the imaginary mess, this magma of words. To pick up a gun is so much easier. You don't have to think. You just do it. You kill, you're killed. That's all.

But I want to understand. Why this bloody mess? Why such misery? Why? It's been years since I've been able to curl up on my sofa and forget that someplace in the world bodies are burning, people are ripping each other apart, people are starving, people are humiliated, imprisoned, raped, tortured. At the very moment I am trying to find a comfortable position on the sofa, mouths are opening and screaming and I try to plug up my ears because I don't know what to do for them. I want to understand. *(Her tone shifts.)* Yes, I'm scared. Yes, I'm afraid of dying. I don't want to die for nothing. I don't want to die before I've written. I don't want to die before I've understood.

MOTHER   There's nothing to understand. It's human destiny.

MONIQUE/KAOKAB   *No, no, no.* Destiny is an easy word. I want happiness to be possible. I want to change our destiny. Christ, will I ever finish this fucking play? Will it ever be over?

MOTHER   What are you talking about?

MONIQUE/KAOKAB   About this goddamned life that no one can live anymore. Never a moment of peace, a time to rest, that's over for everybody, whether their country is at peace or in the middle of a war. And I'm not just talking about myself! Our thoughts are constantly short-circuited. Our planet, a thousand times more complex than my computer, where every little flea, every ant, every human being, every tree has its place, we're all stuck in this together… I want happiness to be possible.

MOTHER   Happiness!

MONIQUE/KAOKAB   *(with unleashed fury)* Yes, happiness, yes, the simple pleasure of living, of just feeling alive, like a stupid cat arching its back as long as it can still move. We know too much and not enough. Closing your eyes hurts as much as opening them. My neighbour may live on the other side of the earth; he's still my neighbour. My eyes open and I don't know what to do. There's too much to do. Every country at war is my country…. I want happiness to be possible.... I don't want the awareness of others to stop us from having a life. Happiness is nothing to be ashamed of. You have to breathe in life, like the tree sucks water from the ground.

MOTHER *(cynical)* So that's why you never came to see us.... You were afraid of losing your little piece of happiness?

MONIQUE/KAOKAB *(furious)* You are really a pain in the ass. You don't understand anything. You talk about compassion and you can't even put yourself in my place, not for one second. Understanding means reaching out to someone, hugging them close, even in your mind. You don't have room for that, you're so full of your own suffering and you won't give up an inch. You're proud of it. It makes you tall, superior. It gives you every right. You talk from the lofty heights of your grief as if you were the only one who'd ever lost anything. Draped in your flaming red robes, you suffer. You didn't want to wear black, because you refuse to face the facts. *(pause)* It's time to mourn, Mariam, that means leaving a little opening for life to return, stop blaming everybody for your pain, that means accepting life, even with the missing pieces.

MOTHER Never, you hear, never.

MONIQUE/KAOKAB You have to. So do I.

MOTHER Do as you please. I can never accept this.

MONIQUE/KAOKAB Mariam, life isn't a contest with a prize for the one who suffers the most. If that's what you think, rest assured, many suffer, too many, and they don't all have the satisfaction of locating the wound. They are bleeding inside.

MOTHER So am I.

MONIQUE/KAOKAB You know where it comes from, you know why, you're luckier than us. All those you see out there walking calmly through the falling snow, they don't know why they suffer, but they do.

MOTHER Nobody here knows what it means to see your country on fire, nobody knows what it means to see your child buried alive.

MONIQUE/KAOKAB You think they're stupid assholes? They know. They're just trying to forget. Life is hard enough as it is. You should understand, in our language "*insen*" means "human" and "forget," the same word. If we couldn't forget, just a little, we'd die or go crazy, if we let ourselves feel to the fullest, we'd die or go crazy. We forget, we have to forget... but we don't know it's useless. We're still eaten from the inside, we still can't live our life, we still ache with solitude. Sure, we forget, but it's of no use.... Whatever we do, an invisible thread is spinning between you, Samira, and all of us... *(her eyes closed as if praying)* I want to reveal this invisible thread. I have to write the invisible.

Scene Five

SAMIRA is walking on a tightrope above the audience.

SAMIRA   Everything was okay when Amal was alive. It was still okay then. We could see each other when school wasn't closed, and we could talk as long as the telephones weren't cut off. It wasn't so bad. You can get used to anything, or almost. I wanted to make a movie about that. I had my topic... two friends who accomplish an impossible feat, who, working together against all odds, keep their good humour. I didn't want to do a big Hollywood production, just a simple film about how two ordinary girls manage to overcome anything, absolutely-lutely anything, just because they love each other. I didn't need to invent a lot, just condense our lives, shorten our conversations. We'd see the streets of the city with lots of kids playing, the houses, the lovely old homes that were left, and the ugly new ones they kept building to replace them. Some wounded people maybe, but no corpses... they rot too fast and smell even faster. We'd have some beautiful close-ups of Amal, with her long, black hair shining in the sun. A neat little film, low budget, easy to shoot. Amal would have the star role. Maybe I'd have a stand-in for me. It's hard to be behind the camera and in the picture. Woody Allen does that, but he has a lot of experience. This would be my first film.

My mother was happy I was going to be a director. She doesn't like to read, but she loves to watch movies. My father thought it was a man's profession. Like war? I asked him. He dropped the subject. What I like about my father is he doesn't try to prove he's right when he knows he's not. He's really cool. He just said, "*Inshalla*[17], we'll see." He was hoping someday the *(spelling the word out)* W-A-R would leave us in peace. Dream on. One of them lasted a hundred years. Just one silly war. I learned that in school. I learned about the Vietnam war in the movies. The Americans came back in pieces and then made movies about it. Others did, not the ones in pieces.

You can't make movies when you're in pieces. Just look at my mother.... She won't make a movie about the war. But my aunt will. Yet... I don't know if movies or plays or books can change anything... I don't know. I haven't been here long enough. Did one ever make a tank turn back? Or stop a bomber from unloading its crap? Has a single bomb ever changed its mind because of a film, a play, or a book? No?... I didn't think so. It helps the guys who write and direct and act, yeah, it helps them let off steam.

People in Europe and America have made movies about us, but we never saw any of them. They say it's to "alert public opinion." *(a laugh)* Alert public opinion.... From up here that's the biggest joke of all.

Blackout.

The notes of a nay or Arab flute solo are heard in the dark.

---

[17]   *Inshallah.* [God willing.]

Scene Six

Night. MONIQUE/KAOKAB paces the floor and then returns to her desk where a game of solitaire is laid out. The MOTHER joins her.

MOTHER   You can't sleep?

MONIQUE/KAOKAB   I can't write. So I'm playing solitaire. It helps pass the time. Watch time passing. Stop time. It inspires me.

MOTHER   One of those queer writer's habits?

MONIQUE/KAOKAB   If you want to call it that…. Every time I lay out the cards, the possibility of a new life opens. The worst thing is stagnation. You have to keep the movement going, any movement, even if it makes no sense. In solitaire you have what is hidden and what is given, what you have to grasp immediately and what takes more patience. I've been playing at least thirty years and I have never seen the same combination appear twice, never the same life. The end is always the same, of course. The most enviable life or the most wretched, they all wind up in the flocks of the dead. That's the rule. So I shuffle the cards again. Someday I'll write a story about each set. A book for each life. They're all worth it.

MOTHER   Spread out the cards. Show me Samira's life.

MONIQUE/KAOKAB   Samira is dead. You can't go on living as if she were alive.

MOTHER   Don't worry about that. It's my problem. I just want you to tell me the story. Isn't that your job? You bring things to life, places and people to life, so go ahead. Tell me the story of Samira's life.

MONIQUE/KAOKAB   I never learned how to tell stories. I just learned how to write… in a foreign language, remember?

MOTHER   Just between us. I'm not going to record your words…. Just to pass the night away.

MONIQUE/KAOKAB   Storytelling and writing are two very different things.

MOTHER   If you wish, I will open the game. I will tell your story.

MONIQUE/KAOKAB   *(in a bad mood)* I already know my story.

MOTHER   But I don't. So I will tell it and that way I can learn it.

MONIQUE/KAOKAB   I'd rather play solitaire.

MOTHER   Play while I tell the story. Once upon a time, in a country far away, a country with no borders and no name, a little girl…

MONIQUE/KAOKAB   *(She cuts her off with a surly voice.)* You're wrong. My country had a name.

MOTHER   Go on with your solitaire if you like, but don't interrupt me. In a country with no name, and no borders, a little girl was born. She had no name. She was the eighth girl of the family. The eighth daughter! All her sisters had been given the names of their grandmothers and great-grandmothers. There was one great-grandmother whose name had not been taken, but no one could remember it because she had died very young, may God forgive her. So all the inhabitants of this country, although they had many other things to do just to stay alive, God willing, braving the locusts, which, without pity, ravaged the crops, confronting the invaders who, with even less pity, ate everything the locusts, by the goodness of their souls, had forgotten… so all the inhabitants of this country, from the youngest to the oldest, searched, from morning to night, searched without resting to find the name of the forgotten great-grandmother. And the little girl, who had no name, may God help her, waited and waited. Then one day when she—

MONIQUE/KAOKAB   I'm going to bed.

MOTHER   You're giving up. You're afraid to tell Samira's story, aren't you?

MONIQUE/KAOKAB   But she's dead!

MOTHER   That's exactly why you should tell her story.

MONIQUE/KAOKAB   It won't bring her back to life.

MOTHER   *(in pain and anger)* No, it won't bring her back, but I need to hear her name spoken by someone besides me. I don't want to be the only one who remembers she existed, that she was alive, so alive, so beautiful it made you breathless, so funny she could make a foreigner forget his own country. Sparkling like the morning dew. Her voice cut through the darkness of our lives. She was alive and they killed her, they killed my child…

MONIQUE/KAOKAB   *(taking her in her arms)* Stop torturing yourself. Stop. You can't ask the world to suffer in your place, nobody can remember in your place. You are your own memory and you will die with it.

MOTHER   *(crying out)* No. I don't want her death to be lost. I want her death to serve life. I want her body mixed with my tears to nourish our memory. I want her blood to give birth. I want… I want… I want…

MONIQUE/KAOKAB   So do I, *ya oum Samira*, but what can—

MOTHER   *(with great force)* Kaokab, if you don't want to tell her story, then write it. Write, I don't care in what language, just write.

MONIQUE/KAOKAB   *(helplessly)* I've tried… I have… I can't do it. Everything I write is trivial compared to the knot in my stomach, compared to the lava drowning the world. I know that memory can only be carried down through art, literature, true art, but I just can't find the way.

MOTHER   You have to. That's all. You have to.

MONIQUE/KAOKAB   I can't... I can't.

> *The MOTHER runs to the desk. She ruffles through the papers feverishly.*

MOTHER   All these words? In all these words there must be one shaped like a knife, one that is stronger than the silence of death.

> *The MOTHER grabs a page and begins to read.*

I learned of war through a distorting lens
from images dreams nightmares and guilt
I learned of war through each of my own who displaced disoriented exiled
one after another
and those who could not escape
and those who lived with blind hope

I learned of war by turning away
I learned of war by refusing to see or to hear
I learned of war by covering my ears
and pretending to go on living
I learned of war through denial and tearing up the newspaper
I learned of war in spite of my constant refusal to learn
I learned of war on my childhood
on my peaceful red village
shattered to pieces occupied territory

I learned that innocence was dead forever
that eviscerated bodies can be used for barricades
piled one on the other in a reeking mountain

Sitting at my desk
I wonder what they did with all the smelly corpses
I wonder sitting at my desk can you be numbed to the stench of the corpses
does a heart smell like a foot, an eye, or a gut
do the flies, the roaches, the rats wait until the soul breaks free and rises
can the soul find its way through the smoke of the street
or does the soul suffocate too

Sitting at my desk clutching to my indispensable
objects, I wonder do dogs and cats still live in the streets
of Beirut Babylon Bethlehem
do dogs and cats like to lick human blood
have the dogs and the cats become used to the sound of bombs
of machine guns of children crying of the wounded screaming
of a woman wailing the loss of her first born
does the wailing change when it's the third or the fourth

child who gives up the last drop of blood to the pavement
does the father, the mother, the grandmother have any tears left
where is the hidden fountain
does a day come when the body hands in its resignation saying
"sorry I don't want to fight anymore"

Is life stronger than death
do flowers still grow in tin cans along the balconies
of Bethlehem Baghdad Beirut
are there any windowpanes left
are there still children playing in the streets
do they wait until the corpses are removed or do they use them as
toys, playing at war or building empires,
constructing fortresses of human flesh

Are their blocks their dolls their balls and their trucks
forever stained with blood
in the streets of hundreds of towns zillions of
flies have sucked the blood of millions of boys killed by their
brothers while their sister sat at her desk, writing or not,
weeping in silence

In the streets of hundreds of towns scorching the world
rats and flies and roaches and bugs of all kind
are licking their chops preparing to feast

In the aseptic offices of a few dozen cities they're licking
their chops, rats of all kinds,
counting their yen their marks their dollars and pounds

In the streets of hundreds of Babylons throughout the world
flies rats and roaches suck on the toes of children who cannot
swat them away and meanwhile I write or I don't,
I weep and say nothing

In the houses of hundreds of cities children open their toy
chests and scratch their head choosing a game that will distract
them for a few minutes and meanwhile I write or I don't
I weep and say nothing
and in those cities bright coloured garbage cans
the pantry of a million anonymous people
without name, or address, or country,
they are silent as I am today,
I have stopped writing, I have stopped crying I
say nothing.

> *A long pause. MONIQUE/KAOKAB returns to her game of solitaire. The
> MOTHER stands staring at her. She seems naked without her rug in her arms.*

Where's Samira in all that? I didn't see her.

MONIQUE/KAOKAB   She was in every single word.

MOTHER   But I want to hear her name. I want you to talk about her, not your silly writer's problems.

MONIQUE/KAOKAB   Do you really want me to tell Samira's story?

MOTHER   Yes, I do.

MONIQUE/KAOKAB   The real Samira? Your child? My child? The child of the whole planet?

MOTHER   Yes, that's what I want.

MONIQUE/KAOKAB   *(firmly, enunciating each syllable) Ya oum Samira*, your daughter Samira, our child, held her head high, kept her eyes wide open and marched straight through the minefield. She chose her own death. *(The MOTHER's head reels under the shock.)* Samira chose her own death.

MOTHER   *Khawta bil marra!*[18] *Khawta bil marra!* You are crazy! You are completely mad!

> The MOTHER picks up her rug and heads for the door. MONIQUE/
> KAOKAB holds her back. She tries to wrench the MOTHER's rug away.
> They struggle.

MONIQUE/KAOKAB   Samira didn't want to die piece by piece, eaten away by fate. She wanted a real death. She wanted to make a choice, just once in her life, to decide her goddamned destiny.

SAMIRA   Yes, I said no. No more hope. Hope had become a bad habit.
Like a drug that's lost its effect.
I said no when my friend Amal died. Course I'd seen dozens die. But Amal's hit me head-on, crushed my lungs, slashed my heart open, cut off my feet, ripped out my tongue.
Amal decided for me. Did *she* have a choice?
I lived in the muck. To go on living was to give up. I decided to die. I broke the contract I had with life. Life never kept its part of the bargain, I don't see why I should have.

MONIQUE/KAOKAB   When Amal died Samira knew she couldn't go on. To go on living would have been to give up, to—

MOTHER   —Who is Amal?

MONIQUE/KAOKAB   *(without missing a beat)* Her friend who was killed, tortured, raped, torn to pieces. The one they had to tie together to bury. Samira saw her with her eyes open…. She saw Amal…

---

[18]   *Khawta bil marra!* [You are crazy!]

MOTHER   Samira had friends, many friends who died. None of them were named Amal.

MONIQUE/KAOKAB   Her name isn't important. Her name was Amal, Amira, Anne, Suzanne, Salam, Sylvia, whatever.

MOTHER   No, there's no "whatever." If you don't know anything, then keep your mouth shut.

MONIQUE/KAOKAB   But you wanted me to—

MOTHER   *(furious)* To speak is not to lie. To write is to tell the truth.

> *MONIQUE/KAOKAB grabs her papers as if she were looking for the truth. She begins to read. Her voice changes little by little. She begins to resemble Samira.*

MONIQUE/KAOKAB   That morning I left for school, like any non-normal day when there was a ceasefire. My mother had made aarouss, she always said "aarouss" like in the village, not sandwich like everybody else in town. Bread and black olives with a little olive oil, the same kind we ate every single day. We complained sometimes, just as a game. "Oh no, not olives again!" "If your grandparents didn't have the olive trees, I don't know where we'd be today. Noushkor Allah, we still have olives, noushkor Allah. And they're good for your health."

But nobody said anything that day. I hadn't said anything for a long time. I waited for the bus with my brothers and sisters, as usual. Mother watched from the balcony, as usual. We lived on the fourth floor. I looked up... for the last time.... I'd been walking around with my eyes shut for months.... I saw my mother bend down and run her hands through the perfume plant she'd brought from her village... she caressed the leaves and brought her hands to her nose. She stayed that way for a long time with her eyes closed, breathing the perfume.

All of a sudden she opened her eyes like a bee stung her, she saw us, she turned toward me, she looked at me...

MONIQUE/KAOKAB & SAMIRA   She looked at me... *(rapidly)* and then we climbed on the bus.

SAMIRA   There was a ceasefire that day... the nine hundred and forty-second one.... Nobody thought it would hold, but everybody pretended it would... you had to lie to yourself to.... I don't know whose plan it was that day, whether it was an American plan or Russian, Zionist, Baasist, Falangist, or whatever... a ceasefire of the allies or the enemies.... We didn't even know the difference between allies and enemies anymore. We didn't know who was calling the shots. The devil himself seemed to be holding the camera. Wide-angle shots, three-hundred-and-sixty-degree panoramas at breakneck speed... only the devil could move that fast. Human beings, with or without Satan, have always been more gifted for war plans than for peace plans. I mean even in the movies, look at all the special effects and stuff used for the big blasters.... For a movie about life... all you need is a little camera, a few spots to light the actors' faces. *(pause)* I decided to do my own film, to call my own shots, to see with my own eyes... or close the lens when I wished. I wanted to see from above, below, all sides, close-up, zoom in, zoom out, distant shot and fade-out...

MOTHER   No. It's not true. Samira loved life too much to...

MONIQUE/KAOKAB   Maybe that's why she did it. She loved life too much. So she took the plunge.

MOTHER   No no no no no no no. They killed her. They killed her. They tore the life from her body.

MONIQUE/KAOKAB   You're right, they killed her. If Samira had lived someplace else, she wouldn't have marched toward the music or the bombs, that music she knew so well. She wouldn't have run from street to street looking for the death machine. No, Samira, like so many others who love life too much, who will not settle for anything less, would have gone home, locked the bathroom door, filled the bathtub with hot water, taken a shiny little object that makes no noise, and sunk into the scalding water.... She sank into the heat... peacefully... *ya oum Samira*, your child, my child, our earth child was swept away in the steaming lava.

MOTHER   You really want to finish me for good.

MONIQUE/KAOKAB   No, I just want to understand. What holds us to life... with all its misery? Why one day do we decide that's enough? Why do we draw the line that specific day? Why do we cut the thread that instant? We could have done it a thousand times before. Why do we say, at that instant, we cannot, we will not go on?

> *Disarmed, ravaged, the MOTHER walks around the room.*
>
> *MONIQUE/KAOKAB picks up her rug and unfolds it slowly. She sets out a brass tray filled with apples on the rug. She gestures, inviting the MOTHER, and then sits on the rug. After a long pause the MOTHER joins her. The two women look at each other a long moment. MONIQUE/KAOKAB holds out her arms. The MOTHER offers her prayer rug. MONIQUE/KAOKAB cradles the rug and sings.*
>
> *During the following scene and accelerating until the end of the play, bodies fall from the drawers and the bookshelves. They fall around and sometimes touch the two women who become increasingly serene. The bodies fall into a mountain of inert flesh and then rise, scale the walls, and fall again. The "Abou Zoulof" melody that MONIQUE/KAOKAB initiates shifts and swells until the end of the play.*

(singing)

Haiyhat ya bou zoulof
Aayni ya moulaya
Ya alb safeyr ma 'aou
Ta trajey'ao leya
La tahzaney 'al heyjr
Ya 'ayney la 'dhoubey
Mahma yagheyb el badr
Wa 'ateymo el droubey. [19]

MOTHER   *(smiling sadly)* So you haven't forgotten everything…

> *MONIQUE/KAOKAB smiles. A pause. She gestures to ask permission to open the prayer rug. The MOTHER nods. MONIQUE/KAOKAB unfolds the rug, admires it, strokes it tenderly.*

MONIQUE/KAOKAB   It's beautiful.

MOTHER   Samira always kept it with her.

MONIQUE/KAOKAB   It's beautiful.

MOTHER   Yours too, it's beautiful.

MONIQUE/KAOKAB   It's the one my mother brought with her when she came. It was a wedding present from her parents. We slept on it over a year. Then we got beds. *(pause)*

Would you like an apple?

MOTHER   I'd like some grapes from our fields. I'd like to eat them with my hands full of dirt, sitting on the ground, watching the horizon slip far, far away, beyond the third mountain. I want to be a child again. I want to erase everything and start all over.

MONIQUE/KAOKAB   Look at this apple. Isn't it lovely? It grew here. Try it at least.

MOTHER   How can anything grow under all this snow?

MONIQUE/KAOKAB   Snow melts. Winter always comes to an end.

MOTHER   You believe that?

MONIQUE/KAOKAB   Everything comes to an end.

MOTHER   Samira's life, did it come to an end?

MONIQUE/KAOKAB   Samira's life was stolen from her. That's not the same thing. It's an abnormal cycle… which has lasted a few eons.

---

[19] "Abou Zoulof" is a Lebanese folk song with a plaintive melody. The first two lines are opening calls that cannot be translated. Loosely translated, the following lines are: "My heart goes with him/ To bring him back again to me/ Don't be sad because of this exile/ My eye does not melt away/ In spite of the waning moon/ And the darkening path."

MOTHER   Kaokab, tell me, do you think it will end one day? Is there any more room in our bones and our hearts for suffering? Does pain also die and make room for something else?

MONIQUE/KAOKAB   Everything has an end. I think so, *ya oum Samira.* If a book is written, then begin another. You can't erase the first one, start from zero, be little again. You have to go on. Keep growing. Keep learning. Stick your foot in the crack, which will somehow open things up. We are all very vain… me especially. To think that I can carry down my memory or that of my own is the height of vanity… but I have to try. I don't want to be crushed. Pain is everywhere, but so is life, it's irrepressible, here, there, everywhere… despite the odds…. I don't want to drown… go under, maybe, but come up again…. I want to write as long as I am alive.

> *She holds out the tray again. The MOTHER takes an apple, rolls it in her hands, brings it to her nose, and breathes deeply with her eyes closed.*

> *The bodies continue falling, rising, scaling the wall. SAMIRA's voice rises over the music.*

SAMIRA   In my mother's belly I learned to count, to sing, to get used to things. In the belly of the earth I am learning how to laugh. All by myself. I am learning the game of patience. *El sabr meyfteh el faraj.*[20] Is patience the secret to finding the light?

> *The lights come down.*

> *The music continues.*

> *The end.*

---

[20] An Arabic saying, *El sabr meyfteh el faraj* means "Patience is the key to deliverance," or "Patience is the key to the light."

A Line in the Sand

by Guillermo Verdecchia
and Marcus Youssef

Guillermo Verdecchia and Marcus Youssef

A writer of drama, fiction, and film; a director, dramaturge, and actor, Verdecchia's work has been published, anthologized, seen, and heard on stages, pages, screens, and radios across the country and around the globe. Born in Argentina and educated in Canada, his theatre is characterized by an acute interest in geopolitics, representation, and cultural conflict, as well as a metatheatrical exploration of form and performance styles. He is, with Daniel Brooks, the co-creator of *The Noam Chomsky Lectures* (shortlisted for the Governor General's Literary Award for Drama), a play without characters or plot based on Chomsky's (and Edward S. Herman's) critique of the political economy of human rights and the political economy of the mass media. His one-person play *Fronteras Americanas*, for which he received the Governor General's Literary Award for Drama in 1993, is a theatrical meditation on hemispheric identity. *The Adventures of Ali and Ali and the aXes of Evil*, co-created with Marcus Youssef and Camyar Chai, is a hyperkinetic, postmodern, transnational cabaret that makes hummus out of the war on terror, while *bloom*, which he created for Modern Times Stage Company, bends gender and recent history to revise T.S. Eliot's *The Wasteland*.

From 1999 to 2004, he was Artistic Director of Cahoots Theatre Projects, a Toronto-based company dedicated to producing new intercultural Canadian drama. While there, he served as dramaturge on dozens of plays, produced several new plays, and directed M.J. Kang's *Dreams of Blonde and Blue*, Rahul Varma's *Bhopal*, and *Ali and Ali*. He directed Sunil Kuruvilla's *Rice Boy* for the Stratford Shakespeare Festival in 2009.

In addition to the Governor General's Literary Award for Drama, Verdecchia is a four-time winner of the Chalmers Canadian Play Award, a recipient of Dora and Jessie Awards, and sundry international film festival awards for his short film *Crucero/ Crossroads* made with Ramiro Puerta. His critically acclaimed collection of short fiction, *Citizen Suárez*, is published by Talonbooks. He lives in Toronto, where he is completing a Ph.D., with his partner Tamsin Kelsey and their two children, Anaïs and Theo.

A recipient of both the Alcan Performing Arts Award and the Chalmer's Canadian Play Award, Marcus Youssef is best known for his plays, including *Ali and Ali and the aXes of Evil*, *Ali & Ali 7*, *Adrift*, *The Bobsledder of Baghdad*, *3299: Forms in Order*, *Apathy House*, *A Line in the Sand*, and more than a dozen radio plays for the CBC. His stage plays have been produced at theatres and major festivals across North America and Europe, from World Stage to Magnetic North, to the Kennedy Centre in Washington and Teatro Ca'Foscari in Venice and have been translated into Czech and Italian.

In addition to his plays, Marcus's fiction and non-fiction have been broadcast on CBC radio and *The Roundup* (where he was writer-in-residence) and have been published in *Grain*, *The Vancouver Sun*, *This Magazine*, *Geist*, *Vancouver Magazine*, *The Globe and Mail*, and *Crank Magazine*, which Marcus co-founded with Matt Hern in 1999. As a director Marcus's 2009 production of *Are We There Yet?* won three Jessie Richardson Theatre Awards in the Young Audiences category, including Outstanding Production and Outstanding Direction. Marcus also hosts, lectures, and reads at universities and literary/political events across the country. He has been an Assistant Professor of Theatre and Development at Concordia University and in 2009 was elected to the executive of the Vancouver municipal political party, the Coalition of Progressive Electors. Marcus is a graduate of the National Theatre School of Canada and holds an M.F.A. in Creative Writing from the University of British Columbia. He is currently Co-Artistic Producer of Neworld Theatre in Vancouver.

A Line in the Sand, co-written by Guillermo and Marcus, deliberately conflates the First Gulf War on Iraq and the 1993 torture and murder of Shidane Arone, a sixteen-year-old Somali, at the hands of Canadian soldiers on a humanitarian mission. Like much of their work, *A Line in the Sand* rejects the "necessary illusion" that Canada is a nation of peacekeepers and interrogates the role of media representation in geopolitical relations.

For

Souad and John Moussa, in memory

—M.Y.

Alejandro and Roberto Verdecchia

—G.V.

Thanks to: Karim Alrawi, Robin Benger, Mordecai Briemberg, Dennis Foon, Urjo Kareda, Laila Maher, Doug and Janette Pirie, George Youssef, Roleene Youssef, Norman Armour and Darren Copeland at Wireless Grafitti, Roy Surette at Touchstone Theatre, and Donna Spencer at the Firehall Theatre; friends on and around Commercial Drive.

Special thanks to Tamsin Kelsey for tremendous support, patience, and more; to Amanda Fritzlan for love, wisdom, and level-headed advice; and Zakaraiya Youssef, born the night of our first preview.

The authors also wish to acknowledge the invaluable contributions of the actors who performed in the Vancouver and Toronto productions.

A Line in the Sand was first produced in Vancouver at the New Play Centre in April 1995 with the following company:

MERCER	Vincent Gale
SADIQ	Camyar Chai
COLONEL	Tom Butler
NORMAN	Norman Armour
MARCUS PATRICK YOUSSEF	Marcus Youssef

Directed by Guillermo Verdecchia
Stage Managed by Michel Bisson
Designed by Adrian Muir

• • •

The play was revised and presented in Toronto at the Tarragon Theatre in April 1996 with the following company:

MERCER	Vincent Gale
SADIQ / ACTOR 2	Camyar Chai
COLONEL / ACTOR 1	Tom Butler

Directed by Guillermo Verdecchia
Stage Managed by Kristen Gilbert
Designed by Glenn Davidson and Sue Lepage

The text that follows is from the Tarragon production.

Characters

MERCER, a Canadian soldier, approximately twenty years old.

SADIQ, a Palestinian boy, approximately seventeen years old.

COLONEL, a Canadian soldier, at least forty-five years old.

Setting

The play is set in the desert just outside of Doha, Qatar, during Operation Desert Shield in the Persian Gulf in the late fall of 1990.

A LINE IN THE SAND

ACT ONE

Scene One

MERCER is alone in the sand. His gun is out of reach. He splashes water from a canteen onto his face. SADIQ enters.

SADIQ   Hey.

Mister. Man.

Hey. Military man.

MERCER stops.

MERCER   Paul James Mercer. Private. Third Battalion, Royal Canadian Regiment. I am serving with the multinational coalition—

SADIQ   It is okay. I have no gun

MERCER   Who are you?

SADIQ   No one. I come in peace.

SADIQ sets his large nylon bag down and MERCER grabs his gun.

MERCER   Get your fucking hands in the air!

SADIQ   Please, please, it is okay—

MERCER   I said, get 'em in the air!

SADIQ   Don't shoot!

MERCER   Shut up! Who the fuck are you?

SADIQ   Mohammed Sadiq Hamid. Not soldier—Palestinian. Look, look, nice, nice, no gun, no gun…

MERCER   You're trespassing. This is a militarized zone under the jurisdiction of the United Nations.

SADIQ   No soldiers here. Only water and sand.

MERCER   It's close enough.

SADIQ   As you say.

MERCER   So fuck off.

SADIQ   Please, just small moment…. It's okay, I got what you want.

MERCER   Why's your English so good?

SADIQ   I study extra in school.

MERCER   What for?

SADIQ   My uncle in City of Kansas. Owns many homes. Soon I will go. To America.

MERCER   You Palestinians are the guys we're supposed to watch out for. Might try to car bomb our air base.

SADIQ   Not me, Military Man. I don't care about that.

MERCER   You part of the uprising, that—uh—in-ti-faggot thing?

SADIQ   Intifada.

MERCER   Whatever the hell it's called.

SADIQ   That is West Bank, Israel. Is one thousand kilometre from here.

MERCER   Saddam is going to get his ass kicked, you know.

SADIQ   You are right. Big tough American soldier like you—must win for sure—

MERCER   I'm not American, kid, I'm Canadian.

SADIQ   Oh. Canadian. Yes! The peacekeepers. *Frère Jacques, Frère Jacques. Dormez-vous….* They teach us this song in school…

MERCER   Oh, yeah.

SADIQ   *Oui.* It is big part of your culture, yes? You speak French, yes?

MERCER   No, I'm from Vancouver.

SADIQ   I could not live like that, all the snow…. I like sun—get dark in the Canada for eight months in year, yes?

MERCER   No.

SADIQ   You lying. I know, we learn all about the Canada. Special textbook donated from your government. We look in book and laugh at clothes you people wear. You cut big bear open and climb inside.

Your skin is like snow, Canada. Maybe you going to melt.

So tell me, what would you like. I got much for sell to Canadian soldier.

MERCER   Like what?

SADIQ   *(cautiously pulls photographs from his bag)* Pictures, photograph, look at this.

MERCER   *(relaxes, finally puts his gun down)* Holy shit.

SADIQ   Good hey? Very popular with American soldier. Good for Canadian, too huh. And this.

MERCER   Fuck—where do you get this?

SADIQ   My boss, Salim. He is big merchant, buy from Americans in Cairo. They sell to US Army. For men on base. Is good for Canada too, hey. You like?

MERCER   Fuck, this heat.

SADIQ   It's okay, Vancouver?

MERCER   Yeah, yeah. I'm fine.

SADIQ   *(hands MERCER water bottle)* Here.

MERCER   Fucking desert. Fucking sun.

SADIQ   Very good price.

MERCER   How much you want?

SADIQ   How many?

MERCER   Just the ones I saw—

SADIQ   Twenty dollars.

MERCER   All right.

Here.

They exchange.

SADIQ   What is this? This purple, with bird eating fish. Is no good.

MERCER   It's two ten-dollar bills. Twenty bucks.

SADIQ   Ha. You can't fool me, Vancouver. I must go to City of Kansas. Need hard money to get there.

MERCER   That's as hard as you're going to get. Canadian dollars.

SADIQ   Is no good to me.

MERCER   Why the fuck not?

SADIQ   Salim, my boss, he say everything must be American dollars. When I start, I sell cigar to skinny black soldier for Bangladeshi dollar, Salim just laugh. Make me pay.

MERCER   Well, Canada's not fucking Bangladesh, pal.

SADIQ   Very big price—from Cuba.

MERCER   I'll give you forty. It's worth like thirty-five US.

SADIQ   Now we talk turkey.

MERCER   Right on, brother.

SADIQ   You want more? Different? I have cigar, cigarettes. Marlboro. American Camel.

MERCER   Don't smoke.

SADIQ   Radio? I have radio.

MERCER   Got one.

SADIQ   CD. Michael Jackson.

MERCER   No.

SADIQ   Tape for video—Madonna. "Like a Virgin." Nice shirt, blue jean from Guess, what you want, I can get.

MERCER   I got everything I need on the base.

SADIQ   Canada Dry One.

MERCER   How'd you know that?

SADIQ   I know many things.

MERCER   Right. You staying here?

SADIQ   No, I go to Kansas.

MERCER   I mean here, the beach. You staying?

SADIQ   You want I should stay?

MERCER   No, I want you should go.

SADIQ   This beach private of GI Vancouver?

MERCER   Look, nothing personal. I'm just getting a little bored. This is my time off.

SADIQ   Is okay, I have work to do. You want more picture you know where to find.

Scene Two

SADIQ   Welcome back, Canada Dry One.

MERCER   How's it going?

SADIQ   Special today— *(holds up perfume bottle)* Obsession. Very nice for send to girlfriend.

MERCER   No, thanks…

SADIQ   Yes, you very smart. Not real Obsession, is only from Cairo.

Pause.

You want more picture? Very expensive. More than before.

MERCER   Right.

SADIQ   For you, I get real good. Best price.

MERCER   Yeah? Let's see.

> *SADIQ pulls out photographs. MERCER studies them intently as SADIQ shows him each one.*

No. No. No. Yes. No. No. Yes. *(beat)*

This woman—she looks dead.

SADIQ   Pretend. Acting.

MERCER   How do you know?

SADIQ   Salim, my boss, he say no one gets hurt.

MERCER   Better than the real thing, eh?

SADIQ   I do not understand.

MERCER   Just a joke, kid. How much for the three?

SADIQ   One hundred US dollars.

MERCER   Forget it, man.

SADIQ   What you say, boss. *(He begins to put the photographs away.)*

MERCER   I'll give you fifty. Canadian.

SADIQ   Purple fish? For beg and steal from Salim? Then I never go to Kansas.

MERCER   Seventy-five.

SADIQ   Ho, for you, okay. Seven five.

MERCER   Special offer, huh?

SADIQ   What?

MERCER   You're giving me a deal, eh?

SADIQ   What is your name?

MERCER   Mercer.

SADIQ   Mercer. I am Sadiq.

MERCER   Sadiq?

SADIQ   Sadiq. Yes, we make deal. Seven five purple fish.

MERCER   Here, Sadiq.

Hands SADIQ money.

SADIQ   Look, I have nice envelope for picture. Customer is always right.

MERCER   Yeah.

Pause.

What are you doing?

SADIQ   Look at water. Beautiful.

My brother is over there. *(He points.)* In West Bank. I not see since I am twelve. You have brother?

MERCER   How old are you?

SADIQ   Sixteen.

MERCER   Sixteen, huh?

SADIQ   And you?

MERCER   I'm twenty.

SADIQ   I am seventeen very soon. One—two month. You skinny to be soldier.

MERCER   What?

SADIQ   You very skinny. Americans soldier much more, you know, with beef. Canadian soldier is much less beef, yes?

MERCER   Well, I don't know if skinny is the word I'd use but—we're not all the same, you know.

SADIQ   You—different. How you different?

MERCER   I don't know.

I went to university.

SADIQ   I do not understand.

MERCER   Most of these guys, they join up 'cause they got nothing else. Or they want a free education. Not me.

SADIQ   Why you join?

MERCER   I wanted to get my shit together. I was at Queen's University. What a fucking waste of time.

SADIQ   School. Puh. School is no good.

MERCER   You're telling me.

SADIQ   My brother real good in school. Always top. Now he is in prison.

MERCER   Oh yeah?

SADIQ   Here I learn real life. But my father, he know I not go to school, he would break my throat.

MERCER   Fuck. When I quit school and joined up, my father freaked.

SADIQ   Freak?

MERCER   He got really angry.

SADIQ   For why?

MERCER   He's a government big shot. Makes him look bad, his son's a stupid soldier.

SADIQ   Yes. You like me.

MERCER   What?

SADIQ   You... like... me.

MERCER   No I don't.

SADIQ   No, I say, "You like me."

MERCER   I don't even know you.

SADIQ   No, no. Like me. For angry father you join army—come to Qatar. Me also. Work for Salim and go to Kansas.

MERCER   No. I didn't join because of him.

SADIQ   Then why you join?

MERCER   I told you. I wanted discipline.

A few months ago there was this thing that happened in Canada with our Indians, they blockaded this town—I watched it on TV at our base in Germany. This soldier—some stupid private—standing at the barricade while this Indian's calling him the worst kind of shit. Guy's spit landing right in his face—soldier didn't move a muscle, not even a twitch. Two inches away, injun's screaming, calling him goof, fuck-wad, cocksucker—

But nothing could touch that guy. That's why I joined.

SADIQ   Why Indian so for angry?

MERCER   Oh, fuck, I don't know. It was some fucking golf course they wanted or something.

SADIQ   And mother? She afraid you go to war—be shoot and killed?

MERCER   Fuck off.

SADIQ   Why you anger, Vancouver? The heat not good to you. You should go slow. Rest. Stay in base.

MERCER   You should fuck off.

SADIQ   I go. You want more picture. I come back three days.

MERCER   I won't be here so don't fucking bother.

Scene Three

SADIQ   You say you will not come back.

MERCER   Changed my mind. Okay?

SADIQ   Okay.

MERCER   Look, I'm sorry I weirded out on you last time.

SADIQ   I have pictures. I have made selection.

MERCER   Oh yeah?

SADIQ   Yes. *(shows MERCER pictures)*

MERCER   Fuck.

SADIQ   You soldiers stay here a while, I make it to Kansas City no time. Flash. Six months.

MERCER   Must be your personal stash.

SADIQ   I do not understand.

MERCER   Ah, c'mon, don't tell me you don't sneak a quick pull over these in the back of your boss's tent.

SADIQ   I not look at picture. They are not for me.

MERCER   I can't get 'em out of my head. During exercises, on watch—I get up in the middle of the night, sneak 'em out of my tent in my shirt. I go to the fucking latrine for Christ's sake.

I haven't seen my girlfriend in a long fucking time. Based in Germany. But these pictures, they're something else.

SADIQ   Top quality.

MERCER   How much for these?

SADIQ   Today, for you—fifty purple fish.

MERCER   Deal.

SADIQ   Deal.

MERCER   Listen, these are way better than what we can get on the base. It's all *Playboy* and lacy shit. I'll meet you here once a week and buy the hardest stuff you can get your hands on.

SADIQ   You buy every week?

MERCER   Yeah.

SADIQ   Yes, this is good, Mercer.

MERCER   Good. It's a deal then.

SADIQ   Deal.

MERCER   Great.

SADIQ   Very good.

You are not so white today. Gold, like the sun. Look. I am so brown. Your nose straight. And your hair. Harrison Ford.

One time I go to the hair cutter in my neighbourhood, in Doha. Stupid ass. Say I want him to make my hair straight. Like movie star I tell him. I have money. I will pay you to do it. I know it is possible. I read about it in magazines. But he laugh at me, says, Sadiq, you always want to be somebody else. You should know, he says, all the other boys, they laugh at you, so worried about how you look, talking about America and movie stars. I do that to your hair, your father, he would kill me. He will say I am traitor to the Arabs, to Palestine, make people not go to my store.

MERCER   Here.

Hands SADIQ money.

SADIQ   More purple fish?

MERCER   Don't tell anyone. Other soldiers.

SADIQ   What?

MERCER   About this. What I told you before. Everything.

SADIQ   Yes. *(He pockets the money.)* We have secret.

Scene Four

SADIQ   My uncle and his wife, when they get to America, right away, they change their names. Here, they Souad and Maher Moussa, but there, no, they Sue and Mike Marshall. He play baseball. In big league.

MERCER   Your uncle plays pro ball?

SADIQ   Yes?

MERCER   Your uncle—he plays professional baseball?

SADIQ   Oh, no. Mike Marshall play baseball. Pitcher for Twins of Min-e-soda. My uncle, Maher, he name himself for Mike Marshall. And Souad, she wanted to name Talullah, like Tallulah Bankhead, star from movie. But Maher is big guy, say to Souad—Mike Marshall wife name Sue Marshall, good for her, good for you, too.

Many years Uncle Mike work very hard for rich American serving dinner in hotel restaurant. Souad clean room. They save all their money, buy house in bad part of city. Then they rent to black people. Make more money and buy more house. Keep going until Maher, he is Mike, rich guy in Kansas. Salim, he promise I make enough selling to soldiers during the war, he will send me to uncle in America. He will make sure.

MERCER Sadiq.

SADIQ turns to face MERCER. MERCER takes photograph.

SADIQ You have camera.

MERCER I do.

SADIQ Why?

MERCER To take pictures. You know.

SADIQ Of?

MERCER Everything. The desert.

SADIQ You have flash build in?

MERCER No.

SADIQ Is no good. Salim, my boss—

MERCER I know he's your boss, you say that every time you say his fucking name.

SADIQ Salim, he have small camera, like this. Excellent picture. Flash build in. Motor for film. All automatic.

MERCER Those are just for snapshots. They're toys.

SADIQ Take good picture. I see them. Good colours, bright. Flash for inside.

MERCER This camera lets me control everything. Shutter speed, aperture. Those little ones—say you're backlit, right? You're in front of a window and there's a lot of light streaming in. Well, with those little ones the camera gets confused and underexposes your face. It comes out in shadow.

SADIQ No, he have flash build in.

MERCER Right.

SADIQ Is good camera. Take good pictures.

MERCER Well, this one takes better pictures. Trust me.

SADIQ Okay. I trust you.

Here. Take picture of me.

SADIQ begins to pose; MERCER takes photographs. SADIQ's poses are based on magazine images, impersonating models, movie stars, etc. He takes off his shirt for the last pose or two.

MERCER   I should get going.

SADIQ   You go back to base?

MERCER   Yeah. So…

SADIQ   Here. *(gives MERCER envelope)*

MERCER   Great. And this for you. *(pays him)* All right, I'm outta here. See you in a week.

SADIQ   Wait, Mercer.

You must go back now?

MERCER   Yeah, I got work to do. I'm not on holiday, you know.

SADIQ   For you. *(offers MERCER another envelope)*

MERCER   What? What's this?

SADIQ   For you. Extra.

MERCER   I haven't got any more money.

SADIQ   No. Just for you. Free. A gift. Today, I do very good, sell much. I make you a gift.

MERCER   You sure?

SADIQ   Yes.

MERCER   What's the catch?

SADIQ   I do not understand.

MERCER   What do you want in return? What's the catch?

SADIQ   No. Gift. To you. From Sadiq.

MERCER   Why?

SADIQ   What why? You understand gift, Vancouver?

MERCER   Yes. I know what a gift is.

SADIQ   Okay.

MERCER   Why?

SADIQ   Why not?

MERCER   *(accepts second envelope)* All right.

SADIQ   Stay a little.

MERCER   And do what?

SADIQ   Tell me of America.

MERCER   I gotta go. I'll see you in a week.

Scene Five

SADIQ   *(sings)* Rudolph the red-nosed reindeer. Had a very tiny nose. And if you ever saw it, you would even say it glows.

    We see on TV with Salim.

    Merry Christmas, Mercer.

MERCER   It's not till next week.

    Pause.

SADIQ   Tell me about base. Canada Dry One.

MERCER   What about it?

SADIQ   What you do.

MERCER   Sweet dick.

SADIQ   Sweet?

MERCER   Nothing. It's totally boring.

SADIQ   You lying. Top secret. I see jeeps, many soldiers run, planes. You practise?

MERCER   Yeah, we practise, neutralize fucking sand dunes. Broman's always cooking up some stupid little exercise to keep us busy. Now that everything's all set up there's nothing to do.

SADIQ   Nothing?

    A pause, MERCER watches the waves.

    On base you have telephone?

MERCER   Yeah, of course. We have lots of phones.

SADIQ   In America, everyone have two telephones in house. In cars too. My family, never a telephone.

MERCER   Oh well.

SADIQ   Tell me about America.

MERCER   Shit, Sadiq. Just shut up for a minute.

SADIQ   Tell only a little.

MERCER   I'm not American.

SADIQ   But still you know. Tell me.

MERCER   Okay. First, it's not what you think. It ain't like TV.

SADIQ   Salim, my boss, he have CNN. We see all sides about America.

MERCER   Yeah, well, don't believe everything you see. This place you think you're going, it's not real, it's in your head. Your uncle Mike, I don't know what he told you.

SADIQ   Uncle Mike say any person work hard in America they can be rich. Like him.

MERCER   Fuck that shit. The guys in my regiment, most of their families got nothing. On welfare or farmers working their asses off. Everybody's got guns in the States, they're fucking maniacs. In Canada we got health care. In the States, you're poor and you have a heart attack, they don't fucking care, they'll turn you away from the hospital.

SADIQ   My Uncle Mike, he say only lazy people are poor in America. If you work you can be rich.

MERCER   What's this thing with being rich? Money doesn't help, you know. You think that having two TVs is going to do anything for you? Having a car, two cars, big cars, a big house, lots of telephones, you think that's gonna solve your problems? No way, Jose. Let me tell you.

SADIQ   I want to be rich.

   Beat.

Everybody want to be rich.

MERCER   Not everybody.

SADIQ   You know hungry. Yes? You know hungry? No. Look at my shoes, Vancouver. Two years, same shoes. My father, he always moving, work different country, dream of his homeland. Little money he make he give away. To PLO. Stupid poor man work for rich fat man. All I remember, poor, hungry, the same the same the same. I want more. There is more to live.

MERCER   Okay, okay, whatever.

SADIQ   I work make dream come true. I quit school. I will go. You rich, Vancouver. You not know work. You know nothing. You are a child.

MERCER   Hey, I work, asshole. You don't know shit about me or what I've done. You're the child around here.

SADIQ   Is true. Little baby.

   Silence.

Mercer—I get angry, no reason. Sorry.

MERCER   Stop fucking touching me. You're always touching me.

SADIQ   I apologize. I do not want anger to you.

> *A pause.*

My father this morning, he find hashish I have for to sell. He learn I not go to school. He shout and shout at me. I say nothing. He is a fool. I am angry to him not to you.

MERCER   That's a total sob story. My heart bleeds.

SADIQ   You forgive?

MERCER   Massage my feet.

SADIQ   Rub feet? Yes? I know how to good. I do for my sister. Her, how you say, blood… too close?

MERCER   Don't talk.

> *A silence.*

SADIQ   I apologize?

Is good rub?

MERCER   Give me the pictures.

> *SADIQ gives MERCER envelope with pictures. Continues rubbing his foot. MERCER looks at pictures.*

SADIQ   Is good rub?

You should see my father, Mercer. His hands are black from oil. And the smell.

There are four hundred thousand people here in Qatar. Three hundred thousand like my father—idiot foreigner work to make oil men rich. Before they find oil here, these rich men, you know what they do? Dive for pearls. Yes. Jump off old boats, swim and dig and hold their breath until they go blue. Every day, up and down, up and down, dig, swim, dig, swim. But now they are rich.

My father says I am a fool. We need these men. They are our friends. These rich Arabs will help us win our home. Oh, he is thick. There is no oil in Palestine, only sand. When Palestine comes we will only stay here, like the Pakistanis and Indians he works with, so far from our home it will not matter that we have one.

My father knows I will go to Uncle Mike in Kansas City. Fly across the ocean. TWA. If he tries to stop me I will say—look how much money I make working for Salim. And you know how I get it? Yes. Just like they say. From American soldier. GI Joe. Bombing and killing your brothers and sisters in Iraq.

I live in Qatar. In America I will be born.

MERCER   Kiss my foot.

Scene Six

MERCER   Sadiq!

SADIQ   Mercer, hello. You are waiting?

MERCER   A while. I couldn't get away yesterday. Fucking Broman. So I came today. I didn't know whether you'd come by.

SADIQ   No.

MERCER   What?

SADIQ   I am here.

MERCER   You are. Me too.

SADIQ   Yes. Here we are.

MERCER   So you got some?

SADIQ   What?

MERCER   Pictures.

SADIQ   You want more picture?

MERCER   Yeah. We have a deal.

SADIQ   No. No picture left.

MERCER   Why not?

SADIQ   All sold. Very popular with soldier. Salim, my boss, he sell out.

MERCER   None?

SADIQ   You have many picture already.

MERCER   We made a deal.

SADIQ   I have cassettes. Music. Metallica. Guns to Roses.

MERCER   I don't want any fucking cassettes.

What fucking good are you? Jesus, I've been waiting out here for a fucking hour. You don't have any left.

SADIQ   No. I say already. No more picture.

MERCER   Bullshit. Let me see your bag.

SADIQ   Why?

MERCER   Let me see.

SADIQ   You don't believe?

MERCER   No. Show me.

>   *He tries to grab bag.*

SADIQ   No.

MERCER   Open it!

What's this? Bullshit. Don't have any pictures. What are these eh? Lying little fuck.

SADIQ   No, not for sale.

MERCER   I'm not buying. I'm taking.

SADIQ   Mercer, pictures, pictures. No good. Only picture. Why you want so many pictures?

MERCER   What do you think, raghead?

SADIQ   You want for fuck? Pictures?

MERCER   That's right. I want for fuck. You know what that is?

SADIQ   Why picture?

MERCER   'Cause that's what I like.

SADIQ   You like.

MERCER   Right.

SADIQ   Why you do this to me, Mercer?

MERCER   I didn't do anything.

SADIQ   Why you ask me to rub feet?

MERCER   What?

SADIQ   I go now.

MERCER   No, hey look. I'll pay you for these. Don't get all fucking touchy. You're the one that fucked up not me.

>   *MERCER pays him. SADIQ starts to go.*

Where you going? Stick around.

SADIQ   You have pictures. What else you want now?

MERCER   Nothing. I don't want anything.

SADIQ   Okay. I go.

MERCER   Hey, fuck. Relax. Let's have a smoke or something.

SADIQ   I have no more hash. Look if you don't believe.

MERCER   No, okay. I believe you. Why you in such a hurry all of a sudden?

SADIQ   I have work to do.

MERCER   Fuck that. Come on, this is my time off.

SADIQ   So?

MERCER   So tell me something.

SADIQ   What?

MERCER   I don't know. You usually have a million things to say. Tell me about your family.

SADIQ   Why?

MERCER   'Cause I want to know.

SADIQ   No, you just want pictures.

MERCER   Okay, fuck off then.

SADIQ   No, you fuck off. This is my beach too.

>   *Silence.*

We are six in my family. Father, mother, two sisters, brother, and me. I am youngest. My sisters both married. Fatma, she is teacher. Leila, she have four children. I am uncle. Mother is dead. My brother, Hanni, he is killed in prison. Choke on tear gas, die. Three years ago. So we are only four. But sisters are in West Bank so we are only Father and me.

MERCER   Holy shit.

SADIQ   I very missing Leila, Fatma. Already four year. You have brother sister?

MERCER   No, just the three of us.

>   *A pause.*

Two of us actually. Now.

My mother just died. Just before I met you.

SADIQ   Mercer... I am sorry.

MERCER   You didn't do anything.

SADIQ   For mother.

MERCER   She was in the hospital for a long time. A mental hospital. Twelve years. I only ever saw her at Christmas. She was a mess. She's better off dead.

The service was packed. Some church. Dad and all his big-shot buddies from the ministry pretending they gave a shit. Telling me they were sorry. She was fucked. I wouldn't have recognized her if she'd climbed out of the coffin and told my father and me to go fuck ourselves. Jennifer was there, couldn't look at her. I always told her my mother was dead. Dad didn't say a word. Trying to act all serious and sad but inside he was dancing.

SADIQ   When my mother die, I am little boy. No one tell me. For two, three week they say she is gone to her sister for visit. I find out from boys at school. Then I am angry. At mother for going. Then I am older, I get angry to father for tell lie.

MERCER   Yeah.

My father was an asshole. Never around. Always at work. When they put my mom in hospital he sent me to boarding school. I was ten for fuck's sake.

SADIQ   Is okay.

MERCER   What?

SADIQ   To be sad.

MERCER   Well I'm not. I'm not anything. It's like nothing there. Like a hole. It's just a hole. And it fucks me up 'cause my mother is dead and I don't give a shit and you're supposed to give a shit when your mom dies but I don't.

SADIQ   Where?

MERCER   What?

SADIQ   The hole. Here? (*indicates MERCER's abdomen*)

MERCER   Yeah. (*SADIQ puts his hand on MERCER's stomach.*)

SADIQ   I know. You empty. Me too.

MERCER   Yeah. Nothing.

SADIQ   I know. We are child.

MERCER   Yeah.

SADIQ   You hurt.

MERCER   (*a whisper*) Yeah.

SADIQ   I know. Is okay.

Scene Seven

MERCER   Sadiq, you should go to Canada. Not to the States, go to Canada.

SADIQ   No, my uncle can bring me to America. I have no person in Canada.

MERCER   My dad, he's a big bureaucrat, he could do something I bet, he could get you in. Whatever. As a refugee or something.

SADIQ   Where I live in Canada, Mercer? In house with you and your father?

MERCER   No. I don't think so.

SADIQ   Me too, I don't think so.

MERCER   But we could work something out. I don't know. You could visit at least. You'd like it. You ever seen snow?

SADIQ   Snow? No.

MERCER   Oh, yeah, come to Vancouver. I'll bring you. Sadiq, I live on the ocean. And mountains. Trees, Sadiq, trees so big, you—

SADIQ   Is too cold.

MERCER   No, no, not where I live. I'll show you, I'll take you. It's cool, not too hot, not too cold. You can smell the ocean in the air. And there's these big trees covered in moss, the colour of rusted copper. It's quiet. And the waves. They're not like here. They crash all white onto the rocks. And there are purple starfish. And birds flying. Hawks and eagles riding thermals and seagulls. And there's these arbutus trees—their bark, it's the colour of your skin. And far off, far, the peaks of the mountains are white and the snow is there.

You have to come and visit.

SADIQ   Will you go back to Canada after this?

MERCER   After this?

A silence.

Crazy fucking world, eh?

I don't know. I guess. Depends on what happens. I guess I'm supposed to go back to Germany but, eventually, yeah, I think I'll go back to Canada. I don't know.

A pause.

SADIQ   The war—when will it come?

MERCER   Fuck if I know. Soon I hope. Deadline's in four days. Then it's up to the Americans.

SADIQ   Will you fight?

MERCER   No, no we don't do that kind of shit. We're the peacekeepers. Don't even know if our Hornets are gonna be allowed into combat. Typical Canada. Join the army but you ain't allowed to fight.

SADIQ   They have no choice.

MERCER   What?

SADIQ   They are not like you, Vancouver. Not want to be here.

MERCER   Who?

SADIQ   The Iraqis. The soldiers. They must sign up with army or go to prison. They have little food, just want to go home.

MERCER   No way, Sadiq. They're crack troops, elite. The Republican Guard, they beat the fucking Iranians, for Christ's sake. And you know how crazy they are.

SADIQ   No, I do not.

MERCER   You see on TV when the Ayatollah died? All those fucking people. Like a million or whatever, grabbing at his coffin. Fucking weird, man. Our prime minister—Mulroney, if he died—I don't think anybody'd notice.

SADIQ   You are a child.

MERCER   Don't call me that. I know you're an Arab but you gotta face the truth. It's like their—whadya call it—gee-had or whatever. It's a fucking holy war. If they get killed fighting us they go straight to heaven.

SADIQ   You think we just want to die? Because we are Muslim. We don't have wives? Families? Children?

MERCER   That doesn't matter. To them fundamentalists, life is worth like nothing. Less than nothing. They'll blow themselves up over anything. I mean, there's always some kind of war here, all the time.

SADIQ   From England and France.

MERCER   What?

SADIQ   For oil, come and make big mess.

MERCER   You can't go blaming your problems on everybody else.

SADIQ   Libya, 1986.

MERCER   What?

SADIQ   Americans bomb Tripoli. Many people dead. And Lebanon.

MERCER   I thought you didn't care about any of that shit. C'mon, Sadiq, you're out of here. You're going to Kansas.

SADIQ   This is my home. My people.

MERCER   It's not a personal thing, Sadiq. I'm just doing my job.

SADIQ   Good job.

MERCER   Hey, I didn't think this fucking thing up, you know. It's the way things go.

SADIQ   Destiny.

MERCER   Yeah. Fate. Life.

SADIQ   It will not happen.

MERCER   What?

SADIQ   The war. Everything.

MERCER   Yeah, maybe not. Who knows?

SADIQ   Me. Tell me again, Mercer, the purple fish and the eagles with the snow so far on the mountains where I visit you.

ACT TWO

A slash (/) indicates that ACTOR 2 begins speaking at that point. The use of italic type is intended to suggest text that is under (lower in volume than) ACTOR 2's text.

ACTOR 1   At 10:10 p.m. on January 16 of 1991, Prime Minister Brian Mulroney made the following speech to the House Of Commons:[1]

Mr. Speaker, honourable members will know that military action began in the Persian Gulf today, / *as announced at 7 p.m. Eastern Standard Time.*

ACTOR 2   Population of Iraq: 18 million.

Cost of one Tomahawk missile: $1.4 million US.[2]

ACTOR 1   *President Bush called me beforehand to apprise me that he had authorized such action. We understand at the moment that the participants of this first wave included forces from the United States, the United Kingdom, Saudi Arabia, and Kuwait.*

ACTOR 2   Estimated number of Tomahawk missiles fired at Iraq during first two weeks of war: 240.[3]

ACTOR 1   The fighting is a direct consequence of Saddam Hussein's determination to maintain his brutal occupation and illegal annexation of Kuwait in defiance of world opinion. He has chosen to ignore the numerous opportunities that were open to him to withdraw. He has had 167 days / *since his illegal and brutal invasion of Kuwait on August 2, and forty-eight full days since the United Nations Security Council passed resolution 678 on November 29…*

ACTOR 2   Duration of Indonesian occupation of East Timor: 20 years.[4]

Number of UN-sanctioned wars to liberate East Timor: 0.

Duration of Israeli occupation of West Bank: 28 years.

Number of UN-sanctioned wars to liberate West Bank: 0.

Number of good Arabs in movie *True Lies*: 1.[5]

---

[1] This speech is taken from Hansard for January 16, 1991.

[2] "High-Death Weapons" by Michael T. Klare, originally published by *The Nation Magazine*/The Nation Co. Inc., June 3, 1991. Reprinted in *It Was, It Was Not*, ed. Mordecai Briemberg, New Star Books, Vancouver, 1992, p. 46.

[3] "High-Death Weapons," Michael T. Klare, p. 46.

[4] Indonesia invaded East Timor on December 7, 1975, ten days after East Timor declared its independence from Portugal. At least 200,000 people, representing one-third of the population of East Timor, have died as a result of the Indonesian occupation. Indonesia is a core recipient of Canadian aid. See also: Noam Chomsky's *Year 501: The Conquest Continues*, Black Rose Books, Montreal, 1993.

[5] Starring Arnold Schwarzenegger, a well-known Republican, and seen by millions representing a multitude of political persuasions.

Estimated number of bad Arabs: 763,000. [6]

Lyrics to opening number from Walt Disney's *Aladdin*: Altered following protests from the American-Arab Anti-Discrimination Committee, citing the perpetuation of the stereotype that the Arab world is a place of deserts, camels, where one's ear might be cut off if one's face is disagreeable. Lyrics not quoted here for fear of litigation from Disney Corp. You don't, as they say in entertainment law, mess with The Mouse.

ACTOR 1   Diplomacy has been given every chance to end this conflict peacefully, but regrettably has failed in the face of Saddam Hussein's intransigence. [7] That same intransigence and his indifference to the suffering of his own people, especially the children, / *made it clear that sanctions alone were not going to force him to leave Kuwait...*

ACTOR 2   Estimated number of Iraqi children under the age of five dead as a result of the war, in the year following cessation of bombing: 150,000. [8]

Number of babies in Kuwait City incubators killed by Iraqis: 0. [9]

ACTOR 1   We have joined with other UN members in expelling Saddam Hussein from Kuwait by force. At this moment our CF-18s are flying combat air patrol in the Northern Persian Gulf, / *protecting Canadian and allied ships and personnel in the Gulf and the Arabian Peninsula...*

ACTOR 2   Number of CF-18s based in Persian Gulf: 24. [10]

Cost to taxpayer to purchase one CF-18: $35 million. [11]

Percentage of Canadian defence budget spent on peacekeeping: less than 1. [12]

---

[6]   Authors' estimates.

[7]   This is standard rhetoric and of course, completely untrue. There were numerous attempts from different parties to negotiate a peaceful end to the conflict. All of these efforts were blocked by the US and, with few exceptions, dutifully ignored by mainstream media. See: *Journal of Palestine Studies*, Volume XX, Number 3, Spring 1991. See also *Desert Shield to Desert Storm* by Dilip Hiro, HarperCollins, 1992.

[8]   A Harvard medical team that visited Iraq stressed a direct correlation between bombing damage to Iraqi infrastructure (power generating plants, for example) and the breakdown of public health (contaminated water supplies, etc.). They estimated that at least 150,000 children under the age of five would die from infectious diseases in the twelve-month period following the cessation of bombing. (*The Globe and Mail*, May 22, 1991) According to the UN, ongoing sanctions against Iraq have resulted in approximately half a million deaths.

[9]   This story was brought to us by Hill and Knowlton, the PR firm hired by the Kuwaiti government after the Iraqi invasion. See among others, "Public Relations" by Johan Carlisle, *Covert Action*, Spring 1993, Number 44, p. 19.

[10] "Ottawa Sending CF-18 Fighter Jets," *Vancouver Sun*, Sept. 15, 1990.

[11] "Forces' Hardware Geared for Defence," *Vancouver Sun*, Jan. 16, 1991.

[12] From Stephen Dale's "Guns 'n Poses, The Myths of Canadian Peacekeeping," *This Magazine* Mar–Apr 1993, Vol. 26 No. 7, p. 12.

ACTOR 1   I profoundly regret, as I am sure, do all members of this House, that it
has come to this. It is with no satisfaction that we take up arms, because war is
always a tragedy, / *but the greater tragedy would have been for criminal aggression
to go unchecked.*

*I am sure that the safety of the Canadian service men and women in the Gulf is
uppermost in the minds of all members. Our hearts go out tonight to those families
with loved ones, fathers or mothers, sons and daughters, and brothers and sisters,
on duty in the Persian Gulf. These courageous men and women are braving great
danger in the defence of the values and interests of their entire country. They have
our gratitude and respect, and especially tonight our prayers...*

ACTOR 2   One thing the Middle East and Somalia have in common: Western
support for dictatorships. [13]

Another thing the Middle East and Somalia have in common: huge markets for
Western arms.

One more thing the Middle East and Somalia have in common: oil. [14]

Estimated number of Iraqi soldiers killed during Gulf War: 100,000. [15]

Number of American soldiers killed: 144.

Number of these American soldiers killed by friendly fire: 60.

Preferred weapon for attacking dug-in troops and heavy fortifications: Fuel Air
Explosives.

Research for Fuel Air Explosive probably carried out at: McGill University,
University of Toronto, University of Ottawa, University of British Columbia. [16]

Example of Fuel Air Explosive: Big Blue 82. The Big Blue 82 is a 15,000 pound
bomb, which explodes in a massive fireball. The pressure effects of Fuel Air
Explosives, such as a Big Blue 82, approach those produced by low-yield
nuclear weapons. [17] If one were dropped on the theatre right now... this entire
neighbourhood...? poof.

[13]   The West has supported, in various ways, despots: Siad Barre of Somalia, Saddam Hussein
of Iraq, King Fahd of Saudi Arabia, Amir al-Ahmad al-Sabah of Kuwait, among others.
[14]   See "Adding Humanitarian Intervention to the US Arsenal" by Alex de Waal and Rakiya
Omaar in *Covert Action*, Spring 1993, No. 44, p. 4; "Gravy Train: Feeding Pentagon by
Feeding Somalia" by Stephen Shalom in *Z*, Feb. 1993, Vol. 6, No. 2, p. 15; and "Somalia: The
Cynical Manipulation of Hunger" by Mitchel Cohen in *Z*, Nov. 1993, Vol. 6, No. 11, p. 33.
[15]   US government estimates.
[16]   Stephen Dale, "Guns 'n Poses," p. 16. Also graffiti on McGill campus.
[17]   "High-Death Weapons," Michael T. Klare, p. 47.

ACT THREE

Scene One

A tent. MERCER sitting in a chair. The COLONEL enters. MERCER jumps, unsteadily, to attention.

COLONEL At ease, Mercer. I got a pile of papers here to organize, so if you'll just give me a second. I'll tell you, there's more goddamned paperwork in the Forces than I don't know what. But if you don't fill out the forms, you don't get paid. So, I fill out the forms. I filled out forms all the way here. That generator make enough noise for you? Should we tape-record this?

A squadron of planes takes off. The noise is deafening and lasts at least a minute. COLONEL and MERCER both react to noise. The COLONEL continues talking although we can't hear what he is saying. The noise ends.

Here we go.

Reading.

I didn't know who he was or what he was doing there. Raymond said they caught him sneaking around the camp. It's pretty hard to say what all happened or in what order. By the time I got there, he was already pretty bad. Raymond was there and MasCorporal Fortier. The Arab was—his head was all cut and bruised and looked like his legs were bleeding too. He was tied up. Raymond hit him with his riot baton and the Arab would scream Canada Canada Canada. Raymond laughed and said they'd been training him.

Somebody had a pistol out. It was lying on the table. They untied him, the Arab, they were poking him with the batons and making him walk around. He got over by the table and reached out to the gun. I grabbed his arm and tried to take it from him. We were pulling away at each other and the gun went off. It just went off. I didn't even know if it was loaded. I didn't know he'd been hit. He fell down. I can't say that I pulled the trigger. I don't know. He fell down and then Raymond and Fortier, or one of them, checked him and said he was dead. I don't remember much else after that.

That's your statement. As taken by Lieutenant Broman. Those are your words.

MERCER Yes, sir.

COLONEL A fight. In the sand. You walked into this, he tries to grab a gun, you fight, a mistake, the gun goes off. He dies. That's basically what you're saying here.

MERCER Yes.

COLONEL Mercer, I have no opinions on the subject and nothing in particular that I want to hear but you are going to tell me exactly, precisely, all the nitty-gritty little fucking details of what happened.

MERCER   It's pretty m-m-much... like that.

COLONEL   That what?

MERCER   Sir... like what you read, sir.

COLONEL   What I read doesn't tell me anything, Mercer. Just an outline, the surface. A couple of people in a dark tent. I want you to fill in the details.

　　　A silence.

　　Okay, let's start with something simple. What do you think of niggers, Mercer?

MERCER   Sir?

COLONEL   Niggers. What do you think of niggers? You have anything against them?

MERCER   No sir.

COLONEL   Pakis? Jews? Indians? You got anything against them?

MERCER   No sir.

COLONEL   Would you describe yourself as a racist?

MERCER   No. I wouldn't, sir.

COLONEL   I'm just asking because it turns out that Raymond, he's one of these White Power guys. Just want to know if you have anything to do with any of that.

MERCER   No sir.

COLONEL   Did you know that about Raymond? He talk to you about that at all?

MERCER   Yes sir.

COLONEL   He did? What did he say?

MERCER   I don't remember exactly, sir. I never paid much attention.

COLONEL   He talk to you about Hitler and the purity of the race thing?

MERCER   Sometimes, sir.

COLONEL   But you never paid much attention.

MERCER   I always thought Hitler was an asshole, sir.

COLONEL   You think Raymond was an asshole?

MERCER   No sir.

COLONEL   But you weren't interested in that sort of thing?

MERCER   No sir.

COLONEL   You know if anybody else is into that stuff?

MERCER   Can't say, sir. Don't know.

COLONEL   Just Raymond then. Far as you know. What about religion?

MERCER   Pardon me, sir?

COLONEL   I want to know what religion you are, Mercer. For the forms. You NFR?

MERCER   Yes sir.

COLONEL   But you were brought up, what, Protestant?

MERCER   Yes sir.

COLONEL   You a lapsed Protestant then?

MERCER   Sir?

COLONEL   Just a little joke. You believe in God though, Mercer?

MERCER   Uh… haven't given it much thought, sir.

COLONEL   You haven't. Big idea. God. Takes some thinking. Not the kind of thing you can just decide about in a few minutes, eh Mercer. Right now though, would you say you're atheist or agnostic? *(a pause)* An agnostic would be somebody who—

MERCER   Is this for the forms, sir?

COLONEL   Just idle curiosity, Mercer.

MERCER   Right now, sir, I'd have to say I'm an atheist.

COLONEL   No faith, eh? No Big Plan out there as far as you're concerned. No Big Guy with a Big Beard.

You had any sleep?

MERCER   No sir.

COLONEL   You want to get some air before we start?

MERCER   No. Thank you, sir.

COLONEL   Something to eat?

MERCER   No sir.

COLONEL   Coffee? Smoke? Go ahead. Do you smoke?

MERCER   No sir.

COLONEL   I used to. Quit. About seventeen times. You don't want anything?

MERCER   Not really, sir.

COLONEL   Where you from?

MERCER Vancouver. I'm from Vancouver, sir.

COLONEL Nice there. Mountains and everything.

MERCER Yes sir, it is.

COLONEL Rains a lot.

MERCER Fair bit.

COLONEL Doesn't get hot like this I bet?

MERCER N-n-n-o sir.

COLONEL Sun's a bitch, isn't it?

MERCER Sir?

COLONEL Sun's a bitch. Get it? Sun's a bitch?

MERCER Ha. Yeah. Sun's a bitch all right, sir.

COLONEL Vancouver.

MERCER Yes sir.

COLONEL I was in Vancouver few years ago. Got that nice market down there on that island.

MERCER Granville Island?

COLONEL Yeah. That's it, that's by that goddamned clock, isn't it? That Gassy Clock thing that goes off every fifteen minutes. Screeches like air brakes. Idiot tourists all gathered round the bloody thing, taking pictures.

MERCER I… n-don't know that clock, sir.

COLONEL What part of town you live in?

MERCER W-w-west Vancouver, sir.

COLONEL What do you do there? You run around that sea wall thing?

MERCER That's pretty far from where I live, sir. Don't do much. Used to ski a bit.

COLONEL Skiing. Skiing's nice. Whistler?

MERCER That's right, sir.

COLONEL You engaged?

MERCER No sir.

COLONEL Just noticed your ring.

MERCER Just a ring, sir.

COLONEL You single then?

MERCER   Yes sir.

COLONEL   Family out there too?

MERCER   My father.

COLONEL   Right. Shit, I'm sorry. Your mother passed away. I'm sorry. Recent wasn't it?

MERCER   Yes sir.

COLONEL   That's too bad. Terrible. *(pause)* How's your father taking it?

MERCER   My father, sir?

COLONEL   How's he taking it? Big blow for him.

MERCER   Yes sir.

    A silence.

Wasn't exactly a surprise, sir. My m-mother'd been sick a long time.

COLONEL   That's always hard. Maybe better that way though. Would you say?

MERCER   Maybe sir.

COLONEL   Your father, Mercer. What's he do?

MERCER   He's in government, sir. Associate Minister, I'm not exactly sure, Department of National Defence.

COLONEL   He's sort of my boss, isn't he?

MERCER   I guess.

COLONEL   Paul James Mercer. Born 1939, in Gatineau, Quebec. Graduates at the age of seventeen, second in his class, from Upper Canada College. Full scholarship to McGill University. Bourassa Fellowship in Government. Law degree at twenty-four. Marries Susan Wainwright, 1963, a psychology M.A. at McGill. First and only child, Paul Junior, born April, 1970. Susan becomes chronically depressed after the birth. Paul rises in the civil service. In 1989 is promoted to Assistant Deputy Minister with responsibility for UN peacekeeping operations.

Homework.

MERCER   Yes sir.

COLONEL   You get along with your dad, Mercer?

MERCER   Sure. Pretty much.

COLONEL   What about your mum?

MERCER   I did, I guess.

COLONEL   They tell me you're a good kid. Quiet.

> *Pause.*

You went back for the funeral.

MERCER   Yes sir.

COLONEL   How was that?

MERCER   Sir?

COLONEL   How did you feel? At the funeral.

MERCER   Pardon me, sir?

COLONEL   Were you upset? Did you cry?

MERCER   No sir.

COLONEL   No? Did you love your mother?

> *A silence.*

Mercer?

MERCER   …Yes sir.

COLONEL   How long was it since she'd lived with you and your father? You were what, six or something?

MERCER   I was n-n-nine, sir.

COLONEL   Nine. So you remember her?

MERCER   I remember some.

COLONEL   What exactly?

MERCER   I remember her. How she'd look at me sometimes, smile and then keep on looking as if she could see right through me. I remember how she cried and cried one time after coming home from the hospital, she just cried because she spilt sugar all over the place when she was trying to fill up the sugar bowl. I remember lots.

Do you want me to tell you more?

COLONEL   No. That's fine. Was it hard for you to come back here? After.

MERCER   Not really, sir.

COLONEL   How've you been feeling?

MERCER   Sir?

COLONEL   In the past while, since your mother's death. All these things, you know, one on top of the other, would you say you've been under some stress?

MERCER   I don't know, sir.

COLONEL   Were you upset at all, in any way, by your mother's death? Anything. I mean.... Dreams or whatever. It must have been pretty tough for you in some way.

>   *Silence.*

Even if you didn't really know her, she was your mother. I mean, it's possible that at the time, let's say at the funeral, you didn't feel anything, you were in a kind of shock, but after, later, maybe weeks later, you feel something. Anything. Not quite right. Would you say that you've been yourself since you've been here?

MERCER   I don't know. It's different, but...

COLONEL   Different?

MERCER   Well, the heat, sir. And the sand. I've never seen anything like this. But I'm a soldier, sir.

COLONEL   What does that mean to you? Being a soldier.

MERCER   I follow orders, sir. Discipline sir. Control. Keeping the peace... fighting for what's right.

COLONEL   Whose orders you follow?

MERCER   Officers' sir.

COLONEL   Your officers give orders to mistreat that prisoner?

MERCER   Prisoner?

COLONEL   The Arab, Mercer. Did you receive orders as to how to deal with him?

MERCER   It was understood, sir, that, uh, p-p-p-prisoners were to be taught a lesson.

COLONEL   How was this understood?

MERCER   It was, sir. It just was.

COLONEL   Did anyone in particular say anything specifically about what should be done to the prisoner?

MERCER   I don't think so.

COLONEL   Let me ask you again. Whose orders specifically do you follow?

MERCER   Sir, my my my superior's.

COLONEL   You always had a stutter, Mercer?

MERCER   Sir?

COLONEL   Stutter, Mercer. You always stuttered? You have problems expressing yourself?

MERCER   No. Sir.

COLONEL   Good. Now, where did you get this idea? Did anybody say anything to give you the impression that the prisoner was to be maltreated in any way?

MERCER   I don't think so, sir.

COLONEL   Your section commander, Sergeant Carrier? He say anything?

MERCER   I don't think so. No, sir.

COLONEL   Lieutenant Broman? He say anything to that effect? You telling me this comes from higher up, trooper?

MERCER   I couldn't say, sir.

COLONEL   Mercer, are you stupid or are you just pretending? You said it was understood that prisoners were to be taught a lesson.

MERCER   I… nnmbelieve so, sir.

COLONEL   You believe so. How exactly was this understood?

MERCER   Sir. I assumed, sir, that seeing as how—as how—mmmng—h-h—the p-prisoner was being… questioned… by the others that it was all right.

COLONEL   A sixteen-year-old kid, Mercer. He was beaten black and blue. He was bound and beaten with a riot baton. Nine teeth broken. Two ribs cracked. Index and middle fingers of his left hand broken. Left foot crushed. Human excrement dumped on his head. Cigarette burns to forearms and pectorals and you assumed this was all right? It was understood that this was all right? Where the hell would you get that idea? You learn that in basic? You learn that in Cub Scouts? Your father teach you that?

   Silence.

   Answer the qu-qu-question, Mercer.

MERCER   No sir.

COLONEL   You maybe aren't seeing things too clearly. I don't give a shit who your daddy is, he's 11,000 kilometres away anyhow. You are up to your goddamn eyeballs in some heavy, heavy shit and the only motherfucker can get you out is me so you better start playing ball. Stop trying to shit me. I'm your friend, you moron. I can help you out of this mess, but don't you dare lie to me.

   So, let's start again. What happened in that tent?

MERCER   It was an accident, sir. The gun—

COLONEL   Accident? What? He was burned by accident? He broke his foot by accident? Shit fell on his head by accident? Don't jerk me around, you pissy little insect. You fuck me around any more and I'll do everything in my power to make sure that you don't get a court martial. You'll get a civilian court and all kinds of press coverage and they will eat you alive. They will put you away for fucking ever. Do you understand what you're up on? Torture. Fourteen years. Manslaughter, if they don't nail you for murder. Kiss your life away.

Or maybe you're planning to save us all the trouble. You gonna do the same as Fortier when I turn my back? You planning on hanging yourself tonight?

I'll be honest. I look at you and Raymond and Fortier and I want to puke. You understand? You're a mess and you haven't even seen any action. You embarrass me. You insult the uniform, the forces, all the men who ever served. You're no better than a handful of fucking delinquent punks. Your whole platoon is unbalanced. You're a fucking disgrace, Mercer. Combat? I wouldn't even assign you to peacekeeping duties. Shit, I wouldn't want you as a school crossing guard.

MERCER   I wasn't there the whole time. I wasn't. They found him. They got him. Not me. I walked in on it.

COLONEL   Okay. What happened?

MERCER   I heard all this noise, shouting, laughing, screaming like an animal. And I went in the tent. And I went in. And there was Sad—he was tied up, his face all busted, bleeding, and there's blood all over his eyes and he didn't see me. Didn't recognize me at first. I walked in and there he was. I couldn't nmbelieve it and I was just scared. I couldn't figure out what the fuck was going on. I just seen him. That afternoon and—and and and unng he was fine, everything was fine, he was like always, he was like always and now there—bleeding and screaming.

I didn't want them to know. So I tried to make a joke out of it. Raymond, he said my name, he said M-m—Mercer and then he heard it, he heard my name and—saw me then. He looked and saw me and he tried to call me, name, but his lips were too swollen or his broken teeth and he couldn't. I saw it, I saw, him trying, and he's there crying and nothing I could do. Raymond said, "Watch this," and he hit him, hit mmmmng with the riot baton and Sa—Sa... he screamed, "Ca—Ca-Canada Canada Canada," and I, that's when I made the joke, I said, "Looks like a good trophy you got there." And Raymond said I should try it, so so so I did. I did. I hit him. I hit him, so, because. I hit him. I didn't know why was he there, nothing. I couldn't believe.

Then. I don't remember. It went on forever. It took forever. He was bleeding so much. No one came in, n-n-no officers. They said he was sneaking around the camp. He was trying to steal something. Nnmm—but that's not true. I mean it's not true. He came, I know why. He was curious, he was always curious. About the camp. He said he was gonna. Come. To see me. He—he—he told me before. I thought—kidding you know. I mean. I told him. He couldn't. He couldn't just come. I don't think he understood really why. He was just a kid.

COLONEL   You knew him.

MERCER   Yes. He—he saw me. He heard my name. He tried to call…

COLONEL   He tried to call you but he couldn't. He was too badly beaten. Right. And you were scared. You didn't know what was going on. You were shocked to see him there.

>   *A silence.*

Mercer?

It was a terrible shock to see him there. You were frightened.

>   *A silence.*

I know, it's a crazy fucking situation. World's gone fucking nuts, Mercer. Things aren't what they used to be.

Canada's going to ratshit in a handbasket. Whole country's going to ratshit, Mercer. There's no political will.

Look at this situation, look at this.

Canada, we send our men, our equipment. What do we send? Three ships. Thirty years old. Ancient. Useless. What's the point? Supposed to have been modernized years ago. But no, Ottawa wants to save money. Send the men in to do a job but don't give 'em the equipment to do it with. It's nuts. It's criminal.

Oka. Christ what a nightmare. What a bloody nightmare. Just between you and me, right, 'cause I get the feeling you understand what I'm saying. You call in the army 'cause it's armed insurrection, right? But do you let them do anything? No. You tie their hands. And the men stand there and take the shit and get garbage thrown at them and Indians point guns at them and they can't do anything but take it. Now, I ask you, what is that? What is that, Mercer? It's shit.

Let me tell you, Mercer, sometimes, sometimes I think about chucking this whole thing. Still, I'm short time now. Might as well ride it out. Pension.

Oka. Oka Oka Oka. And the press? Jesus. A field day. The liberal press. *The Globe and Mail.* Feminist newspaper.

You read the papers, Mercer?

I had a stroke a few years ago. This side of my body doesn't work as well as it did. I'm supposed to take it easy. Don't know how to. Never have, don't intend to start now. My doctor's worried I'll have another. My wife's worried I'll have a coronary. I figure when your number's up, your number's up. Till then you do what you gotta do.

>   *Silence.*

Shall we press on, Mercer?

MERCER   I told you. I told Lieutenant. I told everything. There's nnnnothing more. Why? I don't know why.

COLONEL   I don't care about why, Mercer. Why is for psychiatrists. The fact is it happened. I need to know details, how, when, who shot him…. Details.

How did you know him? How did you meet him?

MERCER   I just did. I just met him. Sir.

COLONEL   Where?

MERCER   Out there.

COLONEL   Where's that?

MERCER   About a mmm… a mile from the base, sir. It's a place I go to be alone.

COLONEL   What happened?

MERCER   Not much. We… uuh, talked. I'm thirsty. Sir?

COLONEL   You talked. What about?

MERCER   Don't remember, sir. The heat. Canada.

COLONEL   This Arab, he was just hanging—?

MERCER   Uuumg…. Sadiq.

COLONEL   Sadiq. That's his name?

MERCER   Sadiq.

COLONEL   What did you think of this Sadiq, Mercer? You liked him? You like him? He give you anything?

MERCER   No sir. I, uh, he was selling… he he he had… these… things to sell. I bought one.

COLONEL   What?

MERCER   No. N-n-nothing. Just… pictures.

COLONEL   He was selling pictures. What kind of pictures?

MERCER   Photographs.

COLONEL   Photographs. You interested in photography, Mercer?

MERCER   Sometimes.

COLONEL   These photographs? *(pulls out SADIQ's envelope)*

MERCER   I don't know why I bought it.

COLONEL   That's fine. I understand. You don't have to explain that to me. It's Jennifer, isn't it? Your girlfriend?

MERCER   Yes sir.

COLONEL   Been a while since you've seen her.

MERCER   Yes sir.

COLONEL   Perfectly natural. Have some water. Help yourself.

So this guy is just peddling black-market goods then. He sell you anything else?

MERCER   No. No sir.

COLONEL   Okay, so you meet this guy. He sells you some pictures. You talk. Visiting. Cultural exchange like. I'm glad you told me and nobody else needs to know about that. You're doing real good. Just a few more questions.

MERCER   What does it matter? Big deal? Who cares? He's n-n-nobody. He's only a fucking Arab. That's what we're here for. To kill a bunch of Arabs. He doesn't count. He's here illegal anyway. Who needs to know?

COLONEL   Mercer. We all have to agree. We need to be sure about what happened that night. You understand? A lot of people back home have questions about this. They need some answers. Good answers. This isn't just about your ass, Mercer. Lot of asses on the line now.

Why did he come to the camp, Mercer? What did he want?

MERCER   I told you. He was curious. That's all.

COLONEL   Did he resist at all?

MERCER   I wasn't there when they found him. I don't know what happened.

COLONEL   He was shot in the back. Who shot him? It's important, Mercer.

MERCER   I don't know. I can't tell you anything. It's all mixed up. Nothing happened. I don't know anything. It can happen like that. It gets in. It gets in, in in and you're gone.

COLONEL   What gets in, Mercer?

Silence.

Son, I want you to know something. This is not a personal thing. It's just the way things are done. You understand. Professional. I don't say I approve. I say it's unfortunate.

It's stupid. It's all timing. Look, this guy died at the wrong time is all. In a day or two when the war breaks out, 'cause it will, trust me, if this guy got killed, who the fuck'd know? Who'd care? Come on. It's fucking hypocrisy.

But there's a few more things. A few things that have got to be cleared up. 'Cause Raymond says you shot him. I don't believe him myself. But that's what he says. It looks like, you know, he was running away and that's why he's shot in the back. But by the time you got there this Sadiq, he was in no condition to run, was he?

That's what I thought. Why would Raymond lie to me? You think he did it?

Silence.

I'll have to talk to Raymond some more. Tomorrow I guess.

You can't keep it in forever, Mercer.

What do you believe in? I was brought up Catholic myself. I don't believe at all really, but still I have this suspicion, a doubt you know, that maybe there's something to all this about heaven and hell. Wouldn't that be a fucking nightmare. If it was true? Eternity, eh. Shit.

The funeral was in a church, right? Must have been strange.

What did you do while you were there? Hang out with your father? Get some skiing in? Actually, I read the psychiatrist's report. You went to that Eddie Murphy movie the night after the funeral. What was the movie? *Another 48 Hours*? I hear it's funny. Haven't seen it myself.

You sure as shit aren't making my job any easier, Mercer.

What do you worry about, Mercer?

He pulls out another envelope.

I got some other photographs here. Tell me about these. That's Fortier there. That's Raymond. This must be Sadiq. Who took these? Sixteen photographs here. Who took them?

Silence.

All right, Mercer, you don't want to talk? That's okay. You can just nod your head. How's that? You don't have to say a word.

You took them?

MERCER nods yes.

Was it your idea? Raymond's idea?

MERCER nods yes.

You sure about that?

MERCER nods.

These supposed to be a joke? Like a safari or something?

MERCER shrugs.

Didn't you think? Didn't anybody think? The last thing we need is photographic evidence of this. You took this? This one here with the baton between his teeth and Fortier pulling him by the hair. You took this one?

MERCER nods.

Was this before or after he was shot in the legs?

What about this one? Close-up of Sadiq's face with a 9mm. Browning shoved in his mouth. You take that? You remember taking that?

MERCER nods yes.

You sure? Whose hand is this in the photo, Mercer?

MERCER shrugs.

Look close. Recognize that hand? Course you do. It's yours, Mercer. Same ring. That's your hand holding your Browning in the Arab kid's mouth.

What are these pictures called? What is the common term in the regiment for this type of picture? It's called a hero picture, isn't it? I've heard them described by everyone I've talked to as a hero picture. Picture's worth a thousand words, eh Mercer?

What do you feel when you look at that, Mercer? You get off on it? You feel anything? Nothing at all? Like at your mother's funeral? Would you say there's something wrong with somebody who can't feel anything for his dead mother?

MERCER refuses to look at the photo.

You getting confused, Mercer, that's it. You need to see a shrink probably. You need psychiatric care? You're going mental like your mother, is that it?

Pause.

Where'd the camera come from?

Was it there in the tent?

MERCER shrugs.

Whose camera was it?

Silence.

Whose camera was it? Where'd you get the camera?

What the fuck do you think you're doing, Mercer? You think you're smarter than me? What the fuck is your problem? Look at me, boy. You think you can get away with something here? You think somebody's going to remember you did them a favour by not talking?

Produces camera.

The camera you took the photos with belongs to Martin Broman. Do you know who that is? Who is that? Would that be Lieutenant Broman? Right. Lieutenant Broman. Your platoon commander.

COLONEL takes photo of MERCER. Flash.

Okay. We'll put this shit away. Let's forget all this shit for now, okay? We forget the photos, you don't have to look at them anymore. I know it was Broman's camera. No big deal. I'll manage that.

It's Broman's fault. I know that. It's his responsibility. And I am going to make damned sure that this whole thing gets nailed to his sorry, fat, pimply, queer ass.

Okay, look, we trade, okay? I told you. You tell me. Exchange. Fair trade. Fair enough.

An extremely long silence.

Did you shoot him, Mercer? I know you hit him with the baton. Tell me, Mercer, did you shoot him?

You can tell me. I understand these things. I volunteered in Vietnam, Mercer. US Marines. So I have seen a thing or two myself. Close up. I understand what can happen. Trust me. Help me out, Mercer.

I know you can help me. You want to help me. Because you knew him. You were practically friends. We need to know what happened, Mercer, so we can do something for his family. Right?

He must have had some family. He was somebody's kid. Sixteen, that's just a boy. You have to tell me, Mercer. So I can do something. So I can help them. So I can help you.

Mercer, I'm going to tell you something. A story.

We had these things, M-26 fragmentation grenades. VC used to rig them up, delay, drop one into the gas tank of a jeep and they'd blow the whole thing up good and proper. It was like ten grenades put together when you did that. I had two friends went that way. Bert and JP, they climbed into the jeep, swung it around, Bert was leaning on the horn and I was coming up the street towards them. I was unwrapping a pack of cigarettes and reaching for my lighter, and I remember so clearly because when the jeep blew I was confused, I thought that my lighter had done it, somehow. But it was a flash. I watched it blow. Saw them fly apart.

All afternoon, there'd been this kid hanging out. He was ten, maybe older, little. Ten or twelve. He stuck with us all afternoon. He was laughing, making jokes, getting beer, asking questions. All afternoon. It must have been him, slipped it in the tank. You have to wonder what the hell it takes to make a ten-year-old blow up a jeep. That was the day of my nineteenth birthday. Every night that week I dream about boys coming up to me selling cigarettes, and when I look it's a grenade.

It's a week after. We're coming upriver through these hamlets that've been neutralized. It's quiet as shit. We're tired as hell. We all just want to sit, rest, eat. We're poking around, slow, make sure the place is secure. I'm way out on the edge of the village, pretty far from everybody else. Standing in front of a hut, it's burned, still standing. All alone. I'm just staring at it, thinking about a shed we had out back at home that looks nothing like this one. There's a noise. Like coughing. So in I go. Very slow. Very quiet. There's somebody in the corner. A boy, he's maybe ten years old. I'm so tired I think I'm dreaming, hallucinating. He gets up. He starts to get up. I put a couple of shots in his legs. He falls. Screaming gook. I just stood there looking at him, Mercer. Telling myself it's not the same kid. Then I put another one in his gut. And one more in his chest. Took him a long time to die.

Turned out he was blind. From the chemicals. Or whatever.

There was no reason to shoot him. I had no reason. He was unarmed, blind, a boy.

Just like the movies, eh Mercer? Kid goes to war, sees terrible things, ends up doing terrible things. Boo hoo. But all's fair in love and war and ain't it a crying shame?

Bullshit. Bull fucking shit.

It's not that simple.

We are a part of something, Mercer. Something that asks us to do certain things, expects us to do certain things. You hear what I'm saying? We follow orders, right? You've got your orders. I've got mine. But we agree to follow those orders. We make decisions, Mercer. We are a part of it. Look at us here in this tent. What the fuck are we doing? What's going on here? It's all a flaming pile of shit, Mercer. And we're a part of it.

Mercer, listen. I made a decision when I killed that boy. I made a decision after. I became a professional soldier. I thought I'd put it behind me. I take the bus to work sometimes, Mercer. But I still dream about kids with bombs for hearts.

I know.

MERCER   I don't think you do, sir.

COLONEL   Then I'm asking you please to tell me.

MERCER   You can't touch me now. Or him. Sadiq. It doesn't matter. It's over.

It gets in. It got in.

I kissed him. I sucked his cock. We—he. We fucked. He melted me like an explosion, like a Big Blue 82. He evaporated who I was, disintegrated me. He put his hands on my stomach and that hole in my gut… he filled it up with his brown hands.

I broke his teeth. I cracked his ribs. I kissed his lips.

Put that in your report, sir. There's nothing else. That's all. It's over.

> *Jets fly by again. Landing perhaps. The COLONEL slowly packs his briefcase, speaks briefly to MERCER, though we cannot hear what he is saying. He exits, leaving MERCER alone in the tent. The generator putt-putts, then silence.*

Scene Two

> *MERCER in Vancouver. A phone rings and rings and rings. MERCER regards it then finally answers.*

MERCER   Hello?

Jen. Hi.

I'm okay. You know. Bit surprised. I mean, I was thinking of calling you but I wasn't sure you'd want to. Talk to me.

Pretty fucking weird. I don't know. I thought there'd be a lot bigger deal in the papers and that but there was hardly anything.

It was…. The desert was wild.

Not much. Lying low. Watching TV. Been going for drives around. Down to the water and that. It's nice up here. Quiet. Like always. I've got the house to myself.

How are you? How's school?

Good.

I don't know really. Just try and chill. Get my shit together. I want to go back to Germany.

I'm just trying to take it one day at a time. Getting my shit together.

Yeah well, something happened. It's over. I have to deal with it and if other people want to be freaked out about it that's their problem. Life goes on.

I'm not saying you. No.

> *A long pause.*

Thanks. Thanks.

> *SADIQ appears.*

Next week. I'm not into it right now. Coffee. Second Cup. Next week. You're on.

Okay. I'll call you. Monday or something.

I will. Promise.

You too. Bye

> *MERCER hangs up the phone. He does not acknowledge SADIQ in any way.*

SADIQ   Mercer. You cannot touch me now. I am too far. You have left only pictures. Photographs. Can you see me?

I have surprise for you. Guess where I go? Not America, Mercer. I am in Sudbury. Ontario. Canada. Cold. When I come to my room it is full of clothes and parka. I am wearing my new sweater. Stanfield's. Very nice, very warm.

In Palestine, you know, boys like me, smaller too, throw rocks. Intifada. Israeli soldiers come and break hands of boys. Some boys die. Not just boys, everyone fight. You think it is crazy but no. They have reasons for to fight in Palestine, the mothers and fathers and children and the children to come. They are fight for a home, for to survive.

You come to Qatar, to Kuwait, Mercer. Why? Why you fight here? Not only you, whole world. Come. Why? You do not know, you go only where they tell you.

Who tell you to hit me, Mercer? Why you burn me? Do you know what reason? He break my foot, the big one, blond hair straight. You say nothing. Do nothing. I ask why for what reason?

You are no reason. You are an animal, you Canadian peacekeeper, you are shit, a beast. If I could reach that gun, I would like to kill you and all your friends. He deserve to die, that one hang himself. You too.

You tell me of Canada and your father and you lonely and the hole in you. You hurt. You cry. Do you cry for me, Mercer? Who cry for me? My family, sisters and mother and father too. But they do not matter to you. Death mean little to us you say. But no. We laugh like you. We bleed like you. We die like you. We deserve to life like you.

Now.

Now. Everything is different. The bruises and burns. They are gone. I am new again. Forgetting. Time. Not forgive. No. But I do not wish harm to you. I have only one picture of you, Mercer. I see you as little boy.

When I go to base that night I tell them I am looking for a child. It is our secret.

Today, I am very hungry. I have my first doughnut, I sneak in the back of Tim Hortons. Long john. I think if I am not the way I am, dead, it would make me very sick, military man.

I miss the sun, the heat. Here everything is clear.

> *The end.*

The Monument

by Colleen Wagner

I against my brother
I and my brother against our cousin
I, my brother, and cousin against the neighbour
All of us against the foreigner

—Bedouin proverb

A voice was heard in Ramah,
Sobbing and lamenting
Rachel weeping for her children,
refusing to be comforted
because they were no more.

—Jeremiah 31:15

Colleen Wagner

Colleen Wagner, playwright, film, and short-fiction writer, was born in Elk Point, Alberta. She currently lives in Toronto, where she teaches screenwriting in the department of film at York University. Before she began writing, Wagner studied at the Ontario College of Art and at the University of Toronto, working as a designer and actor. She has been playwright-in-residence at numerous theatre companies across Canada. One such residency took her to New Brunswick, where she now has a summer home.

Her first work for the stage, *Sand* (co-produced by Toronto's Nightwood Theatre and Factory Theatre), about a woman's return to her family's desolate farm, was shortlisted for best international play at the Royal Exchange Theatre in Manchester, England in 1989. *Eclipsed*, which examines a couple's attempts to keep their son alive after he has been diagnosed with a fatal disease, was staged at the Canadian Stage Company's Word Festival in 1991. *The Morning Bird*, an exploration of domestic fear on our neighbourhood streets, was performed in 2005 at the Notable Acts Summer Theatre Festival in Fredericton, which Wagner co-founded, and was translated into French by Maurice Arsenault for a production at Théâtre populaire d'Acadie, Caraquet, New Brunswick, in 2009. *Down from Heaven*, a social satire set during a pandemic and food crisis that explores the collapse of civil society during an emergency, premiered at Imago Theatre, Montreal, in September 2009. Her most recent play, *Home*, which is about an aging father and his son who return to their homeland after years of living in exile, explores repatriation, memory, language, and ownership. It premieres in February 2010 at the Bus Stop Theatre, Halifax, Nova Scotia.

Wagner spent a year between 1991 and 1992 travelling through Southeast Asia, where she became aware of escalating civil strife and the death of students and citizens protesting for democracy, fairness, and justice. Despite her experiences, she claims that she never intended to write *The Monument*. When she returned to Canada, however, a seminal moment came when she noticed a photograph in a Toronto newspaper of a Somalian man being dragged across the street by a length of barbed wire tied around his neck. Pressed to submit something for a commissioned deadline, she wrote the opening monologue of *The Monument*, but feared it would be too shocking and she tossed it in the garbage. She couldn't shake the voice of this character, however, and wrote the play in a furious three weeks. Then spent a year revising the last scene.

Wagner wanted *The Monument* to speak to the "universal" theme of war and genocide and thus deliberately left the setting and the characters' nationalities ambiguous, but individual productions have situated the play in war-torn countries such as Sudan, Rwanda, China, Romania, Bosnia. The play centres around Stetko, a young soldier convicted of war crimes. Stetko is the boy next door, raised by respectable parents but he has been caught up in the political events of a war he never understood. Like the good son, he obeys his superiors only to find that, at the conclusion of war, he has become the scapegoat for crimes "everyone was doing." Shortly before his execution, he is approached by a woman who suspects he knows the whereabouts of her missing daughter and arranges his release. *The Monument* charts the visceral journey of two characters and, through their journey, examines the ambiguities of morality and justice, the paradox of a soldier today, and the length that must be traversed to reach potential reconciliation. The play resists easy answers, questions the notion of forgiveness, and situates the drama beyond the conventions of "revenge" plays.

The Monument premiered as a co-production between Necessary Angel Theatre and the Manitoba Theatre Centre and opened at Toronto's Canadian Stage Company in 1995. It has since been performed nationally and internationally and translated into French, Mandarin, German, Portuguese, Romanian, and Kinyarwandan. It was also the first production by a non-black writer at Toronto's Obsidian Theatre Company. It was voted best play in China in 2002 and has since been published by the Publishing House of China University of Media. It premiered in Rwanda, a country emerging from genocide, in 2008 and Wagner attended a number of performances and talkbacks. She was particularly interested in the reaction of audiences who are still coping with genocidal issues. Many felt that she wrote the play about Rwanda, that she had somehow smuggled herself into the country during the genocide to write their story. However, those in China felt the same. They would comment that China has thousands of years of history of war. It is a powerful and transformative experience to witness theatre that speaks so viscerally to an audience.

Wagner has completed a screenplay adaptation of *The Monument* and is currently a recipient of a SSHRC research/creation grant to develop a new work that explores a modern, female-centred heroic myth gathered from the stories of women and girls who have survived trauma in African countries emerging from war.

In memory of my mother,

Lucille Anne Wagner (née Caskey)

Acknowledgements

There have been so many people who supported this project. Many have already been thanked, but I wish to make special mention of the following: Iris Turcott and Candace Burley for nurturing this play from its first thirty pages; Don Kugler and Richard Rose for believing in me for all those years, and for having the courage to produce the play; Rosemary Dunsmore and Peter Van Wart for their exceptional help and friendship; Dave Woolacott, who has supported and encouraged me through many creative projects and to whom I owe a special thanks; Jane Leis and Dianna Laanamets, who gave me a space to write and unconditional love; and Walter Muma, for the trees.

I also want to acknowledge and thank the Canada Council for the Arts, the Ontario Arts Council, the Banff Playwrights Colony, the New Play Development Centre at Canadian Stage Company, Necessary Angel Theatre, and Northern Light Theatre for their assistance in the development of the play.

—C.W.

The Monument premiered in January 1995 at the Canadian Stage Company, Toronto, in co-production with Necessary Angel Theatre and the Manitoba Theatre Centre. It was produced in Manitoba in February 1995 with the same company:

MEJRA   Rosemary Dunsmore
STETKO   Tom Barnett

Directed by Richard Rose
Set and costumes by Charlotte Dean
Lighting by Kevin Lamotte
Stage managed by Naomi Campbell

• • •

A second performance was presented at Northern Light Theatre, Edmonton, Alberta, April 1995 with the following company:

MEJRA   Maralyn Ryan
STETKO   Kurt Max Runte

Directed by DD Kugler
Set and costumes by David Skelton
Lighting by Stancil Campbell
Sound design by Dave Clarke
Stage managed by Susan Hayes

• • •

The play was performed at La Mama, Melbourne, Australia, July 1995 with the following company:

MEJRA   Brenda Palmer
STETKO   Bob Pavlich

Directed by Laurence Strangio
Set and costumes by Anna Tregloan
Lighting by Richard Vabre
Stage managed by Jeni Hector

CHARACTERS

STETKO, nineteen
MEJRA, fifty

THE MONUMENT

Scene One

STETKO is strapped to an electric chair. A single bulb above him provides the only light. He appears small in the vast darkness. He speaks to spectators sitting in a gallery behind or around him. We cannot see the gallery or the spectators.

STETKO   The one I liked the best was seventeen, maybe eighteen.
And pretty. With watery eyes.
Like a doe's.
She was like that.

I was her first.
I mean, she was a virgin.
A man can tell.
She said she wasn't, but the way she bled—
and cried—
I knew.

I didn't mean to hurt her.
Every time she cried out I pulled back.
I wanted it to last.

   Pause.

I don't care for orgasm like some men.
They only think about coming. They rush through like they're pumping iron, just wanting to come.
Not me.
Once you come that's it.
It's over.
And there you are facing the same old things that were there before you started.

I don't care for the world much.

(laughs) 'Course it doesn't care much for me either.
So big deal, eh?
It don't care for me, I don't care for it…
Big deal.

The doctors—make me laugh—they're trying to figure me out.
Why I'm like this.
Nobody agrees.
Dr. Casanova— Yeah! Casanova! I think he's joking when he tells me his name.
I laugh in his face.

He stares back.
He's got eyes like a chicken's.
Beady.
And small.
So I don't say nothing.
We have 106 sessions and I don't say anything. Not a word. We stare at each other for one hour, 106 times.
He thinks I'm a "passive aggressive."
I think he's fucking nuts.

They bring in another doctor.
A woman.
She comes with a bodyguard.
'Cause I'm dangerous.
That's what the bodyguard said.
"Dangerous."
I say to her, "Wanna fuck?"
She says, "And then go to the forest?"
I know what she's doing—egging me on.
Trying to trick me.
Get me to talk.
I look at her and I think, this doctor has never done it except in a nice soft bed and she doesn't do it much, and she doesn't like it when she does do it.
She's got a tight puckered mouth.
I said to her: "Is your ass like your mouth?"
She says, "No. One exhales, the other inhales. Don't yours?"
She's funny. So I talk to her.
Except,
I don't tell her where the bodies are.

I don't remember.

   Pause.

I tell her about my girlfriend.
My girlfriend's a virgin.
She wants to do it but there's no place.
She lives at home.
Whenever we'd go into her room her mother would listen at the door and open it all of a sudden and poke her head in. "It's too quiet in here," she'd say. "If you got nothing to say then you can join us in the living room. If you do have something to say, say it and come out here. It's not good for people to spend too much time alone together when they've got nothing to say." She should talk. I don't think she's said two words to her husband since "I do" at the wedding.

We couldn't do it at my place 'cause I was in the army.
Some men would bring their girlfriends to the camp and would do it while
others watched.
I can't come when people are watching. And the men never let you forget it
when you don't come.
So I never brought my girlfriend.

I never took her to the forest.

I think she's watching.
I don't want her to think I'm nervous.
I didn't eat or drink since yesterday.
I don't want to mess my pants in front of her.

After I was arrested she went to the camps where the women were held.
They told her that I'd been there and raped twenty-three girls.
At first I told her it wasn't true.
It wasn't really.
I mean I had to.
The other men forced me.
First time I said no they stripped me naked and laughed at me—said I had no
dick, said I turned into a girl all of a sudden, that maybe they should do it to
me.

So I did it.

I couldn't come.
So they rubbed my face in shit and made me do it till I came.

I faked it.

She just laid there looking at me.
She didn't care. She gave up.
She didn't even blink when I was doing it to her.
Just laid there like she was dead.

After it was over they told me to kill her.
I had to. I had lowest rank.
We took her to the forest and I shot her with my machine gun and hid her body
under a log. It'd been raining and she was covered in mud. Somebody might
have mistaken her for a dead pig.

That was the first time I did it.
Sex.

I didn't mind killing her 'cause she knew I faked it and I didn't want her telling
anyone.
It was like that.

We went to the prison camps about every three days after that and would pick out women and we'd all do it then drive them out to the forest. We'd rape them again then kill them.

Everybody was doing it.
I don't know why.

That's where I saw the one I liked.
In one of the camps.
I was the first.

I got nothing against those "people" personally.
I was seventeen.
I had to enlist. If I didn't they'd think I was a sympathizer and they'd kill my family.
Only soldiers were getting paid.
My brothers and I were the only ones in the family making any money.
I drove a cab before, but with the war nobody was taking them. Besides, only the army could buy gas.

So you do what comes up.

Who knows what that will be, eh—what life brings?
You're born.
You die.
And in between you try to live a little.

Maybe it's fate, eh?—our lives.

> *Pause.*

I'm not proud of what I did and I'm sorry my girlfriend found out.
I'm sorry we couldn't do it before I die.

> *Pause.*

I did to the one I liked what I wanted to do to my girlfriend because I knew my girlfriend wouldn't let me do it to her.

It was getting harder and harder to get it up.
I knew one day I'd get caught faking it.
So I took this girl to the forest after we raped her.
I got to drive alone.
The others thought I was taking her there to kill her.
I tied her up to a tree so she was just off the ground and started talking to her.
I told her about my girlfriend, about me driving cab, and about my uncle, who has a still out back of his house, and how he's always dodging the authorities and selling to them at the same time. I tell her she's pretty,
that she reminds me of my girlfriend.

My girlfriend's studying to be a nurse.
She says she wants to put some good back into the world.

I would too.
If I knew how.
Who wouldn't, eh?
If they knew how.

   Pause.

So I take all her clothes off and she's crying and begging me not to do it.
I want to
but I don't.
Her crying doesn't stop me.
I can't get it up.
I can't do it anymore.

That's what I really regret.
That I didn't do it with my girlfriend before I got caught. I think I could have
come with her.

The woman doctor, Nika, Dr. Nika—she wouldn't tell me her first name—said
that was reserved for friends. Obviously I wasn't one of them.
I don't know what she told the authorities, but next thing you know I'm being
tried for war crimes.
Makes me laugh.
If war is a crime why do we keep having them?
Why isn't everybody arrested?
They show us porno films and tell us doing it to women is good for morale and
they bring women in and then after the war is over they tell us what we did is a
crime.
After it's over you find out there were rules.
Like no raping women.
(*ironic*) No massacres.
Just good clean fighting—as if it were a duel, as if it were honourable.
As if you were brave.

Men aren't brave. We're all so scared we're going to die we do anything to stay
alive. We'll shoot a guy in the back. We'll creep into his bedroom in the middle
of the night and shoot him in his sleep.

And we'll rape his wife and daughters.
Nobody's going to stop you.

Some of the men said we shouldn't kill the women. We should get them all
pregnant with our babies and that's how we'd win the war.
Create a new race.

I heard some men were keeping women till after they got them pregnant. Seven, eight months. Too late for them to do anything about it.

It's a very good way to wipe out a race. Take away their women and get them pregnant. Their own husbands don't even want them after that. And what's she going to do, kill her own baby and be completely alone?

They're doing it to our women too!

I never did that.

I don't care who wins the war.
It was just a job.

I guess rape is just part of it.

> *MEJRA enters. She's dressed in black and stands to STETKO's right, which makes it difficult for him to see her. She looks at him impassively.*

> *Long, long silence.*

Are you the executioner?

> *No response.*

I guess it's only fitting that a woman do it.

> *Silence.*

Women can't rape men.
Too bad, eh?
There's probably a lot of women who would if they could.

> *Silence.*

I'm as ready as I'll ever be.
I guess.

I suppose going for a piss before we begin is out of the question.

> *He laughs. She remains silent.*

I'm not going to say I'm sorry if that's what you're waiting for.
What difference would it make?
It won't bring them back.
It won't undo what I did.
It won't make me a better man.

MEJRA Won't it?

STETKO Ah, she has a tongue.

> *Pause. He strains to see her.*

(*derisive*) I'm sorry.
Feel better?

MEJRA   Should I?

STETKO   Isn't that what forgiveness is all about?
I say sorry and the world forgives me.

I'M SORRY.

> *Silence.*

I don't mean it, of course, and so how can I expect forgiveness.

MEJRA   Is that what you want?

STETKO   I want to do it with my girlfriend.
And I want to take a leak.
My life is simple.

MEJRA   So take a leak.

Do you think we haven't seen a man pee his pants before?

If you were a dog you could pee down your leg quite easily.
But you're not a dog, are you? And so you can't pee your own pants.
You're too dignified for that.
You may think other people act like animals, but not you. You're a good person.
A good dog, who has only had a bad owner.

STETKO   Are you a doctor?

MEJRA   No.

STETKO   Missionary?

MEJRA   No.

STETKO   A mother?

MEJRA   ...no.

> *Silence.*

STETKO   And you're not the executioner...?

MEJRA   I'm your saviour.

STETKO   Oh yeah?

MEJRA   Yes.

STETKO   Maybe I don't want to be saved.

MEJRA   That's up to you.

STETKO   What do you mean?

MEJRA   I can have you released.

STETKO   Is this a joke?

MEJRA   No joke.

STETKO   You can set me free?!

MEJRA   On condition.

STETKO   What condition?

MEJRA   You must do as I say for the rest of your life.

STETKO   Do as—just do whatever you say?

MEJRA   Yes.

STETKO   Like… anything?

MEJRA   Everything.

STETKO   No deal.

MEJRA   As you wish. *(begins to exit)*

STETKO   Wait!
What if you asked me to kill myself?

MEJRA   Then you would have to do it.

  Silence.

STETKO   Would you?
Is that it? The state's too bankrupt to do it? It's a new way to save money—get
the prisoners to do it themselves.
That's it, isn't it?
They're too cheap.
Maybe the power's been cut off, eh.
What a laugh!

  Silence.

MEJRA   It's up to you.

STETKO   What kind of choice is that?

MEJRA   The only one you have.

STETKO   One choice is no choice.

MEJRA   You have two.

STETKO   I do it or they do it.

MEJRA   They do it or you obey me for the rest of your life.

  Silence.

STETKO   Why would they do that?

MEJRA   If you want to find out you'll have to postpone your death.

STETKO   What if I don't do as you tell me?

MEJRA   What do you think—that you'll get away with it?
Run and hide
—like a frightened dog?

Where can you go?
Everyone knows your face.

You're the most hated man in the world.

STETKO   Is that true?

MEJRA   What do you think?
You kill twenty-three young girls and people will love you for it?

STETKO   So why do you want to save me?

MEJRA   You'll have to agree to the conditions if you want to find out.

(checking her watch) It's time.

> *STETKO experiences a few frantic moments. MEJRA begins to leave.*

STETKO   Sure!
Okay.
What have I got to lose.

> *Lights out.*

Scene Two

That night. STETKO fingers the last morsels of food from a bowl and sucks his fingers clean.

STETKO   *(after a satisfying burp)* Very good.
Prison food is the worst.
Sometimes I wouldn't eat it.
I left some in a corner once. Even the rats wouldn't touch it.
But today I might have.

MEJRA   Freedom makes everything look good?

STETKO   Even makes you and your scowling face look good.
So, you live here?

MEJRA   Yes.

STETKO   No husband about?

MEJRA   Killed.

STETKO   I lost a brother.
And sister.
Do you have any beer?

MEJRA   Yes, but none of it is for you.

STETKO   Aah. I see.

MEJRA   What do you see?

STETKO   Nothing.

MEJRA   Then why do you say "I see" when you in fact see nothing?

STETKO   It's just a phrase.

MEJRA   It's also a lie.

STETKO   Truth. Lie. What difference does it make?

MEJRA   Don't you know?

> *Pause.*

STETKO   What do you want me to say?

MEJRA   Tell the truth.

STETKO   Everybody said what I did was wrong. That I should die for what I did.
Bad people are punished. Isn't that the truth? Bad people go to jail.
Good people, innocent people go free.
I'm free.
So tell me, am I bad or good?
What's the truth?

MEJRA   You're not free.

STETKO   From my shoes, things look different.

> *MEJRA swiftly picks up a small farm sickle that has been stuck in the ground, and with a single smooth motion deliberately slices off his ear. As he falls to the ground she clamps a collar and chain around his neck and fastens it to a bolt in the ground. He gasps for air.*

MEJRA   Get up.

> *She kicks him sharply. He cries and gasps on the ground.*

Get up!

> *He rises slowly, realizing as he rises that he is bound.*

STETKO   What is this—?!

> *She strikes him across the face and chest.*

What are you doing!?

She slaps his mouth.

MEJRA   *(ordering)* You will be silent.

STETKO   Why are you doing this?

She strikes his mouth again.

MEJRA   You will be silent.

STETKO goes to speak but thinks better of it.

MEJRA begins to beat him, methodically, dispassionately, one open-handed slap after another.

STETKO rages, straining to fight back.

STETKO   STOP IT!

She stops.

MEJRA   You will be silent and you will take your beating like a man.

STETKO   Why should I?

MEJRA   Because that's the deal.

STETKO   Are you going to beat me to death?

MEJRA   I am going to beat you until you fall to the ground or until I'm unable to beat you any longer.

She strikes him and STETKO immediately falls.

Get up.

STETKO   I've fallen.

MEJRA   Get up you coward.

Pause.

Last time.

STETKO reluctantly but obediently rises.

Stand up tall.

He leans into the collar and prepares himself for the beating. MEJRA stands in front of him and begins the beating, a beating that seems to last forever.

The lighting changes to indicate a passing of time into night and a slivered moon. In this light we only see her back and her arms swinging back and forth as she strikes him.

MEJRA stops for a breath.

Get down.

> *He goes to his knees, shakily. She takes off a scarf and bandages his ear. They both fight back tears.*

STETKO   Why did you do that?

MEJRA   Because you don't know the difference between the truth and a lie.

STETKO   I don't even know you.
Do I?
Have we ever met?
Have I—have I ever done anything to you?

MEJRA   You don't know me.
We've never met before.
(finishing the bandaging) Not like a nurse would do it, not like your girlfriend, but it will serve its purpose.

STETKO   Do you know my girlfriend?

MEJRA   I know of her.

STETKO   Because of me?

MEJRA   Of course.

STETKO   She was there, wasn't she?
At the jail?
She must know I'm here.
I'd like to see her.
…can I?

MEJRA   She's dead.

> *Silence.*

STETKO   I know she was there.

MEJRA   You saw her?

STETKO   She said she'd come.
She said she'd see if she could come in with me—near the end.

MEJRA   She was shot on her way to the jail.

STETKO   *(on his feet)* You're lying!

MEJRA   If that's what you choose to believe.

STETKO   Tell me you're lying!

MEJRA   I'm lying.

> *Silence.*

STETKO   Is it true?

MEJRA   Don't you know?

STETKO   *(stunned)* Is she really dead?

MEJRA   You tell me.

STETKO   Show me proof!
The police report!

MEJRA   Why should I?
Why should I tell you, prove to *you*?
Who are you to ask for anything?

STETKO   I have a right to know the truth!

Long silence.

She's alive.
I know it.
You're playing games with my mind.
I know about mind games.

MEJRA   Time for bed.
You sleep out here.

STETKO   Outside?

MEJRA   Outside.

She exits. He stands stubbornly.

STETKO   Fuck you.
Fuck you.

Blackout.

Scene Three

STETKO, shackled, is yoked to a wooden plough. MEJRA is behind, guiding it. The plow is stuck.

MEJRA   Can't you pull harder, Stinko?

STETKO   It's Stetko.
Stet-ko.

MEJRA   I prefer Stinko.

STETKO   I prefer not to pull harder.

MEJRA   You have no say in the matter.

Silence.

He leans into the yoke.

STETKO   It won't budge.

MEJRA   If we can't make something of this land we'll starve.

They look at the charred ruins of the land.

STETKO   Sometimes I think we should all starve.
We'd be better off.

MEJRA   *(laughing)* Stinko, you are so stupid you're funny.

STETKO   Don't call me Stinko, okay?
Please.

Pause.

MEJRA   Okay.

Silence.

He tries again. It won't budge.

STETKO   Maybe nothing will grow anyway.
It's probably been poisoned.
We sometimes sprayed.

MEJRA   There are land mines also.

STETKO   Here?!

MEJRA   Afraid to die?

STETKO   Everybody is afraid to die.

MEJRA   Is that so?

STETKO   Sure.
Except when living looks worse. Then they want to die.

MEJRA   Were the women you killed like that?

STETKO   Some.

MEJRA   All?

STETKO   Some.

MEJRA   Who?

STETKO   I don't remember.

MEJRA   What were their names?

STETKO   I don't know.
Why?

Silence.

MEJRA   Pull.

STETKO   It won't budge.

MEJRA   We have to dig it out.

STETKO   *(in the yoke)* How can I?

Long silence.

STETKO grins. MEJRA begins to dig with her hands. STETKO leans against the plough and whistles a light tune. MEJRA, angry, digs harder, faster.

(looking up) Sunstroke weather.

She looks up at him in anger. He grins back.

Take off the yoke, Mejra.

She resumes digging.

I've met people like you before.
Stubborn.
So stubborn they don't know when they're beat.
When they need the help of others. Even if they don't like those others.

MEJRA   This rock was never here before!

STETKO   Maybe it's not a rock.
Maybe it is a land mine.

MEJRA weeps.

Hey, it's a joke.
It's a rock.

It's obvious it's a rock. I'm joking.

You have to laugh at life sometimes.
Otherwise you go mad.

MEJRA   That's your remedy, is it?

STETKO   *(shrugs)* Got a better idea?

MEJRA swiftly unhooks him from the yoke, cuffs his hands in front, and drags him by his chains to the rock.

MEJRA   Dig it out.

STETKO   How?

MEJRA   With your feet. Your mouth. Your nose.
I don't care.
Just do it.

STETKO assesses the rock for a moment then proceeds to poke with one foot. He whistles a long note.

STETKO   She's a big one.

MEJRA   Dig.

He works harder, using both feet. This motion develops into a kind of Russian jig or march. He sings and kicks at the dirt until he tires.

STETKO   This is sunstroke weather.

MEJRA   For idiots, yes.

STETKO   What's life, eh?
Drudgery, and a few dances in between.
Care to dance, madam?

MEJRA   Dig.

STETKO   Take off my shirt.

It's hot.

I like the sun.
I never saw daylight in prison.
It's the first hot day of the year.

MEJRA strikes him.

MEJRA   Stinko, you are nothing.
No one.
A dog.
A slave.
A murderer.

STETKO   I know what I am.
I know I'm a murderer
and a dog
and a slave.
I don't care.
I'm not proud.
I can be those things.

MEJRA   You *are* those things.

STETKO   So what?
So what do we do with that?
Kill me?
You went to a lot of trouble to save me.
Why? Eh?
What do you want?

I'm your dog and slave.
I'm Stinko the murderer.
So what?

She sits on the rock.

MEJRA   So what.
Right.
So what.
What do we do with dogs and slaves and murderers.

What would you do?

STETKO   Shoot them probably.

MEJRA   Shoot them.

STETKO   Yeah.
It's simple.

MEJRA   Maybe I should shoot you.

STETKO   You like me.

MEJRA   Understand one thing if you can, stupido—I despise you.

STETKO   So shoot me.

Silence.

So use me like a dog and a slave till it's time to shoot me.
Do you think I care. Eh?
What do I have to care about?

MEJRA   Don't look for pity!
Dig!

Pause.

He begins, furious at first, then grins and switches again to his manic dance, singing at the top of his lungs, kicking dirt everywhere until the rock is exposed. He clasps his handcuffed arms around the boulder and heaves with all his might and lifts the rock triumphantly to his chest. He turns as if he would hurl the rock at her, but it's impossible.

Go ahead.
Show me what you're really made of.
Smash my face with it.

STETKO laughs at his own impotence.

Drop it on your foot.

STETKO   (*suddenly serious*) I can't.

MEJRA   Why not?

STETKO   I don't know.

> *MEJRA puts her foot beneath the rock.*

MEJRA   Drop it on mine.

> *He releases the rock immediately. She pulls her foot away in time.*

Try again.

STETKO   *(laughs)* It's too heavy.

MEJRA   Pick it up.

STETKO   You are one strange woman.

MEJRA   Who are you to judge?
Pick it up.

> *STETKO attempts to pick it up but can't.*

STETKO   Impossible.

MEJRA   A moment ago it was possible.
Pick it up or I'll bury you in this field.

STETKO   I can't pick it up now.
I had strength then.
I don't now.
I used it all up.
Who do you think I am—Hercules? I can lift mountains on command?

MEJRA   Didn't you kill on command?

> *No response.*

Which is harder? Killing someone or lifting a mountain?
Is that where your strength is, Stinko?
In hatred?
If you hate enough you can lift a mountain and kill a people, on command.

STETKO   I don't hate them.

MEJRA   You kill people you like?

> *Silence.*

Learn to hate me, Stinko, because you are going to lift that rock on command or be buried alive in this field.

STETKO   I wish you'd never come to save me.

MEJRA   I never came to save you.

STETKO   You said you were my saviour.

MEJRA   I lied.

You know all about lies, don't you?
Haven't you ever said to a young girl, I'll show you the forest.

STETKO   I never!

MEJRA   Someday you'll take me to this forest.

STETKO   What do you mean?

MEJRA   You look nervous.
We all know about the forest.
Dead bodies.
Not your girlfriend though.
She died on the street.
A virgin.

>   *STETKO weeps.*

You're right, Stetko.
I am your saviour.

Now pick up that rock because you owe me.
Pick it up out of gratitude instead of hate.

Go on.

>   *He tries, but in vain.*

Hate works best for you.

STETKO   For you too.
You hate me.

MEJRA   Yes.

STETKO   Why?

MEJRA   I might kill you before I could finish my sentence.

>   *Pause.*

STETKO   You're one of "them," aren't you?

MEJRA   What if I am?

STETKO   My aunt is one.
My father's brother married one.
I used to see them a lot.
Before.

Now everybody fights.
The whole family.

Everyone thinks they're right.
That's why people need someone to take charge.
Keep people in line. Make them shut up and do as they're told.

MEJRA   You?

STETKO   Not me,
but somebody.

MEJRA   Then you'll like our arrangement.
It's a dictatorship.
I'm the dictator.
I tell you what to do and you do it.

STETKO   Sure.
I don't care.
People don't care who's in charge just so long as they don't have to take
responsibility.

MEJRA   I'll take responsibility.
Pick up the rock and drop it on your foot.

STETKO   It's not normal to injure yourself.

MEJRA   It's normal to harm someone else?

STETKO   I've done nothing to you.

MEJRA   (*suddenly angry*) Pick up the rock.

STETKO   I can't.

> *He grins.*

Funny thing about "dictators" eh?
What happens when nobody does as they're told? What's the dictator to do? Kill
them all?
Then there'd be nobody left to do all the dirty work.
Then the dictator isn't a dictator anymore.
Maybe everybody is pretending to be who they are.
Maybe everybody has to believe a lie.

MEJRA   And what lie do you want to believe—that I'm here to save you, or to
bury you alive?

STETKO   (*grins*) I believe you like me.
But you're too old and ugly for a young guy like me.

MEJRA   Too ugly to be raped, too old to be impregnated.
Just right for killing.

STETKO   For sure. We would have just shot you.

MEJRA   I would have considered myself lucky.

STETKO   Strange world, eh?

MEJRA   What will it be?
Choose.

>   *Pause.*

Pick it up.

STETKO   No.

>   *Pause.*

>   *MEJRA starts digging STETKO's grave with her hands*

What are you doing?

MEJRA   Guess.

STETKO   You stupid bitch fucking cunt—

>   *He heaves the rock to his chest.*

MEJRA   *(slaps him across the face)* Don't ever call me that again.

STETKO   What's with you?
I lift it.
I drop it.
Doesn't matter what I do I get slapped down.
You wouldn't touch me if I wasn't tied up.

MEJRA   You wouldn't rape girls if they were armed.

STETKO   *(laughs)* Guess not.
You think I'm stupid?
I know they don't like it.

MEJRA   No they don't.

STETKO   You been raped?

MEJRA   None of your business.

STETKO   I take that for yes.

MEJRA   I don't care how you take it, just understand this, the military is not the only one with power.

STETKO   *(grins)* Untie me, Mejra.

MEJRA   *(grins back)* Not yet, Stinko.

STETKO   This rock is too fucking heavy.

MEJRA   Drop it—except on your foot—
and I bury you alive.

STETKO   What is the point of this?

MEJRA   The right to choose.

STETKO   Hold it, break my foot, or be buried alive?!

MEJRA   I knew you had some potential, Stinko.

>   *She exits.*

STETKO   Don't call me Stinko!
It's Stetko.
Stet-ko Tef-te-dar-i-ja.
Stupid—

>   *He stops short just in case she hears him. He holds the rock as the lights
>   indicate the coming of night. He sings a marching tune, baldly, defiantly.*

>   *Blackout.*

Scene Four

>   *MEJRA is bandaging STETKO's foot. He shivers from cold and shock.*

MEJRA   Papa cut his tail off and he howled and wailed through the night and in
the morning the poison was out of his system.
The shock drove it out of his body.
He was my father's favourite dog.
He used to say "I loved that dog enough to chop its tail off—which is more than
I could do for my children."

STETKO   What if he had died?

MEJRA   Who knows.
We only ever know what does happen.

STETKO   I wouldn't have done that.
I probably would have just watched, to see if he'd make it on his own.
See if he was meant to live.

MEJRA   Who decides that?
Who decides who will live and who won't?

STETKO   *(shrugs)* I don't know.

MEJRA   My father loved that dog.

STETKO   *(grins)* Like you love me?

MEJRA   I don't love you.

STETKO   You sure?

MEJRA   Positive.

STETKO   You live out here alone.
No neighbours.
Nothing.
You see me. Young—

MEJRA   *(bursts out laughing)* You are so arrogant and stupid—
I think all your brains must be in your cock.
And you're impotent!

STETKO   Not anymore.
Last night I had a hard on.
That's why I dropped the rock.
So I could masturbate.

MEJRA   You lie.

> *Pause.*

STETKO   Yeah.
I couldn't hold it any longer.
My back was killing me.
In a way I was relieved when it fell.

MEJRA   Nothing like pain to stop… everything.

I have something for you.

STETKO   A gift?

MEJRA   Sort of.
I found it.

STETKO   What is it?

MEJRA   A rabbit.
It had been caught in a snare and chewed its front paw off to escape.
I was going to kill it for dinner but it snarled at me.
I thought anything that wants to live that badly deserves a chance. So I brought
it home.

STETKO   I had a pet rabbit when I was seven.
Where is it?

MEJRA   There, in the basket.

> *STETKO limps to the basket, opens it, and looks in.*

STETKO   It hissed at me!

MEJRA   Maybe it doesn't want our help.
Maybe it wants to die.

STETKO   Nobody wants to die.

MEJRA   How do you know?

STETKO   ...I saw lots of people die.

MEJRA   The girls?

STETKO   Yeah. Some of them didn't seem to care.
But they probably knew it was for the best. Nobody wants a woman who's been raped.
Husbands walk away.

MEJRA   Mothers never walk away.

> *Silence. STETKO considers this statement.*

That's where men always become confused.
They don't know what to do about mothers.

STETKO   It bit me!

> *He sucks his finger and closes the basket.*

Look at me.
No ear.
Crushed foot.
Bit finger.

MEJRA   Should we kill it?

STETKO   —no.

MEJRA   Why not?

STETKO   It doesn't know any different.
It doesn't know I'm a friend.

What are you smiling about?

MEJRA   I'm not. I'm musing.
We forgive an animal but not a people.

Well, it's yours then.

> *She gives him dinner.*

This is all there is.

STETKO   What is this?

MEJRA   It was growing near the marsh.

STETKO   A man can't live on this.

MEJRA   Eat the rabbit then. That's all there is.

She exits.

STETKO   And what did you have, eh?!
Beer?
Potatoes with gravy?
Some cabbage?
Stewed beef and cabbage with potatoes and paprika, and carrots.
Dumplings.
I'll die on this!
She's going to starve me to death.

The rabbit scratches at the basket. He opens it and looks in.

Where do you think you're going, eh? With three feet.
What a pair.
Maybe if we team up we'll have enough feet between us to escape.

Maybe I ought to eat you instead.
Stay and eat—run and—
and what?
Be eaten?
What a life, eh?
Eat or be eaten.
What a fucking life.
That's it though, isn't it.
At least for you.
I'm a man.
I'm supposed to be above that.

(starting to eat) But I'm not.

He shares some of his greens with the rabbit.

I'm not.

Blackout.

Scene Five

STETKO is bent over, looking closely at a small green growth in the plowed field. The rabbit is beside him in the basket. He straightens up suddenly and runs, still shackled, as far as the chain leash permits.

STETKO   MEJRAA!
Something is growing!

He runs back to the growth and examines it further.

A green thing.
What though?
It's not even in the row.
Maybe it's a weed.
(grins) Maybe it's—rabbit food!
That's what you wish, eh?
Is that what you wish?
A big green salad?
Even if it's a weed?
MEJRAAAA.

It must be a weed.
Nothing else is growing except it.
Do you like weeds, eh?
Would you like to try a leaf or two?

> *STETKO plucks a leaf but the whole plant comes up.*

Oh shit! The whole thing's come up.
Maybe it was dying anyway.
What do you think?
A plant comes up that easy—can't be meant to live, eh?

> *He dangles it over the opened basket.*

Feast your eyes on that.
Do you want it?
Roll over.
(laughs) You're no dummy.
Only dogs roll over for their dinner.
And play dead.
Because you're so smart you can have it.
Don't bite my fingers.
Gently.
You see, even a stupid animal can learn.
Yes, you'll let me pet you as long as I feed you.
It's nice, eh?
Feels good.

> *MEJRA enters with cut flowers.*

MEJRA   Look what I found.
Growing.
Wildflowers.

STETKO   They're nice.
Pretty.

MEJRA   They're weeds really but who names the rose?

STETKO   Huh?

MEJRA   Never mind.
Why were you shouting?

STETKO   Something was growing here too.

MEJRA   Of course.
I planted it this morning.
It's a wild-bean plant.
I found it by the marsh.
A lone survivor.

STETKO   Lone?
The only one?

MEJRA   I don't know how it grew, but there it was, so I uprooted it and brought it here.

STETKO   I don't think it will make it.

MEJRA   Why not?

STETKO   Too hot.

MEJRA   It's not too hot.

STETKO   Too dry.

MEJRA   We'll carry water from the mountains if we have to.
It'll grow.
It has to.
That's all there is.

What's the matter?

What have you done, Stinko?
You look—ridiculous.

She pushes him aside and can't see the plant.

Where is it!?

Did you eat it, you pig?!

STETKO   No.

MEJRA   Did you feed it to that damn rabbit!

STETKO   No.

MEJRA   Then where is it?

STETKO shrugs and looks confused.

Don't you realize that was our chance to grow something?!

STETKO   I'll do without.

MEJRA   You idiot!
We'll all do without!

>   *She sees the rabbit.*

You fed it to the rabbit.
(snatching it) Give me that.

>   *It is a gnawed nub.*

Nothing.
Chewed the vital part first.

>   *She strikes STETKO.*

Shit for brains.

STETKO   I thought it was a weed.

MEJRA   It was!
One we could eat.

STETKO   We'll find something else.

MEJRA   What?

STETKO   —Flowers.
Mix them with something.
Grass!
Roast them.

MEJRA   I can't believe you!

STETKO   I didn't know!
I wouldn't have done it if I'd known.
Why didn't you tell me?

MEJRA   I don't have to report to you.

STETKO   No, but if you'd told me—if you'd said
"Hey, Stinko, I planted a wild bean in the field, don't feed it to the rabbit—"

>   *She realizes his attachment to the rabbit and makes a step toward it.*

MEJRA   Give me the rabbit.

STETKO   *(steps between it and her)* No.

MEJRA   Get out of my way.

STETKO   —No.

MEJRA   Move, or I'll beat you purple.

STETKO   Please, Mejra.
 She's mine.

MEJRA   She's not yours any more than the sun is yours.
 The air
  the water
 this land.
 You own nothing!

STETKO   Then why did you give her to me?

MEJRA   I heard something about your girlfriend.
 She was raped.

STETKO   You lie!

MEJRA   She was shot first.
 Killed.
 Then raped.
 She was lucky, wouldn't you say?
 She didn't have to endure the—what—
 indignity?
 Pain?
 A lucky girl.

STETKO   You lie.

MEJRA   Yes. I lie.
 We all lie.
 Why do we do that, Stetko?
 Why do you lie?

STETKO   I don't know.

MEJRA   Think!

STETKO   Depends on the lie.

MEJRA   You lied about the rabbit.
 You said she didn't eat the green.
 Why?

STETKO   I was afraid you'd hurt her.

MEJRA   Do you think the first lie ever told was to protect another?

STETKO   ...Maybe.

MEJRA   You think we're that noble?

STETKO   Probably the first person to tell a lie did it to save himself.

MEJRA   From what?
What are we saving ourselves from?

STETKO   I don't know.

MEJRA   Think!
What are you afraid of, Stetko?

> *Silence.*

STETKO   What do you want to hear?
I'll say anything.
I don't care.
Whatever you want.
Do you think just because somebody says something they mean it?

MEJRA   You lie to make life easier for yourself?
It's more convenient to go along with the others?

STETKO   Sure.

MEJRA   You raped and killed girls because it was easier than disobeying orders.

STETKO   Yes!
Yesyesyes!
It's easier to obey.
I obey authority.
I obey you.
It's easier.

MEJRA   I guess that's why the soldiers killed your girlfriend first.
It's easier to rape them when they're dead.

STETKO   She wasn't raped!

MEJRA   Yes she was.
Gang raped.
From the back.

> *He covers his ears and sings, wildly fighting tears. MEJRA exits.*
>
> *Lights indicate night and a lambent moon. STETKO stops singing and sobs.*
>
> *Lights out.*

Scene Six

> *The same lambent moon. MEJRA enters with a jar. STETKO stands defeated.*

MEJRA   I brought you a beer.

> *He looks at it, at her, then takes it.*

STETKO   *(ironic, toasting)* To life. *(and swallows a large mouthful)*
It's warm.

MEJRA   Yes.

STETKO   Who cares, eh?
To life!

> *He drinks.*

MEJRA   To life.
To children.
To love.

STETKO   To love.
Who knows about love?

MEJRA   I do.

STETKO   You are the cruellest woman I know.

MEJRA   Kindness is not love.
Besides, I don't love you.

STETKO   You hate me.

MEJRA   Yes.

STETKO   Why do you hate me so much?

> *Silence.*

Why did you bring me here?

MEJRA   Drink up, Stetko.

STETKO   Thank you.
For not calling me Stinko.

Is it late?

MEJRA   Almost morning.

STETKO   You couldn't sleep.

MEJRA   No.

STETKO   Me either.

MEJRA   I know.

STETKO   You watch me?

MEJRA   I just know.

STETKO   Was she really raped?
Tell me the truth, Mejra.

MEJRA   What is the truth?
I tell you your girlfriend is dead.
Raped.
I can't show you the body.
There is no body to be found.

People tell you one thing. ·
The military tells another.

We'll read about the war in the papers—new territories divided among the victors.
New leaders.
Economic decisions determined by outside interests.
There will be medals for the dead soldiers on all sides.
Plaques for the brave and foolhardy.
Monuments for the generals.

What will anyone know about you and your girlfriend?
About me?
About the girls in the forest?

What is the truth?

The truth
is like love.
It defies words.
It's known without "facts."

STETKO   Was she or wasn't she?

MEJRA   She's missing.
That's all we know.
That's the "facts."
Now, what is the truth?
You're a soldier. You know how a soldier's mind works.
Is she alive?
A virgin?

STETKO   Maybe she's hiding.

MEJRA   Yes, maybe she's hiding.

  Silence.

STETKO   Things happen in war.
We're trained to follow orders. Our lives depend on it. It's automatic.
Soldiers aren't supposed to think.
Only obey.

MEJRA   I guess you'll bear the "other side" no ill will if they've captured your girlfriend.

STETKO drinks.

STETKO   Warm beer is better than no beer.

MEJRA   *(ironic)* "Facts" are better than truth.
Revenge is better than sorrow.

STETKO   I hope I never grow old and bitter like you.

MEJRA   Then chances are you'll die young.

STETKO   *(shrugs)* What can I do?
I'm a prisoner.
I do nothing.
I think nothing.

MEJRA   Right.
You're helpless.
I'm helpless.
We're all victims of fate.

She can see STETKO thinking about the issue of fate.

Is war fate?

STETKO   I don't know.

MEJRA   And the girls?

STETKO   *(shrugs)* A girl walks by
and—
In a war
you can get away with it.

Everybody's doing it.
Rape is just part of war.

That's how some men pump themselves up.
Get their adrenaline going.
Makes them reckless.
Fearless.
I've seen men run into the open afterwards, spraying bullets.
Most of them get shot down, but some don't and they come back looking like
heroes.
Everyone cheers.
They get first pick of the women.

I never did it.
Run in the open.

MEJRA   You only shot women.

STETKO   Yeah.
That's how it was.

> *He drinks.*

That was their fate.

MEJRA   They cut her tongue out
and slit her open from her vagina to her navel
and filled the hole with dirt
and pissed on it.

STETKO   I don't believe you anymore.

MEJRA   That's right.
We all know soldiers don't do that to women and children.
Men don't do that sort of thing.
We all know that.
Isn't that the "truth"?

Tomorrow we go to the forest.

> *She exits.*

> *A pale light of dawn.*

> *Blackout.*

Scene Seven

> *They stand in the forest.*

STETKO   It's gone.

MEJRA   She.
She is not an it.

STETKO   She.
She's gone.
Animals must have got her.

MEJRA   This was the first one you killed?

STETKO   Yeah.

MEJRA   Where's the log? You said you put a log over her body.

STETKO   Someone must have taken it for firewood.

MEJRA   No evidence.

STETKO   No.

MEJRA   No one is going to know the truth.
That's the plan, isn't it?
Keep it secret.
No reminders.

Maybe you're lying.
Maybe this isn't the right place.

STETKO   This is the right place.

    Silence.

MEJRA   Do you know her name?

STETKO   I didn't ask.

MEJRA   Missing.
That's her epitaph.
Missing.

Where are the others?

STETKO   I don't know.

MEJRA   You knew where she was, where are the others?

STETKO   I don't know.
This was the first one I killed.
The first always sticks in the mind.
After that it was—
I don't know—

MEJRA   Routine?

STETKO   Sort of.

MEJRA   What about the girl you liked the best?
The virgin.
What was her name?

STETKO   I don't know.

MEJRA   Think!

STETKO   I don't remember.

MEJRA   You don't remember or *won't* remember?

STETKO   I *don't* remember.

    Silence.

MEJRA   Where is she?

    Pause.

STETKO   A different place.

MEJRA   Where?

STETKO   In a grave.

MEJRA   You buried her?

STETKO   We dug a big grave and put lots of them in it.

MEJRA   Where is it?

STETKO   I don't remember!

MEJRA   Take me there.

STETKO   How can I when I don't know where it is?!

MEJRA   What will make you remember?

STETKO   What?

MEJRA   What do I have to do to you to make you remember?

STETKO   Some things are just gone from memory.
Blocked out.

MEJRA   *(hands him a shovel)* Start digging.

STETKO   It's not here!

MEJRA   Your own grave.
Start digging.

STETKO   Things have changed!
The markings are different.
Trees have been cut
and—

      Looking up, remembering.

It was west,
the sun was in my eyes,
it was late afternoon.

MEJRA   Find it.

STETKO   There was a tree,
a large tree,
there were bullet holes in the bark
and a strong branch hung low—
the one I tied her up to.
I see it
but I don't know where it is now.

MEJRA   Then dig.

STETKO   I'm not sure where it is!

MEJRA   Then dig!

STETKO   Come on, Mejra.

MEJRA   *(strikes him)* Find her.

> *Pause.*

> *STETKO wanders in one direction, stops, shakes his head, and then wanders in another direction.*

STETKO   No.

> *He wanders, thinks he's getting close, stops, uncertain. He takes a few steps farther. MEJRA stands impassive and watches.*

> *Meanwhile, the lighting has gradually changed to indicate the passing of time and a change of location. They are now deeper in the forest; it is darker, the shadows are longer.*

> *STETKO stops and looks down.*

This is it.

> *MEJRA comes to the spot.*

MEJRA   Here?

STETKO   Yes.

MEJRA   Are you sure?

STETKO   I'm sure.

MEJRA   How do you know?

STETKO   I can tell.
I can feel it.

MEJRA   Feel what?

STETKO   I don't know.

> *STETKO remembers.*

MEJRA   Tell me.

> *Silence.*

Tell me, Stetko.
They mustn't be forgotten.
Same as your girlfriend.
They must not be forgotten.

Pause.

You liked her the best.

Tell me.

Pause.

STETKO   I was driving the Jeep.
I was laughing.
Finally I was alone.
I got to drive on my own—with her,
this girl.
I felt really good.
The sun was shining the whole time.
I was singing,
I'm finally alone with this girl.
And I'm singing—

He sings a popular song.

I look over at her
and she's not smiling,
just looking straight ahead.
I'd forgot you see,
I forgot what I was supposed to be doing—
killing them.
I forgot.
I was suddenly a free man going for a ride with my girl.

Then everything got serious.
I don't remember anything until we get here
and I tell her to lift her arms up over her head.
And she does.
I tie her hands together and throw the rope over the tree branch.
It's gone now.
Somebody has cut it down.

I pull the rope till she's stretched as far as she can go
and then I pull till she's just off the ground.
She looks so pretty.
Big watery eyes
like a doe's.
I cut her dress—
because her hands are tied and I can't get it off otherwise.
I use my hunting knife.
She's got very white skin.
It's never seen the sun.
She's got a thin line of black hairs that run up to her belly button.

I think it's quite sexy.
I tell her so.
I go up to her
and
put my arms around her
and kiss her neck.
I figure I can do it with her.
I feel her shiver.
I ask her if she's cold.
She says, "No."
I ask her if she's afraid.
She shakes her head
but I think she's lying.
I ask her if she wants me to undress—
maybe she hasn't seen a man before
naked.
She closes her eyes
tight.
So I tell her I won't take my clothes off
and she opens them again
and I can see she's crying.

So I stop
and sit down on a log
or rock
and I tell her about myself
and my uncle.
I tell her about my girlfriend.

I ask her what she wants to be when she grows up.
She says she wants to be a teacher.
I tell her she's just like my girlfriend,
wanting to put some good back into the world.
I tell her I would too
if I knew how.

I tell her she's beautiful.
I tell her I want to do it with her.

I figure maybe I can come with her.

She begs me not to
but I try anyway.

Only I can't.
I can't get hard.
It won't go in.
I can't do it anymore.

It's all over.

Pause.

I don't know what to do.

She begs me to set her free.
And I'm thinking, "What if I do?"
What if I set her free. What will happen?
I'm scared—in case the others find out—
they'd kill me for letting the enemy go.

She says she won't tell anyone.
I notice her hands are swollen and white.
It's getting late,
the sun's going down,
I have to return the Jeep.

So I leave it to fate.
I say, "Let's see if she's meant to live."

I back away
and
close my eyes
and aim the gun
and I say to myself
if I miss,
no matter what,
I let her go.

Pause.

It hit her in the face.

Silence.

I cut her down and dragged her to a grave we'd dug before but hadn't covered
over
and I put her into it
and buried her.

Long, long silence.

MEJRA   Dig it open.

STETKO   What!?

MEJRA   Dig the grave open.

STETKO   She's dead!

MEJRA   Dig it open!

STETKO   I can't.
I'll be sick.

MEJRA   Be sick, but dig.

STETKO   What's the point!

MEJRA   Proof.
We want the "facts."

STETKO   I did it like I said!

MEJRA   Stetko, you will dig open that grave or you will dig your own and lie in it.
Choose.

> *Pause.*

> *STETKO takes the shovel and digs.*

STETKO   It's been a while.
There might not be anything left.

MEJRA   Dig.

> *He digs.*

STETKO   I hear corpses carry diseases.

MEJRA   None worse than any the living carry.

> *He digs deeper.*

STETKO   Maybe this is the wrong spot.

MEJRA   It'll be the right one for you.

> *He digs even deeper.*

STETKO   There were a lot of bodies.
How will I know which is her?

MEJRA   Because her spirit will return and shriek her name.

> *He drops the shovel and scrambles out. MEJRA blocks his way.*

Afraid of spirits?

STETKO   We shouldn't be doing this!

MEJRA   Why?
Afraid to revisit?
Do you feel graves are haunted—
that the spirits of the dead linger on if their bodies have been brutalized?
Murdered?

Dig.

STETKO   It was a war!
   I only did as I was told!

MEJRA   Such a good boy.
   What if you'd said no.

STETKO   They would have killed me.

MEJRA   Me or you.
   It comes to that.
   Me
   or you.

STETKO   War changes everything.
   Once you're in it—
   there are no choices.

MEJRA   Yes there are.
   Dig.

STETKO   Right.
   "Dig."
   Obey or die.
   People will always obey rather than die.

MEJRA   Dig.

STETKO   Sure.
   I'm not proud.
   I'm no hero.
   I'll dig.

   He digs furiously.

   I don't know about life.
   I'm no great thinker.
   What am I supposed to know that would change things?

MEJRA   You should look at every woman as if she were your daughter.

   He stops.

   Every woman
   as if she were your daughter.

   Dig.

STETKO   I can't.

MEJRA   You can
   and you will.

STETKO   (*digs*) Okay.
Big deal.
Big f'ing deal.

I've hit something.

MEJRA   Keep digging.

STETKO   I think (*looking closely, leaping out*) it's a head!

MEJRA   Pull it out.

>   *He looks frantic.*

Pull it out.

STETKO   I can't.

>   *Long silence.*

>   *STETKO walks into the grave and pulls at the corpse.*

Okay!
It's out!

MEJRA   Bring her here.

STETKO   Oh God—

>   *He hauls it up and tosses the small corpse at her feet.*

MEJRA   Who is she?

STETKO   I don't know.

MEJRA   What was her name?

STETKO   I don't know!

>   *Pause.*

MEJRA   Dig up the rest.

STETKO   Oh God!
Fucking hell—

>   *He stomps into the grave and digs.*

>   *MEJRA looks at the corpse and brushes dirt off the decomposing skull.*

MEJRA   How old, child?
You will not be forgotten.

>   *STETKO tosses another decomposed body on the ground. MEJRA goes to it and puts a finger through a hole in the breastbone.*

Was it quick
or did you suffocate in the grave?

Another body, and another are unceremoniously tossed out. MEJRA goes to one and bends low.

Is it you?
(kneeling) Is it you?

She cradles the body in her arms, and rocks, and begins to keen.

STETKO climbs out and observes. When MEJRA finally sees him she stops.

A long, long silence.

Come here.

He does.

On your knees.

He hesitates but obeys.

Hold her.

She offers the body to him.

Hold her.

STETKO reluctantly holds out his arms to receive the corpse.

Her name is Ana.
She was nineteen.
Young-looking for her age.
She wanted to be a teacher—of philosophy.
She respected all religions.
She was brave and kind at once.

She had a thin line of black hair that ran up to her navel.
And watery eyes
like a doe's.

She felt every person had dignity regardless of their race.

She believed love was the answer.
Patience was the teacher.
Compassion was the mirror.
She would say, "I am the reflection of love and trust and joy—all that you are but haven't yet recognized
in yourself."

Silence.

I felt her adjust her shoulder before she entered this world. A world not yet ready for grace and beauty.

I never taught her about evil.
I thought I could protect her by hiding the truth.

Pause.

Give her back to me.

Pause.

*STETKO returns the corpse with as much grace and reverence as he can.
MEJRA stands. Silence.*

You can get up now.

He doesn't.

No longer "missing."

Get up.

STETKO   I can't.

MEJRA   You are going to dig up the rest
and then you have one more task.

You are going to tell the story of the missing ones.
The women and children you killed.
You are going to name them.
We are going to build a monument to the truth about war.
We are going to let the mothers reclaim their daughters.

STETKO   They'll kill me.
Then the truth will never be out.

MEJRA   The truth has a way of emerging.
Nothing can stop it
once it's started.
I may be gagged,
my husband tortured,
my house burned down,
my land stolen,
my children savaged,
but the wind will speak my name,
the waters will tell the fish,
the fish will tell the hunter
"I am."
I am.

Blackout.

Scene Eight

A monument of the dead bodies has been built. The corpses have been seated, stacked in a circle, looking out.

MEJRA is standing by the monument holding the corpse of Ana in her arms. The basket with the rabbit is near the monument. STETKO stands centre stage, holding one of the corpses in his arms. He is uncertain and nervous.

STETKO Uh…

He looks at MEJRA.

MEJRA Name them.

STETKO I don't know who they are.

MEJRA It's time.

STETKO *(looking at the monument)* I don't know.
It's a blur.
You just did it.

MEJRA "I." "I" did it.

STETKO "I" just did it.
I…
killed them.

Silence.

My girlfriend is missing.
She has dark shoulder-length hair.
She wears it in a ponytail.

She has green eyes.
Her name
is Ini.
Ini Herak.

Pause.

MEJRA Name all the girls you killed, Stetko.

STETKO I didn't always ask their name.

Silence.

MEJRA Describe them.

STETKO I can't.

Pause.

MEJRA Begin with the first.

STETKO   I don't know who she was.

MEJRA   What did she look like?

STETKO   ...She was older.
Maybe forty.

After I shot her I hid her body under a log.

MEJRA   Remember her.

He sets the corpse he is holding with the others. It triggers a memory.

STETKO   She had had children. I saw stretch marks on her belly.
She had a birthmark near her left shoulder—a purple one shaped like a kidney bean.

Long silence.

I killed a girl named Mini. Fifteen.
She had a sunburned face.
Luba, maybe twenty-one.
And a young girl with reddish hair. Long. Down to her waist.
A girl named Sara. She wore glasses. She was short and chubby.
A married woman. She had a wedding ring with a tiny diamond set into the band.
Monica. She had a gap between her two front teeth.

A girl with one brown eye and one green one.
Carol. I think she was pregnant.
Eva. She was a swimmer in training for the Olympics.
A girl who said she was a waitress. She dyed her hair blond.
Dark roots were showing.
Misa. Sixteen.
Her older sister.
Twins. Thirteen. They looked identical.
A mother of two boys.
A girl with a scar on her right side.
An older woman who wore a copper bracelet on each wrist.
A girl with a mole beside her left nipple.
A girl with pimples.
A girl with black lace-up boots.
A girl with big soft lips.

He has trouble continuing.

Ana.
Ana.

MEJRA, in a rage, rushes at STETKO with the shovel and strikes him on the back. He falls against the bodies and scrambles behind the monument. MEJRA pursues him and strikes him a single hard blow to the head. He falls still and silent, his feet extending beyond the bodies.

Silence.

MEJRA realizes she has killed him and is horrified. She fights back retching. She looks up and out and realizes her deed has been witnessed. She starts to flee, but can't. It's pointless. She's been seen and the deed too horrible to run from. She wants to scream but can't. She is like a caught animal. She runs back to STETKO.

She decides to bury him, and after glancing around for a suitable spot, proceeds to drag him out by his feet. She begins to dig a hole when STETKO groans. She hears him and rushes to him, grabbing his head in her hands.

MEJRA   Stetko?
Stetko!
Are you—?!

She checks his breathing and unconsciously, ecstatic, hugs him to her chest.

STETKO stirs. MEJRA, aware of her compromise, abruptly drops his head, stands up, apart, and resumes a hardness. STETKO sits up and rubs his head.

Silence.

STETKO   So, you're glad I'm alive, eh?

You're just like me, Mejra.
A murderer.
A slave and a dog.

MEJRA   Don't you compare us!

STETKO   "If you hate enough you can kill a people on command?"
Who commanded you?
You think you're above it all, eh?
Once you got what you wanted from me then you were going to do me in. Just like we do to prisoners.
You'd make a good soldier, Mejra.

MEJRA   I did it for my daughter!

STETKO   I had no daughter.
Only me.
Who are you to say who's more important?

MEJRA   I was doing it for love.

STETKO   That's what the soldiers say.
"Love for my country."

MEJRA   It's not the same!

STETKO We all have our reasons, eh?
We all think we're right.

So, what's the answer,
eh, Mejra?

MEJRA She was innocent!

STETKO War is no place for the innocent.

MEJRA How dare you!

STETKO Going to kill me again?

> *MEJRA stops.*

> *Silence.*

Me or you.
Isn't that what you said?
Me
or you.

Who's it going to be?

Why don't you look at every man as if he were your son?

> *Silence.*

MEJRA Would you have died to save your girlfriend?

STETKO I don't know.
How do we ever know that?

MEJRA I would have cut my own throat to save Ana.
I would have endured rape by every last soldier.
They could have flayed me alive and dragged my wet body through the streets.

STETKO And you would kill for her too.

You can't win a war by dying for the enemy.

> *Pause.*

You willing to die for me, Mejra?

> *She is outraged at the idea. STETKO laughs at her.*

So much for ideals, eh?

It's easy to hate.
Easy to kill once you feed that hate.

Isn't that right, Mejra?

MEJRA You make life unendurable.

STETKO   But we're here.
You're here.
I'm here.
We made it.

MEJRA   Yes.
There's no justice in this world.

STETKO   No.
Dogs and slaves.

MEJRA   Dogs and slaves.

> *Long silence.*

Get out of here.

> *She tosses him the keys to his chains.*

You're free to go.

> *STETKO does not go.*

Go.

> *MEJRA turns to leave.*

STETKO   Where will you go?

MEJRA   Back to the land.

STETKO   Can I go with you?

MEJRA   No.

STETKO   You need someone.

MEJRA   Not you.

STETKO   Who then?

There is no one, is there?
You're alone.

MEJRA   Go home to your family.

STETKO   They might take me back.

MEJRA   So go.

STETKO   Mejra?

> *No response.*

I'm sorry.
I'm sorry for what I did.

> *Pause.*

Forgive me.

MEJRA   How?

STETKO   Pardon?

MEJRA   How can I forgive you?
Show me.
Show me how to forgive.
I don't know how.

STETKO takes an uncertain step toward MEJRA.

STETKO   *(almost a whisper)* I'm sorry.

He unconsciously reaches out a finger to touch MEJRA's hand.

Forgive me.

MEJRA unconsciously makes a movement in his direction.

Slow fade on the monument of MEJRA and STETKO in a moment of possibilities.

The end.

Palace of the End

by Judith Thompson

Dedicated to

the memory of Connie Rooke
a visionary, brilliant editor, great beauty
and inspiration to women everywhere
&
the thousands of Iraqi children who have endured
unimaginable suffering for so very long

Judith Thompson

Toronto-based playwright, director, professor, and screenwriter Judith Thompson was born in 1954 in Montreal and raised in Middletown, Connecticut, and Kingston, Ontario. She studied drama at Queen's University in Kingston, and graduated from the acting program at the National Theatre School of Canada in Montreal. Considered one of the most dynamic, unusual, and provocative theatrical voices in Canada, Thompson has garnered much acclaim. She has received, among other awards, a Dora Mavor Moore Award, a Toronto Arts Award, two Chalmers Awards, two Governor General's Literary Awards, the Canadian Author's Association Award, the Nellie Award, and the Prix Italia. In 2007, she won the Walter Carsen Prize for Excellence in the Performance Arts. She received an honorary Doctorate of Divinity degree from Thornloe University, and she also earned a Distinguished Professor Award from the University of Guelph, where she has taught since 1992. In 2005, she was appointed as an Officer of the Order of Canada.

Thompson followed her first play, *The Crackwalker* (1980) with *White Biting Dog* (1984), which won the Governor General's Literary Award, as did her collection of plays, *The Other Side of the Dark* (1989). *I Am Yours* (1987) garnered the Floyd S. Chalmers Canadian Play Award, as did *Lion in the Streets* (1991). Since then, Thompson has written *Sled* (1997), *Habitat* (2001), *Capture Me* (2004), and *Enoch Arden in the Hope Shelter* (2005). She initially wrote the play *Perfect Pie* (2000) as a short monologue for television in 1993, and she has also produced a number of radio plays, one of which, *Tornado*, won the Best Radio Drama award in 1988. She was nominated for Genie Awards for her screenplays *Perfect Pie* and *Lost and Delirious.*

In 1991, Thompson adapted and directed Henrik Ibsen's *Hedda Gabler* for the Shaw Festival, which was then staged by Volcano Theatre in 2005 and at the Mainline Theatre in Montreal in 2008. Toronto's Tarragon Theatre staged her translation of Serge Boucher's *Motel Hélène* in 2001.

In 2008, Thompson created *Body & Soul.* The play consists of stories Thompson painstakingly drew out, edited, and wove together from the "real-life" experiences of women ranging from forty-eight to eighty-one; these non-actors performed their stories to live music at Toronto's Young Centre in the Distillery District. In 2009, Thompson revised the work by introducing a new cast member and darker, more complicated stories; the play was remounted at Tarragon's Extra Space Theatre, produced by Judith alongside Lois Fine and Brenda Surminski.

Also in 2008, Thompson became the first Canadian to win the prestigious Susan Smith Blackburn Prize, given annually to recognize women from around the world who have written works of outstanding quality for the English-speaking theatre. (Thompson had previously been nominated for *Habitat.*) Organizers called the provocative and timely *Palace of the End* (2008) a "theatrical Guernica." Nominated for the Governor General's Literary Award in 2008 and awarded the Amnesty International Freedom of Expression Award in 2009, this is Thompson's first overtly political work in her three-decade career. The play had its genesis when, in 2004, Ross Manson, artistic director of Toronto's Volcano theatre, asked Thompson to write a ten-minute piece for the Wrecking Ball, a political theatre cabaret. Although she had never considered writing a play about a real person before, she was fascinated by the story of Lynndie England, an American soldier court-martialled for the sexual torture of Iraqi detainees in Abu Ghraib prison. Thompson then produced a monologue titled "My Pyramids," a reference to England's penchant for forcing Iraqi prisoners to form human pyramids, which premiered at the inaugural Wrecking Ball cabaret that winter.

The following summer, Volcano toured an expanded version to the Edinburgh Fringe, where its rave reviews encouraged Thompson to add the two additional monologues on real-life figures. The second monologue features Dr. David Kelly, a British microbiologist and weapons inspector who exposed his country's "sexed-up" justifications for the invasion. His comments caused a major political scandal, and four days after appearing before a government inquiry investigating his claims, Kelly was found dead in the woods; he had apparently committed suicide. The third and arguably most powerful monologue features Nehrjas Al Saffarh, a mother of four and a member of Iraq's Communist party who survives torture by the secret police under Saddam Hussein, whom the CIA helped bring to power, in the 1970s in the former royal palace that gives the play its name. Thompson based Nehrjas's monologue on a written account of her experiences, which a friend translated from Arabic.

Two of the monologues from *Palace of the End* received their first reading in Florence, Italy, in 2006. In 2007 the full play was produced by 49th Parallel Theatre at the NoHo Arts Center in Los Angeles, a company founded by Canadians Sara Botsford (who directed the performance) and Chris "CB" Brown in order to enhance Canadian cultural presence in Los Angeles. The play received its Canadian premier at Toronto's Canadian Stage Company in 2007; it featured Genie and Gemini Award-winner Arsinée Khanjian, best known for her work acting in Atom Egoyan's films, in the role of the Iraqi mother. In 2008, *Palace of the End* was staged by the Epic Theatre Ensemble in New York, who originally commissioned Judith to write the second and third monologues; by Edmonton's Theatre Network, and Manchester's Royal Exchange Theatre. The play continues to be performed frequently: in 2009, Vancouver's Touchstone Theatre (in association with Felix Culpa and Horseshoes and Hand Grenades) and the PAL Theatre in Coal Harbor mounted productions, as did Calgary's Downstage Theatre, with Sharon Pollock directing the role of Nehrjas.

Thompson is donating her royalties from the published version of the play to the Iraqi Al-Amal Association, a charity formed in 1992 to help improve the medical, social, cultural, and economic conditions of the Iraqi people. Thompson encourages her audiences to make contributions to the association.

Thompson continues to work on theatre motivated by socio-political issues. She is currently working on a play about Omar Khadr, a twenty-two-year-old Canadian who was, at the age of fifteen, captured by US forces in Afghanistan. Accused of murder as a war crime by throwing a grenade that killed a US Army medic in July

2002, Khadr has since been detained at the Guantanamo Bay detention camp, although the evidence against him has yet to be proven. A small piece of this new work, which weaves together Khadr's story with that of a disabled CSIS agent who interviewed Khadr, was presented, as part of the Wrecking Ball political cabaret, to protest cuts in funding to the arts across the country on the eve of the 2008 federal election.

Playwright's Note

Each of these three monologues is based on news stories or research on events involving the real person named as the speaker, but the persona or character of each speaker has been created by me, and everything other than the real events springs from my imagination.

"My Pyramids" was inspired by the media circus around Lynndie England, the American soldier convicted of the sexual torture of Iraqi detainees in Abu Ghraib prison.

"Harrowdown Hill" was inspired by the well-publicized events surrounding the public life and solitary death of Dr. David Kelly, the British weapons inspector and microbiologist.

"Instruments of Yearning" was inspired by the true story of Nehrjas Al Saffarh, a well-known member of the Communist party of Iraq, who was tortured by Saddam Hussein's secret police in the 1970s. She died when her home was bombed by the Americans in the first Gulf War.

Acknowledgements

Palace of the End was commissioned by Epic Theatre Ensemble and received a developmental workshop with the company in June 2006 and a full production in 2008.

Teatro Limonaia in Florence, Italy, produced a staged reading of both "My Pyramids" and "Instruments of Yearning" in October 2006.

Further developed with the Canadian Stage Company, Toronto, 2007.

Special thanks to Rena Zimmerman for dramaturgy help with *Harrowdown Hill* and to Ann Anglin and Julian Richings who participated in the stage readings of the play for ARCfest Toronto, in October 2006.

Palace of the End was first produced by 49th Parallel Theatre in association with Open At The Top at The NoHo Arts Center, North Hollywood, California, in June 2007 with the following company:

SOLDIER   Kate Mines
Dr. DAVID Kelly   Michael Catlin
NEHRJAS Al Saffarh   Anna Khaja

Directed by Sara Botsford and CB Brown

• • •

Palace of the End received its Canadian premiere by the Canadian Stage Company at the Berkeley Street Theatre, Toronto, in January 2008 with the following company:

SOLDIER   Maev Beaty
Dr. DAVID Kelly   Julian Richings
NEHRJAS Al Saffrah   Arsinée Khanjian

Directed by David Storch
Set and Costume Design   Teresa Przybylski
Lighting Design   Kimberly Purtell
Composer/Sound Design   John Gzowski
Stage Manager   Marinda De Beer

• • •

Palace of the End received its New York premiere by Epic Theatre Ensemble (Zak Berkman, Founding Director of Artistic Programming) at the Peter Jay Sharp Theatre, June 23, 2008 with the following company:

SOLDIER   Teri Lamm
Dr. DAVID Kelly   Rocco Sisto
NEHRJAS Al Saffrah   Heather Raffo

Directed by Daniella Topol

CHARACTERS

SOLDIER, female
Dr. DAVID Kelly
NEHRJAS Al SAFFRAH

PALACE OF THE END

MY PYRAMIDS

Music over:

A SOLDIER, Dr. DAVID Kelly, and NEHRJAS Al Saffarh all enter, as if through a looking glass, and take their places.

The SOLDIER, nine months pregnant, speaks facing the audience, to an imaginary Quebec landlady:

SOLDIER *Bonjour, Madame Frenchie. J'm'appelle Evangelique.*

Comment vous appelez vous?

Avez vous une chambre ici pour forty *dolleurs* per *nuit pour une* lost soldier?

Pas de cockroaches *s'il vous plaît!*

(now to the audience) 'Cause I grew up with roaches, dude. Roach shit on the counters every damn morning. Seen roach shit on my toast before! I didn't eat it. Heard roaches poppin every time I went to cook a pizza in the damn oven.

Oh. Speakin of pizza. *(She dials.)*

Hey there hamsom. Well I think you're hamsom. You goin to pick up lunch today? Well damn, it's your turn soldier. Yes it is. You are teasin me, because I'm PRENINT.

Yes he is, he is kickin like a cancan dancer today. Yeh, maybe he's gonna be gay thas okay, every girl wants a gay son to go shoppin with aha course I'm kiddin I would drown him in the river if he was that, without a second thought YAH, well listen are you goin to KFC? Or Jimmy's? Okay. Well get me the chicken burger thing, grilled.

No, I don't. I give ya the money when you bring me the food, loser.

(She sings.) Kentucky Fried Chicken finger lickin good… *(She looks at the computer longingly, makes sounds of an inner struggle.)* Ohhhhh…

Don't do it don't do it do *not* google yourself, girl…

She googles herself, mouthing the spelling of her name as she does. Goes to first site.

Whew! Six hundred thousand on me on Google here. Six hundred thousand.

I guess that'd make me famous. WORLD famous.

She reads.

"Are you looking forward to the release of the photos of that soldier getting screwed? By Froggle."

"She's the hamster-faced twit in the Iraqi prisoner photos. There are pictures of her getting nailed, and it looks like they are going to be released."

She reads.

"Drown the slut in acid, she should be hogtied, damn she's ugly I'd put my wang in her ass she is the ugliest female I have ever seen drown that bitch in acid I'd rather cut her head off and fuck her neck hole, show her a fucking donkey, she's inbred poor white trash from West Virginia! Did she get beated with an ugly stick? That soldier's my kind of girl stupid and willing to please we need more like her and fewer like Hilary and Laura kappa kappa kunts! She's a trailer whore; even a dog wouldn't hump her! She needs her hole beat oh so hard, I think she's HOT! Stupid egocentric pitiful excuse for a human being and worst of all a feminist! I want to fuck her, kill her by fucking her continuously, cut her buttocks into four parts fuck each part fuck to the mouth tear out her vagina."

Whoa. I guess if I was an actor I would call that a bad review. A real bad review.

Long beat.

You must all be liberals, what wrote them comments on me. PEACE PINHEADS.

Pink cotton candy cowards afraid of bein at war.

Afraid of your own SHADOW.

Tell me how much you care about them Iraqi men when they are sawin the head off a one of our boys. Tell me fuckin that.

If all of you was right here in front of me now what I would say to you is one *thing above all:* I am NOT ugly. I am at least a six and a half out of ten I was voted a six and a half outta ten at my school, it was just a real skanky picture. I could shoot that damn photographer! You just take out your driver's licence or your passport and tell me if *you* don't look ugly. I *hate* ugly women, women who don't take care of themselves I am not that woman. I have always took care of myself. And strong? I am like piano wire. I could see if I was *fat* y'all hatin me so much, but I don't have an *ounce* of fat on me.

So what gives? What gives, dudes? I am not an ugly girl and I am definitely *not* nor have I *ever* been a feminist. I hate feminists, man, now *feminists* are UGLY.

Thas why they don't like men, they can't get theyselves a man. Is that why you think I am a feminist because I am a soldier? I am a soldier because I love my country.

Because I grew up singin "God Bless America" every single day of my life.

And pledgin allegiance to the flag...

...every ever-lovin day of my twenty-three years and so when I seen the call, when the recruiters come to town so handsome and real nice talking to me so nice like Tom Hanks style I said "Sure, I'll do whatever it takes to protect my country." I wasn't doin nothing anyways, just working at the Dairy Queen. "Hello how are you today? We got Peanut Buster Parfait, Strawberry Sundees, Brownie Explosion." Hell, I wasn't doin nothing for my country working at the Dairy Queen except makin it fat. And there was no way in hell I was going back to work at that chicken factory. So I signed up that day. *(She sings/chants:)* "I used to be the high-school queen. Now I got my M16." That there is a jodie; a kind of motivational chant we sing in the army. Or: "Walkin tall and looking good, ought to march in Hollywood. Lift your head and hold it high, 3rd platoon is marching by. Close your eyes and hang your head we are marching by the dead." That one is sad, you know, respectful. And then? There is: "Flyin low and feeling mean. Find a family by the stream. Pick 'em off and hear 'em scream, napalm sticks to kids." Shhh. We ain't supposed to say that one no more but we do, 'cause, well it's tradition, just part of being in the Army. And hey, we don't really mean that, most of us love kids, if kids gets hurt, we feel real bad.

> *Pause, does busy work.*

If things don't go well for me in court, I am up shit creek. Me and my boo, up the shitty crik.

I am *no* feminista.

And... I... am... not ugly.

Man I tole my sister when she went on Larry King to tell him that that is a bad picture that I do *not* look like that and she forgot!! My blood just boils thinking that that homely picture is how everyone thinks I look. And that makes Charley look bad, right? That he got it on with a *dog*. Thas why he has cut me off. I've written him fifty-two letters since he went to military prison, but he don't answer them. I tole him in the letter, I will wait for you the whole eight years, you takin the heat for Condoleeza, me and the baby, 'cause the love we found in Abu G. is like Romeo and Juliet.

And we was makin our little GI. I *hate the* media for makin you ashamed. Ashamed of being with an ugly girl. That burns me more than any other part. Your daddy is a war hero. He gonna get a Purple Heart eventually, that's what someone who I will not name in a very high-up position tole me that we would eventually get citations for service to military intelligence and even medals because we are takin the fall. I am willing oh yes I will take the fall for my country any ole day. I am like Joan of ARC being burned at the stake. With them pictures and the whole world wide web hatin me and havin to be a secretary I took the fall but I am not goin to prison I'm going to QUEBEC. Yah, I got a plan to excape to Canada, I'mona lie under a truckload of Hostess cupcakes or field tomatoes and I'm goin into exile like Napoleon; and like Napoleon, I will return one day, an American hero.

I seen an angel.

I had a lot of hash in me but I seen an angel with eagle wings flying, soaring through Abu Ghraib on that night. And that vision assured me that vanquishing the enemy, vanquishing evil was what I was born to do.

None of them higher-ups have spoke to me since it all came crashin down on my head. Since they moved me here to push around paper; I been waitin on their call, but the only person ever calls me is Mommy. And my lawyer. He says I am a scapegoat. And he won't let me up on the stand because I won't act like I'm retarded, which is what he wants me to do, so I won't be held accountable; I'll tell the truth. And that is not what anyone wants to hear.

Wonder if I'll be sentenced to jail for eight years like Charley. It's funny, you know, if things had gone different for me, insteada working in an office and waitin for my trial I mighta had a TV movie made about me, too. She is truly a hero she is, and hey, did you know she's from West Virginia too? Yeah. I reckon Jessica Lynch is America's sweetheart. I am America's secret that got shouted out to the world. And they is not happy about that, not at all.

And that is why they gonna make an example of me.

But one day, I'mona be in the history books. *You wait and see.*

I'mona be a war hero; like Annie Oakley.

I was in that in high school, *Annie Get your Gun*, I was one of the chorus singing; our lead was real good, Lisa? She tried for *American Idol*: "Anything you can do I can do better, I can do anything better 'n you." Or what's that one from *Oklahoma*? "I'm just a girl who cain't say no, I'm in a terrible twist."

I am going to be *remembered*. But first, we gotta find a way to somehow, make them pictures disappear. 'Cause: the thing about them… pictures.

I look at her, me, that homely little private with the thumbs-up.

And the naked Iraqi men,

And…. Well it's like a dream they are telling me I had?

But I don't remember it like that?

And they are sayin: "No this is the dream you had!"

Because they can doctor pictures you know. They can do anything they please.

And those forces that do not want

Girls in the army—wanted the world to see them pictures.

Okay, okay, I'mona be honest with you… in the fact of it.

That is what I did, for one second they said "Give us the thumbs-up, baby."

So that's what I did. For one second of a whole year, dudes. And *that* is what everyone sees? How would you like your weirdest second, like, played out over and over all over the world... for all of time, dude?

Like those dreams about yourself where ya did something WEIRD something you would never do? And ya wake up and ya feel uneasy and you are glad that nobody was lookin in your dream? And ya just wanna forget it and ya do, because dreams, they just disappear, don't they?

   Long beat.

I'll tell you what most people don't know. It got a hell of a lot worse than that.

That is for pussies. So what they were naked? So? They get naked every time they have a shower. So? And as far as me laughin and pointing at the guy's willie? Well tie me down if that's the worst thing that happened to 'em in Abu G. they be lovin it.

But that is not the style of girl I am, okay? I respect men and their privates and I do not nor have I ever laughed at a man's willie. But these are not men, they are terrorists.

And they had intelligence. They knew who was gonna blow up who and as far as I am concerned I was doin what had to be done, *to get to the intelligence* and that is, according to their culture, me laughin at their willies was worse than a beatin *way* worse. I was softening them up; like you might put out hard butter on the windowsill. *I was doin' what I was trained to do!* I had a smile on my face but this was SERIOUS—INTELLIGENCE—WORK.

And I am very proud to say that the naked human pyramids WAS ALL MY IDEA.

Actually, it's the first thing that come to my mind when I walked into that prison and seen all them men that look exactly alike. I know what might be fun: HUMAN PYRAMID WITH NAKED CAPTIVE MEN. Because I always did have an interest in choreography, you know? I see people dance, I wanna go in an mould 'em.

And they might not have liked it, but they have learned something useful. If they teach gym, in a school. Or supervise a cheerleading squad.

We was not entertaining ourselves. We was breaking down the terrorists.

And it worked. We did attain information.

And the other...

Takin the guy around on a leash?

Well he called me a dog.

Yes he did. Just like all you losers on the net. Like all those assholes back in Fort Ashby. He knew a little English and he called me a dog so for once in my life I could fuckin give it to him: *you think I'm a dog? You think I'm a fucking dog, you monkey? Let's go for a fuckin walk you wanna go for a walk?* And Charley and them is laughing and well, I never got laughs before I am not a funny person, and WOW man, getting laughs is the *best high* the guys was laughing dudes, they loved it, so they go: "Put him on the leash." And I do like a sketch, like *Saturday Night Live*, like "Oh my God it's time to take the dog for a walk... hey Mom? Did you take the dog for a walk? *Henry? Henry.* Did you walk the dog nobody walked the damn dog I'm walkin' it. Here dog, ya dirty dog. No treat for you today you been a *bad dog*." And I'm pullin him... I was surprised how different is a human neck from a dog neck. With dogs you can pull and pull and they just keep on going not with humans. They necks is soft.

And... well.... It is a weird feeling—made my breathing go—a little funny. Shallow. My voice kinda got full of breath. And I felt like that—Alice in Wonderland? Where everything was not real and I could walk out anytime and what was behind there would stay there.

I had that over someone else once and that was—Lee Ann Wibby; she was missin a leg? And she wanted friends so bad and she smelled and she was weird and ugly? Now *she* was ugly, so nobody liked her. So we was bored so we axed her to come to the clubhouse and she come with her backpack and her nightie she thought it was a sleepover birthday and we made her strip and bark like a dog and even lick Ryan's dickie, and there was a moment that I realized she would do anything we said. Anything at all. We burned her clothes? And we took her fake leg off, and chopped it up—okay, I know it sounds terrible but we didn't chop up her flesh leg or nothing—and then we tole her to start crawlin home.

   Beat, where she struggles with guilt.

Once in church, we hadda think upon our sins? And I seen her there, she was in the church, and she turn around and she looks at me. And I knew then, that what all happened at the clubhouse had been more than a joke for her. Well sir, I love God with all my heart and Jesus is my Lord so I did pray for forgiveness about Lee Ann Wibby—but dudes, Lee Ann Wibby is an American, she was very VERY different from the APES AT ABU GHRAIB. They was monsters in the shape of human beings. They was prisoners of WAR.

So, there I was, little me, in ABU GHRAIB me who'd been workin in the Dairy Queen in Fort Ashby, who had been fired several times from the Dairy Queen, for messin up the Brownie Explosion and I was the BIG boss of these BIG DEAL TERRORISTS, guys who had KILLED AMERICANS. GUYS WHO WERE PLANNING ANOTHER 9/11, dude, AND YOU ARE UPSET THAT I laughed AT THEIR WILLIES?

   Beat.

Like I said: we did a hell of a lot worse than what you seen. Or what you heard. What YOU seen is tiddlywinks: we made a man masturbate. Ohhhhh. So SCARY!!! SO? So WHAT? So the frick what? I'll tell you I didn't do nothing to them Iraqis that hadn't been done to me many times at the clubhouse. By my friends, and they still my friends. Yeah. I'm not mad at 'em, it was just a little fun.

Some of the churchier girls'd look down on me for that but hey at least I'm BUSY ON A SATURDAY NIGHT, at least I got a date.

   Beat.

See I guess I'm a bit of a martyr. Like them pretty-eye Palestinian girls who wear the scarf and walk into a supermarket and blow theyselves up? THAS what I done; I done blew myself up.

I ain't here no more.

See… they didn't like me at first. Charley, and Bruno, and Francis.

Wayne, Ry, all the guys, I walked in? They started with the comments.

Okay, you know what I'm sayin, like I should be cleanin or cookin and what am I doin in the hardest ass prison how I'm gonna wussy out. They didn't like me, they wouldn't talk to me; they stole my food, they hung me upside down, poured water on me in the night. Then they seen what I could do. They seen I was tough. I was as tough and as bad-assed as they was. I wudn't afraid of no Saddamite. I may be a little girl from West Virginia but once I was out of the gate and through the lookin glass I just thought of bein in the shack with Lee Ann Wibby and I thought of the twin towers and all them people running and I thought I'm takin your soul first. I'm takin your soul down like a big saw can take a hundred-year-old tree down; I'm buzzin you down till you ain't got shit left till you ain't even human. And then I'mona take you down further.

And then, when we good and ready, we blow your brains out.

And we laugh while we are doin it. Make no mistake.

Because we are rejoicing.

In defeating. The enemy.

Of freedom.

   Long beat.

And so Charley and them, they started to think I was okay.

Pattin me on the back, it was like camp.

It was like workin a farm in a way. The animals you gotta just handle.

You gotta do what you gotta do, slaughter the pigs, herd the cattle,

I mean guys like Charley never looked at me back home. Suddenly, a cute guy had a woody for me. I couldn't b'lieve it. I like the way he called me he always said "Private Sexy" like that? With this wicked smile make me melt—so we started doin it up down and sideways, yes, sometimes in front of the RAKEES. Just to fuck 'em up, it made Charley harder when they was watchin and I am NO prude never have been and so he got Ry and Wayne to tape us and at first I was a little shy, but he said "please," he would need it when he was away from me, when he was lonely, he could just pop in the tape and he be fine. So I said, "Okay, for my Romeo," and I let them tape. I just pretended they wasn't there, an I ask you, is there a girl in America that has not been videotaped doin the you know what? It's human nature, innit?

Silence, reflection.

They didn't say a word, man, everyone ax me wha'd they said when you was trippin on 'em but they didn't say—hardly nothing. It was just this silence. Make me feel weird, that silence, you know? This thought run through me once, with that silence? From the History Channel, when the Nazi's there? Made the Jews run. They always had to run everywhere, and so they would run, without sayin anything, with this look on they face that is what the RAKEES had they had that look that is what Lee Ann Wibby had when we was choppin up her leg. Made me feel weird. Made me feel...

One of 'em, who the other ones seem to look up to? I think he was like, a holy man. Ronnie goes to him: "Hey you. Wise man, mullah. Fuck him, fuck your friend there in the butt, man! Do it *now*," and the translator tells him and the guy, he speaks English anyways, right? So he turns around and says, in this soft doctor voice:

"There is no reason for this. This I will not do for your entertainment."

So you know what Ronnie does? He hadda take a shit so he takes it right there in a bucket hands it to the man, the guy who spoke English, and Ronnie makes him... eat his shit! Starts shootin at his feet. "*Eat it, eat it, teacher.*" So he eats... Ronnie's shit and that shit stink, dude. The funniest was Ry; he gets the other Rakee to kiss the holy man with his mouth full of shit? And Manny throws up. Oh my God we razzed Manny about that all night!!

She reflects for a moment, and to her surprise, a feeling of remorse wells up inside her. She remembers the man speaking—both DAVID Kelly and NEHRJAS look at her.

"There is no reason for this. This I will not do for your entertainment." Him sayin that, won't leave my head, you know? I wake up in the night sometimes, hearin him say that. I have to take a Percocet, make that go away.

This paper-pushin is so damn *boring!* I am a mover, dude, I likes to move all the time you never see me sittin any time of day, that's what my mom always said, "That girl don't sit unless she shits." I think I am messin it up, too.

Silence.

"JUMP ON THE CAT."

That's what he said my best friend Ray it was on Easter Sunday? I had on my lilac dress and my little white shoes my hair was permed and I ask him how does he like my new lilac dress innit pretty? He goes: "*Jump on the cat.*" Cat's there, breathin too fast, I don't know what Ray done and I'm like "NO, I don't wanna mess my shoes," he's like "JUMP ON THE CAT."

So I takes off my shoes and...

So soft. Like the Rakee's neck. Like Lee Ann Wibby. Same feeling in my stomach. Same feelin in my heart. Same fast breathin... like the Rakees when we was...

"There is no reason for this..."

I am thinking very serious about splittin, don't tell nobody. I'm goin to Canada. To French Canada just gonna blend right in. In Quebec City won't nobody know me, they like Americans there! I say I run away from the Mafia. I'll get a nice French-Canadian guy, a Pierre, to take me in. An I could have the baby, and we could bring him up Eskimo.

They take me to prison, they take away the baby.

And they take away my baby. Over my dead body.

And I could work in his corner store. *Depanneur.* I seen it in the Quebec dictionary.

I would like that. Sellin cigarettes. And candy bars. And milk. And bread. And the baby grow up to a little French Canadian, but really an American boy, help out his mom. Same customers every day. "*Bonjour, Madame Claudine! Comment savah?*" Nobody knows me. And every morning, when I get up and start the café, I will pledge allegiance to the flag; I will pray to my American God. And I will make American coffee and when I look in the mirror, to wash my face, I will take a minute to go back through the lookin glass. To those secret nights when my breathing went funny and there was dry ice in my heart and I did GOOD for my country. I said NO to the enemy.

I said you don't MESS with the eagle you don't MESS with the eagle, dude, or the eagle tear your eyes out and that's what I did I tore 'em out and I flew, man, for just that night I flew through Abu G. my wingspan like a football field.

And I soared through the air.

Long silence.

Till I crashed back.

Through the lookin glass.

Fade to black.

HARROWDOWN HILL

Dr. DAVID Kelly, a Welsh/Englishman of fifty-nine, a microbiologist, sits against a tree. His pant leg is pushed up, and there is a slash at his wrist, but not much blood. There is a little blood on his knee. His glasses are beside him, on one side, and his watch on the other. There is a bottle of water beside him, and an empty bottle of pills. He sings the first few lines of "The Ash Grove" by John Oxenford.

DAVID   The ash grove how graceful, how plainly 'tis speaking
The wind through it playing has language for me.
Whenever the light through its branches is breaking,
A host of kind faces is gazing at me.

I've solved the riddle.

Can you believe it?

I have been trying to solve the bloody thing,

since…

Oh! Look at that. *(shows leg)* Quite nasty…. I used to scream at the sight of my own blood, as a child, did you? But somehow as an adult, it soothes me—lets me know I'm—not made of… Plasticine—does that sound koo koo?

He breathes in.

Smell the roses on that breeze. Oh they smell so… red, don't they?

You know, this is my first moment of peace since the invasion.

And, in case you're wondering, that's why I am hiding. Hiding in Harrowdown Hill. Sounds like a children's book. Looks like one too, doesn't it? All these ash and oak trees, little woodland creatures running about, wildflowers everywhere, mad scientist hiding.

It's the best hiding place in the world, don't you agree? Ohh! Did you ever play sardines, as a child? I did, it was my favourite hide-and-seek game—how you'd start out all by yourself and one by one they would quietly find you and squish in, and you'd be this big squished group all just breathing, trying not to giggle while the last seeker walked round and round, calling out. I loved that game. I loved… hiding. The idea of being… invisible, you know? There and yet not there? The way I am now.

Oh, they will never find me.

Not behind that thorny thicket.

Not the baddies.

Nor the good…

Until tomorrow morning.

They'll find me about eight o'clock.

And I'll be dead by then.

Dead at first light.

D-E-A-D.

I can't fathom it, can you? I mean, as a scientist, I know it to be true, I know exactly what's going on inside my body, how long it will take for my liver to fail, the loss of blood to have its effect. I know that if I am not found, I will certainly die, and I accept this, fully, but you see... I can't imagine... it. It's the—forever part that stumps me. I mean, it would be one thing if I was dying just for a while, even for five or six years, until this whole mess in Iraq is over, as long as I knew I would be coming back, it would be *fine*, I could cope with that.... The idea of *never ever*... seeing orange juice again, or my daughter's eyes, or wild honeysuckle... the never never neverness of it all, you know?

If someone had told me when I was sixteen, "David Kelly, you will die in a forest when you are fifty-nine, after your fifteen minutes of w*orld fame*"—I wouldn't have believed *either*... the forest or the fame.

Me? The quiet little Welsh boy? How could I ever be of consequence in the world?

Perhaps I'll come back as a great spotted woodpecker, make lots of noise, and fly anywhere I want to. I always did love flying dreams, do you have them? Perhaps it'll be like that.

I'm sure it'll be like that.

Yes.

So it's not so bad for me. It's them.

My wife. My daughters. My sister.

The shock.

The... shock.

The loss, I suppose. The grief.

The tawdry... talk, all the bloody nattering.

"Oh, yes, remember that mousy British scientist Kelly? He killed hisself. Remember? He was the weapons inspector who got himself into all that trouble blabbing to the BBC? Saying there were no weapons of mass destruction in Iraq, calling Tony Blair a stinking liar—they found him, dead, in the forest."

Was it suicide?

Or WAS IT MURDER?

Some will say it was bloody murder, it was MI6, it was the Iraqis, it was the Italian Secret Service, the CIA.

They will cite the email I wrote this morning to my friend Judy. "There are many dark actors playing games." The other emails I wrote this morning show I was fine. I was strong. Very excited to go back to my beloved Iraq. My work is not finished yet. I have no psychiatric history whatsoever. After all I've left no notes. For my family. Whom I love. Whom I… adore…. Why, oh why would I take my own life? Others will say it was certainly suicide. There will be an inquiry, which will declare to the world that yes, of course it was suicide.

That sad little Walter Mitty of a man just couldn't take the pressure. The pills *(He points them out.)* they will say, are proof positive—two co-proxamol will be found in my stomach; they will point out the slashes on my wrist, the ulnar vein cut, the knife that made the slashes, a knife I was given when I was twelve years old… they will say I was a man defeated: the brutal interrogations, the bloodthirsty press, the threat of being terminated. I was depressed, exhausted, and in despair. I was a weak man, a meek man, poor in character, of course I committed suicide.

But almost nobody will believe it. There will be a rock song by a member of the band Radiohead, art installations by angry Germans, television movies, and the Internet will roil with talk of the murder of David Kelly by men in black. That's how I'll be remembered. The mousy scientist who set off a storm. Another casualty of the War in Iraq. After all, what is one fifty-nine-year-old slightly potty scientist? Hundreds of British lads have been killed already. Hundreds of thousands of Iraqis. Why should I make a noise? Many men don't make it to my age anyhow; I've had a good go.

When we are young, our death is impossible… we see our end as a calamity, don't we? Like the sinking of the *Titanic*. Part of the… salve of aging, is that our death starts to make a sort of sense. Like one's child going off to university. Yes, it's a bit sad, but not tragic. It's as things should be.

Evensong from a church in the village—or bells.

Is this too much to ask? That you witness my death?

It's a terrible thing to ask, I know.

But… I am asking.

Because…. Well, I don't want to be alone. Is that weak?

I can't have my loved ones here because, of course, they would revive me.

Do you remember Bobby Sands? He and some other IRA fellows they were on a hunger strike for better conditions in prison, and they insisted their wives and mothers and sons and daughters promise them that when they became unconscious, they would not be revived. An almost impossible promise to make, can you imagine? But the family of Bobby Sands, they kept their word. Maggie Thatcher, of course, didn't give way. And Bobby Sands died.

Does his death have meaning? I believe… that it does. After all, he is remembered.

You see, this might be the only way I can have an impact, the only way I can make up for what I did not do.

Beat.

I'm beginning to think that it's the greatest sin of our time.

Knowing, and pretending that we don't know, so that we won't be inconvenienced in any way. Do you understand what I am saying?

I knew. Oh the things I knew.

And I did nothing.

Can you imagine, knowing, knowing that a man is torturing a child in your basement, and just going on with your life? Knowing it is happening right under your feet, as you wait for the kettle to boil, as you tuck your own children in bed, as you work in the garden the dim light is always there, the muffled sound of her screaming, you pretend to yourself, "It's the crows on the line," but in your belly you know it is her *agony*, he is cutting off her fingers one by one, pulling out her eyes, her teeth, unimaginable torture and this is something you know for certain, others may guess at it, many deny it, but you know it for certain and you don't tell anyone because you might lose something if you do. Your carefree life, your ability to be happy, your job. Your job. And if you lose your job you lose your pension. And you don't want to lose your pension. They said, they admitted they needed to sex it up, for the people, the people of Britain were not going to send their boys to a war they didn't believe in, they would tie them down rather than see them go, they said we had to fill the people with fear, we had to remind them of World War II, they had to understand that the threat of Saddam was like the threat of the Nazis. We all knew that this was not true. We all knew that the *casus belli* was a lie. What could we do, we had no power, we just shook our heads, and scurried away, little mouse men. We were not to talk; we had taken a vow of secrecy, if we wanted to hold onto our jobs, we had to keep our mouths shut. So. I put my head in the sand.

I told myself, "I am for the invasion, Saddam is a monster no doubt about that, regime change is a must. The people will dance in the streets, if only for a day," I told myself: "They are good men, Bush and Blair, and Berlusconi. They want good for the people, they will topple Saddam, give aid to the new government, and be on their way."

I told myself lies.

Have you ever?

Have you ever told yourself an unforgivable lie?

Long beat.

A few weeks before the invasion, a friend of mine, the American ambassador to Sweden, asked me what would happen to me if Iraq were invaded and do you know what I answered? I said I would probably be found dead in the woods. They'll make much of that, after my death. It'll be all over the Internet. And the funny thing is, I can't explain it. I was making a kind of morbid joke. But maybe I knew something that I didn't know I knew, you know?

At the start of the war I would wake up at six, watch the news every morning, from my bed, each day's smooth, velvety-voiced account of bombings, and casualties, and "collateral damage," I watched, hoping against hope that things would... would improve, but it soon became very clear to me that things were far, far, far, far worse for the Iraqi people than even I could have imagined.

What did I do?

Did I go scream in the streets?

Did I write to the papers?

No.

I did nothing. Nothing at all.

I became... clumsy. Yes, that was the only giveaway, I burned myself on the stove, I cut myself chopping onions, and I fell flat on my face on the pavement, I crashed into people in hallways, sat on my glasses, dropped the phone constantly, dropped and broke plates, couldn't eat without dribbling, staining all of my shirts with food, I was in great demand. Flying to conferences all over the world. With stained shirts and broken glasses. The truth about Weapons of Mass Destruction that's what everyone wanted to know, I skirted the truth, bobbed and weaved but I loved to hear my own voice. Loved to be regarded as the expert the world expert on biological weapons; I was even nominated for a Nobel Peace Prize, for my work in Russia ten years before: uncovering Stalinist secrets, disarming the next Black Plague, and that is how they always introduced me, I talked to the press incessantly, my words always precise, witty, always filtered, always bloody lies. Walked through a screen door in Houston, Texas, and fell into a river in Bern. Bit my tongue constantly. That was maybe the worst.

And then one day, one sunny June morning I was in New York City just leaving the UN I received a phone call, from my dear old friend Jalal. He owned a bookshop in Baghdad, called Al Nakhla, in English, the Date Palm Tree, it was my favourite bookshop in the world, and I have been to almost *all* of them, no, I truly have! It's what I do in my downtime, wherever I am—well Jalal is one of the most kind and joyful and learned men I have ever known, he had about five degrees in literature he had thousands of books. And he had read *all* of them. He had books that were hundreds of years old, written in blood; he had giant books it would take three men to lift, tiny books with pages like moth's wings that would fit in the palm of your hand, they smelled of history, books in every language, illustrations that would make you weep, each room had a theme, the art of Babylon, American cowboys, Chinese fantasy, Antarctic cuisine, everything you can imagine, it was a kind of magical labyrinth, and the delicious cooking smells, of kubbeh and mint filling the shop—I would browse for hours, in a kind of trance and then, Jalal would insist I stay to dinner, with his family, oh, you would love his family—Marwa, well Marwa, and she wouldn't mind me saying this at all, is sort of an Arabic Lucille Ball— she would turn the act of getting ice out of the fridge into this huge comic routine, have us all on the floor shouting with laughter—and she was an amazing cook, and their daughter, Sahar. I think she had just turned thirteen last time I saw them, she was obsessed with *Anne of Green Gables*—her life's dream was to dye her hair carrot red and to visit Prince Edward Island, in Canada—we hatched a plan, to bring the whole family on a ship to the island and rent a farmhouse together for a summer, we were really going to do it, and Tabarek—the naughtiest five-year-old boy in the universe had to climb everything he saw—tables, fridges, walls, people, I became... so... so close to this family, bringing gifts for them all, never the right gifts of course, I'm terrible at gifts, being treated to little plays and songs, I loved that family, they became, in a way, my best friends in the world. He said they were watching her. Sahar, his thirteen-year-old, she was a very pretty girl, like a magazine model, I suppose, tall for her age, beautiful smile, a woman's figure but still very much a little girl, a happy child who loved her stuffed animals, and he said the American soldiers were watching her. He said they looked at her like a wolf looks at a rabbit. They were ravenous. There was evil in their eyes, he said, blood. He said he planned to move her the next day, to take her to another town, to stay with her cousins. He wanted to know if I could speak to someone. I said I was sorry, but there really wasn't anyone I could speak to, even if they had been British. And then I reassured him. I told him not to worry; I said they were probably bored young hicks from Alabama who couldn't put two words together. Intimidating young girls—their only entertainment. I reassured him that they were carefully monitored by their commanding officers, and they would never dare approach her. "If you could only see their eyes," he said. Even when he was with her, they would look her up and down, and say what were clearly crude things and laugh. She would go home and cry in her mother's arms. I told him again not to worry. I was sure everything would be fine. Not two days later, according to the *New York Times,* four American soldiers confronted Jalal and his daughter Sahar outside his bookshop. Took them inside. Said they were looking for weapons. For insurgents. "There are only books, please take all the books you want," said Jalal. Once in the shop, two of them took Sahar aside. The other two rounded up Marwa and Tabarek, took them with Jalal into the basement. And shot them. The killer climbed the stairs and said, "I've killed them. They're all dead." And then the four soldiers threw Sahar to the floor, raped the child. Put a bayonet through the child and shot her in the face.

They then set fire to the bookshop.

 He is having trouble breathing.

The press initially said it was the work of insurgents.

"The terrorists." Until two other soldiers from the same battalion as the killers were captured, and beheaded on camera. One of the four killers, tormented with guilt over his comrades' deaths, certain it had been revenge for the murders, confessed. Well. The day I heard what happened to my beloved friends was the day I blew myself up. Was the day I met Andrew Gilligan of the BBC and I told him the truth.

To *hell* with vows of secrecy, professional confidentiality.

To *hell* with my pension.

To *hell* with my life as I know it.

The *truth* the truth must out.

 He yells.

I want to tell the TRUUUUUUUUUUUUTH.

The truth the truth the truth the truth the awful horrible terrible.

Truth truth truth truth truth truth truth.

And out it poured.

Whatever he asked me? I told him the truth.

Yes I had seen the dossier before the invasion.

Yes I had had serious concerns.

And *yes* they ignored them.

And *yes* they *lied* to the *people.*

And *yes* tell the *world.*

And you know how it went, he told the world, he shouted it out but I was his secret, his secret source. And just when he was about to be sent to prison for not revealing his source I did the right thing, I wrote the letter.

The letter to the ministry explaining that I was the source.

I was the source and I was not ashamed. *I am not ashamed.* I naively believed they would protect me: they threw me to the hounds. I was ready. I sat before

Parliament on the hottest day in ten years, I was lashed, I was blasted, I had crashed through the looking glass; I was confused and exhausted, and I could barely be heard. I could not raise my voice. They even turned off the air conditioning so that I could be heard. Everyone was wilting. "Will you speak up please?" I was not capable. I was a tired old man and I wanted to go home. They very nearly defeated me. But do you really think, do you really think I am so pathetically poor in character that I would *kill myself* because the parliamentarians BULLIED me? When I had so much left to do? When I have a family I worship? Listen: Do you say that a soldier who loses his life in the name of freedom, truth, and compassion, has *killed* himself?

When I finally *talked, told the truth,* I knew that I was risking my life. And I knew, absolutely, that it was worth it. I accept what has happened, do you understand?

I accept what has happened. I sat in my chair this morning and I *made a choice.* I made a choice to stop—fighting; to allow whatever was to happen to happen. Because I realized that they would never ever leave me alone. What I had done, in their minds, was treason. I would be like what's his name, that character in Greek mythology that is tied to a rock in the ocean and is doomed to have his liver pulled out by ferocious vultures every day for eternity—they would never ever leave me in peace. The only way to defeat them is to disappear, do you understand? To be present, but invisible. Like hide-and-seek. I'm here. But you can't touch me. I see you, but you don't see me. I am the ghost of Harrowdown Hill.

I hope it's a searcher who finds me. Please let it not be my daughter. She does know my walking routes. We have walked this route together, many a Sunday afternoon, although never this far. Never through thickets. Is that her calling me? Or is that my imagination? Please God let it not be my daughter.

What time is it? Four forty-two in the morning now. The police are everywhere, and I can feel the fear in my family. I hear their worried voices. I am so... deeply sorry that it has to be this way. I hope, I know that they will understand. And one day they will see clearly that although I look as though I've lost, I have won. I have solved the riddle.

A song: there is a song that I need to sing, a song that I used to sing when I walked with my daughter. Searching for buttercups:

A... dahh dahh dumm. Yes, yes, that's the melody. La laaa... yes.

Breathing is quite difficult now. My organs are failing.

Less oxygen in my blood, heart tired out.

Thank you. Thank you for witnessing... it won't be long now.

Within a few hours, my flesh-and-blood body will cease.

But I, David Kelly, I am *here*, and I promise, I will always be here.

He weakly sings:

The ash grove how graceful, how plainly 'tis speaking
The wind through it playing has language for me.
Whenever the light through its branches is breaking,
A host of kind faces is gazing at me.

He falls asleep, into a coma.

Blackout.

INSTRUMENTS OF YEARNING

A beautiful, but haunted Iraqi woman of about fifty sits in a chair by a window overlooking a huge date palm tree. She is a woman who has a strong, buoyant spirit but she has suffered immeasurably. There is a small golden pot of tea and a glass saucer and a tiny glass with a gold rim. She drinks tea as she talks. She smiles at the audience:

NEHRJAS   One of my earliest memories is drawing in my own blood.

Drawing a flower, a daffodil for the school nurse. Looking back, I can't imagine why they were taking the blood of a child at school. It wasn't enough to send to a lab, just enough to draw a daffodil. I drew a daffodil because that is my name:

Nehrjas. "Daffodil" in Arabic.

My Western friends tell me that there is no such name in English, although there are many of flower names.

There is Rose.

There is Dahlia.

There is Lily.

There is Violet.

There is Viola.

I laughed when my British friend said to me, "Now what is the correct spelling of your name, dear." How can you talk of correct spelling when you transcribe Arabic into English? It is phonetics only.

What is fascinating to me is that women are names of flowers, but not all flowers; because if you are English and you are named Daffodil people will laugh. That is what my friends have told me. And if they want to insult a man, say to a man that he is not masculine, they call him "pansy" but not rose. Or tulip. And another thing I have observed is that a woman is never called after a tree. Only a flower. Because the purpose of a flower is to attract a bee.

And the tree,

The tree stands alone.

Blissfully—alone.

The tree provides air.

And shelter.

And food.

So I think all mothers should be given a second name after a tree.

Do you see the tree outside my window? Ah, isn't that a beautiful view? I can see the whole world from here.

This tree, this is a date palm or the Nakhla. So tall, elegant, proud, and beautiful, and how should I say it—enduring much like a woman. A fully grown tree, like a fully grown woman, does not need much of anything, save a little rain now and then. Like me: Some people feel sorry, "She is old, she is over fifty now, can't attract a man," are you joking with me? You think I want to attract a man? Oh yes I am dying to wash his feet and make his bed and cook and clean and soothe him and praise him and say he is so strong and sexy and smart and bury myself alive! Although I loved—adored—my husband, he was an extraordinary man… I will tell you about this later… it was only once I was all alone that I could live in the land of myself. People ask me, "Aren't you lonely, with your husband dead and your children elsewhere? Surely you will die of loneliness." I am not lonely; I am a full-grown tree.

Just as the leaves breathe out into the air and fill it with healing substances I breathe out my memories, good and bad. It is not company I want. It is to bring back what I can never bring back. And anyway: you will know that I deserve to be alone. For I have committed the greatest sin of all.

She takes a drink of water, or does a chore.

So, the date palm tree. When she has age, she doesn't need much. But, when she is young, she requires a great deal of special attention to truly flourish and bear fruit. Like every young girl, like my daughters, oh so much attention or else they wilt like flowers in the heat and have such anger and screaming at their mother. Every year, an—arbourist, is that the word? Good for me, ah?—has to climb up each tree at least four times. I watch them from this window. It is one of my greatest joys. The lowest row of drying leaves must be removed of course, sometimes I lean out and I would say, "You missed one, right there!" and then in April this tree has to be—pollinated. In August, the dangling dates have to be positioned—so they are supported. Otherwise they just—you know—hang down and be ruined.

In September or October, the dates are harvested. Such a happy time. It is an amusing puzzle to me that in the West dates are only eaten by the average person in something you call "date squares." They say they are too sweet and rich for the Western palate and yet what about this "fudge"? When I was in America they sold this fudge everywhere. Is this not over-sweet and over-rich and over-creamy with zero nutritional value?

I don't get it.

English is a funny language. How is it permissible to say the idiom "I don't get it," but if you were to say, "I don't catch it," the whole room laughs.

So. Back to blood. One of the exhibits at the Umm Al-Maarik Mosque in central Baghdad was a copy of the Koran written in Saddam Hussein's own blood. This is ironic. This is blasphemic. Why do not the heavens rain tears and the earth vomit blood at this outrage? The Holy Book written in the blood of the Devil?

I wonder who told him to do that? Or did he think of it himself?

Did a mullah demand of him to do this, as a proof of his love of Allah?

Or did his mother or his wife say to him you must appease the mullahs or they will defeat you? Because they *will* defeat you. If they want to defeat you.

They are as water, which eventually defeats everything.

> *Silence.*

Is there anything more powerful than the love of God?

I want to tell you a secret. Before I had babies I did not really believe in God.

I said that I did. Everyone thought me very religious. I went to the mosque. I prayed five times a day. I observed all the rituals: the food, the dress, all of it.

But in my heart? In my secret thoughts? I did not believe. I thought to myself I thought maybe this is mass delusion. As Karl Marx has said, "the opiate of the people." And then I hated myself for even thinking that: "Who do you think you are," and I would smack myself in the face. I wanted to believe. I prayed to Allah to help me believe in him. I prayed so hard I drew blood from my lip. But He would give me no help. And I felt like an imposter.

Pretending. I would never tell my secret to anyone. Even my husband.

Because an infidel has no friends.

My soul was an empty space. Until

I had my first child… a son,

I looked at him and I saw Allah.

I cannot explain this—it is beyond words.

My faith came back like a great river, which has been dry and begins again to flow. And every time I felt it drying up, because of the terrible the unspeakable things that were happening to my people, I looked at the face of my son, and my faith returned. Listen, no matter how bad things get in your country—I know you have your terrible sex and blood crimes—there are many gang shootings and your prisons are full, but you cannot I do not want to be rude but I am telling you that you cannot even begin to imagine what life was like under Saddam Hussein. To even say his name it makes my stomach sick. And I will not offend any of God's creatures by calling him a beast. There is only one word for such an evil human being. *Shaytaan.* Satan. Because Satan means to me the human embodiment of evil.

And I do not mean by this ignorance.

I remember the day of the coup. I was in a taxicab; he was taking me to school. I was a high-school teacher then, when I was a young mother. The radio was on but I was not listening. Suddenly the cab driver stopped. He got out of the car.

He cried, "All of Iraq is burning," the Baathists, with the support of the CIA, had killed the president and all the ministers.

We were entering the age of darkness.

I laughed out loud when Saddam's statue was toppled. And I cheered when the Devil was turned into the rodent he truly was and captured in the claws of the Eagle. I was overjoyed to see elections: hopeful. I would like to have voted. I thought maybe, maybe there is at last some light. But this moment of light and hope was an illusion, how stupid was I, ah? To think for even one moment that life might be better? That the Americans and their murderous brothers the British cared about us, about our freedom, our children? This hope was a flash, a lightning flash in the pitch dark, and it is gone.

Iraq is once again hell.

Could hell be as bad?

Those who supposedly came to liberate us… it reminds me of a young woman I know who had been taken off the street one day by officials and raped many, many times. At the end of the day they threw her out of the car to the side of the road, in the countryside. She crawled along, bruised and bleeding, half-naked, and soon, a car stopped. A very kind and gentle man with his family stopped and helped her to the car. The wife covered her and they took her to their home nearby and the wife drew a bath for her and said they would call her family while she cleaned herself and rested. As the children played in the house, the man sneaked into the bathroom and raped her again in the bath. She did not cry out because she did not want to embarrass his family. And when her own family arrived, thanking this man so profusely, bringing him gifts—

Those who say they have come to save us have come to destroy us.

So. My sin. *Hal Haram.* The worst sin of all.

On the day of the Devil—the Baathist Coup—they rounded up anybody they believed was a threat. That day, my husband went into hiding. I myself was arrested at work, taken from the school, interrogated, and after a few days released. My mother thank God was with the children. Oh yes! Everyone we knew was put in prison for a time; anybody who was thinking, intellectual, active. Anyone who was political and could be a threat. Anybody who was a member of the Communist Party.

Everyone I knew was a member of the Communist Party. Wait. I can see you are pulling away from me when I say "Communist." But this is not the Communist Party of Stalin, or Mao, or Pol Pot, or post-war Europe, far, far from it.

All of the kind and thinking and peace-loving people in Iraq at that time were members of the Communist Party. You would all have been members of the Communist Party. Oh yes. Ask anyone now. The Communist Party was the only one that welcomed people of all religions and backgrounds. And it was the only party prepared to fight to the death to free the people.

It broke our hearts that the United States land of the free, home of the brave—liberty and justice for all was supporting the coup. After the coup, the CIA gave the secret police a list of the names of everyone in the Communist Party; they were making the Baath army, and their torturers all-powerful we had to be very secretive. We had to let our babies cry at night so that their cries would cover the sound of typing. If the secret police heard typing, they would arrest us immediately. One day they took my little brother. He was a silly boy, he liked to dance with girls and drink alcohol and wear expensive clothing and he was at the university. He was taken. We did not know where he was. We received a phone call in the morning. "We are sending him home in a taxi." We waited all day. The taxi arrived. The taxi driver said *Allah akhbar.* "Thanks be to God"—because my brother was, incredibly, still alive.

We rushed him into the house because if the neighbours saw they would shun us—they would be afraid of guilt by association. And he—he was so badly beaten we couldn't recognize his face, and he, he could see nothing. My other brother cried and my mother said, "Don't cry! This is the way men learn to be men." It seems harsh, but you have to understand the way we lived, and what it was to be a man.

So, the monsters we lived in fear of were the Baath secret police, "Jihaz Haneen." If you can believe it, in English? The Instruments of Yearning. Can you explain that to me please? The torture jail was a fairy-tale castle, from long ago where the king had lived—we had not liked him either, he was Saudi but he was nothing compared to Saddam. The gardens were tended by a master gardener, a true genius of nature. And so the castle was called the Palace of Flowers. Until the Dark Age. When it became the Palace of the End.

"Qasr al-Nihayah." Iraq's own house of horrors; our children weren't afraid of fictional witches or monsters, those stories are only for peaceful places, our children had nightmares about the Palace of the End. "O people of Iraq.... By God, I shall strip you like bark, I shall truss you like a bundle of twigs, I shall beat you like stray camels.... By God, what I promise, I fulfill; what I purpose, accomplish; what I measure, I cut off."

So said al-Hadjadj, the newly arrived governor of Iraq, in the year 694.

So said Saddam.

So said George Bush and Tony Blair.

And here we are. So.

As I said, my husband had been in hiding ever since the coup, as he, at that time, was the great, visionary leader of the Communist Party. Oh yes! He was a beautiful and courageous man. He had a huge popular support, and he was poised to begin a revolution. Yes, it would have taken years, but it would have happened, and so many lives would have been saved. We all believed fervently in this revolution. Watching our friends and loved ones disappear or at best be tortured beyond recognition, it gave us hope. So we would do anything to protect this possibility.

You must understand that countless lives depended upon our success.

Hah. I just thought of an amusing story. A friend of mine who lives in America now, he was in Washington, DC, at a party or event and the wife of US Ambassador to Iraq in the sixties and seventies said of the Baathist coup: "It was a terrible time, my God we lost all our electricity. We had to go around by candlelight and it was freezing at night." My friend just laughed and laughed. He said: "Madam, for you it was electricity. For us it was death."

So imagine me, a young and very beautiful woman. Well it's true. You see me now, in my fifties, I am a handsome woman. But then? *Kullish Helwa!* I have pictures. I had now four children. My son, fifteen, Nahdne. I had a two-years-old girl, Laila, and a precious eight-years-old son, Fahdil, the light of my life, my helper, my inspiration, my mischievous monkey. Also, I was eight months pregnant.

Well. One day, as I knew they would, they came for us. Thank God they let my mother take Laila, but they took Nahdne from school, and me from my home.

I had been boiling an egg. To have with a date. It's true. And in came the thugs.

And you know who they were? You might wonder, who were these secret police? How did they collect so many eager criminals and sadists? Well I tell you they were the local bullies. One of them I recognized, he used to bother me when my brother and I went to the movies. He would harass me, say filthy things, and my brother gave him a warning. That's who it was, the losers, the ones who would torture animals, those people you avoid. So. They took us to the prison.

I remember thinking thank God they do not have Fahdil—he will know when he comes back to an empty house he will know to go to the neighbours. He had been carrying some mail from one house to another. Young boys would always do that for us they were so fast and so small. So we are driving up to the castle.

Like an American horror movie. Now, the castle has three stories. The highest floor is where they would take you to talk. The surroundings were quite nice. A reasonable conversation. If you were willing to talk, then you talked you betrayed everyone you knew, and you were free to go. Sadly, some were so afraid of torture that they talked immediately. I don't judge anyone. Everyone is different, and torture changes everything. Then, if you didn't wish to talk, they would send you down to main floor. It was what we call Torture Lite.

Beatings. Broken bones. Nails removed. That kind of thing. And if you still didn't talk, you were sent to the basement. There were bodies everywhere. Bodies of people you knew. Once you have smelled the smell of death, of mass murder and suffering, nothing smells sweet again, not ever again. The memory—not the memory, the actual smell… remains always, somewhere in every breath you take. So. At first we were sent to the highest floor. And we refused to speak. So after an hour or so we were sent to the first floor. A small room. Me, my fifteen-year-old son. And my torturers. The first thing they did. They held my belly in their hands. They laughed. And they said, "Who did this to you?" I turned to my son. I said, "Do not listen to them. They are half men." And then I said, "It is the child of my husband." And they asked to me, "Where is your husband?" I said that I did not know. They started only by jumping on my feet. And hitting my son's nose with a hammer. They hit him until he could not feel it. So he stopped crying out. And then they stopped hitting him, because they knew it did not hurt anymore.

We were… inside hell now. I only prayed I would not lose the baby. My son and I looked at each other. I knew he would be strong. This went on for hours.

Needless to say I was raped many times in front of my son. They forced him to watch. But he did not see. His eyes looked into my eyes only. So wise for fifteen.

And then, when I thought they will let us go. At this point they did not want to be seen killing women, especially pregnant women, or children. They were trying to win the hearts and minds of the people still. And this is what is taboo in every culture in the world I think. The last taboo. And just at that moment when the head torturer said to me, "We will let you go, but next time…" in through the door comes another with my eight-years-old son Fahdil. They had caught him as he was running with the mail. Someone must have pointed him out to them. Someone had betrayed us. They had blindfolded him. He was very frightened of the dark. They had beaten him about the face even before bringing him in. My son. They let me embrace him once. First: they asked him to tell them where was his father. He said he didn't know. He had been well-trained. Then they began to beat me again. And rape me again. To scare him into speaking. To protect his mother. But he knew. I turned my face to him to make sure he was alive and you know what he did? He smiled at me. He kept smiling to give me courage. And he was eight years old.

> *Fi 'aalamen azlamat marayaahu*
> *Ayyu nashidehn lam yanbajas 'aassalan*
> *Wa anta tafar fi sanayaahu*
> *In a world whose mirrors are dimmed*
> *What song did not flow with honey*
> *If you were to smile your praise upon it?*
>   —Nazik al-Mala'ika: a great Iraq poetess

So. They began to torture my son Fahdil. They said all we want to know is where is your father. You tell us you can have bread and water. About six hours later. He said he would tell them. I was almost relieved. But then he told them a lie. They gave him bread and water while the others went to find my husband.

He whispered to my older son that the reason he told the lie was although he knew they would keep beating him, he thought that the bread and water would give him the strength to keep the secret to endure more torture. And so they came back. And so beat him more. I was tied up, on my back, forced to watch, as was my older son. Well Fahdil lied three times. Three times he got bread and water. But the third time, they were onto his trick. They were furious. Now they beat him hard, with the full strength of men. He said to my older son, "I'm dying," he said, "I feel death around me. I want you to take care of my mother and little sister." They thought what more can we do? What can we do to break down this child and his mother?

Meanwhiles, they had taken away my older son, Nahdne, I did not know where. What they did then? Do you notice I have no fan here in my apartment? And it is forty degrees outside and probably forty-five in here?

There was a fan in the torture room. Right above me where I was tied.

They grabbed little Fahdil by his shirt. He was able to look at me one last time, my precious boy, he looked into my eyes with his beautiful sorrowful eyes and he smiled. I said, "I love you, my son." He did not scream, he did not even whimper. My son was more brave than many full-grown men, and he was eight years old. They turn him upside down, and then they tie him to the ceiling fan—upside down. They tie him to the ceiling fan and they turn it too fast. So my son. Is spinning. He is spinning round and round. I cannot put into words the feelings inside me.

I was praying and he was praying. We were in the hands of the devil no doubt but we had faith that we would be delivered—faith was all we had. And neither of us will speak. If we give in, we are giving not only our lives but the lives of millions. It would be like giving up Nelson Mandela, you understand? It would be like saying yes; you can go and murder these million children. To save ourselves. And I knew, I was quite certain they would not kill us because it was so deeply in my culture to never harm a pregnant woman or a child. I thought we will survive this. My son will be known forever as the most heroic child who ever lived. He will become a great leader. But he kept spinning.

My son who loved to write stories and draw pictures of animals. Who named our black-and-white cat "Jawhar": "Precious"... loved geckos, gave every one he saw a name, and you know in Iraq they are everywhere, but he had a story for each one, and always hoped to see a cheetah, for there are a few cheetahs in Iraq he would pray to Allah to see a cheetah and have a running contest for he was a very fast runner... spinning upside down over my face. And still, I did not speak. The baby was turning and turning inside my belly. I fainted many, many times that day. After hours and hours of the spinning. My son, of course, was unconscious. And they threw him on the roof. It was cold then. It was winter. He had no coat, of course. And they carried me up to an attic room, just underneath the roof, and tied me down. And still I did not speak. For days and days I lay there, the only thing keeping me breathing, was that I could hear my son coughing on the roof. That gave me such happiness, to hear him cough. I knew he was sick. He probably had even pneumonia, but the coughing meant that he was alive! And as long as he was alive when they let us go I could nurse him to good health again. I was sure they would try to look like good-hearted men, and at the very last minute they would let us go. I was so sure. And that is why. I did not speak. Every hour was like a day, every day like a year, his cough was stronger and louder and then it began to get weaker.

And weaker.

Why did I not speak then?

And weaker still.

And then he did not cough anymore.

Long beat.

They came in, laughing.

"We found your husband anyway you foolish woman. And oh... we are sorry about your son, we were going to let him go today, but he must have had a weak constitution. He is with Allah."

The Palace of the End.

A long silence.

Succour? Is that the word? For sustenance of the soul? Oh! Alliteration. Like Shakespeare. I like that in English. Not the same in Arabic. Impossible to explain. So. My succour these days is poetries. I am not talented to write it. But I am talented to learn! I have learned much Iraqi poetry by great Iraqi women. I have memorized by heart. I say it out loud. Every day. To my date tree. To the dead who are all with me. To my father, to my mother. To my husband.

And always, of course, to my son.

Long silence.

You might be wondering after that, "Does she still believe in Allah? If she found Allah in the face of her son where is He now? Where are her rivers of faith?"

Isn't my date tree so beautiful? There are more than three hundred varieties of dates. Can you imagine? When I was pregnant with my oldest son I wanted to try every kind of date. But I stopped at one hundred. Yes. *One hundred.* Actually, they all taste pretty much the same but don't tell an Iraqi I said that!

You know that for hundreds, thousand of years, the dates, together with camel milk was the diet of the Bedouins, just as potatoes was the diet of the Irish.

To harm this tree, it is unforgivable. A military saying from ancient times:

Do not kill a woman, a child, or an old man. Do not cut a tree.

What happened to that? That is only a joke now. That is "collateral damage."

One of the sights that made my blood freeze during the long Iraq-Iran war in the 1980s was the orchards of date palms with all trees—with their tops taken off. Bare.

Now the US army has torn down thousands of trees on the road leading to the airport. For security they say. But a palm tree is not like your maple tree or your evergreen it cannot hide anybody.

Sound of a bomb.

Of course my faith was gone. The riverbeds were dry. But my soul was not empty and I will tell you why. Many nights I had a dream, that when I would finally die, which happened in the first Gulf War when I was killed, right here, by an American bomb, I would finally again see my son. I knew that he would smile to me just as he did on my darkest day, a smile that said: forgive. Forgive yourself, Mama, because I forgave you. And he takes my hand and together we fly. We fly around Baghdad putting the crowns back on all the date palm trees.

It is very nice, this flying. Just the same as in your dreams. Only better. So we flew. For a while. But after a while he said, "Mama, you must go back to Baghdad—and watch over our people, with all the other ghosts. Me, I am a child, so I can go to paradise now. But you, you must watch, because the worst, Mama, the worst is yet to come…. You must watch until there is finally peace. But I will wait for you." And so I am here, watching. With the thousands of other ghosts who are watching with me. There are more every day. Do you see them all? They are everywhere, all around us. And when there is finally peace,

Fahdil will come again and we will fly together, we will fly through the crowns of the Nakhla and into the eyes of Allah.

> *More music, and the three performers stand, somehow communicate with each other, and walk off.*

> *The end.*

Scorched

Incendies
Translated by Linda Gaboriau

by Wajdi Mouawad

For Nayla Mouawad
and Nathalie Sultan
one an Arab, the other a Jew
my blood sisters both

Wajdi Mouawad

Playwright, actor, director, producer, adapter, and translator, Wajdi Mouawad was born in a tiny Lebanese village, Deir el Qamar (the Monastery of the Moon), in 1968. When civil war broke out, his parents were forced to flee the war-torn country, but not before Wajdi, who was only six, witnessed an attack on a bus full of civilians, an event he recreates in *Scorched*. After spending several years in Paris, the family moved to Montreal. In 1991, Mouawad graduated from the acting program at the National Theatre School of Canada, French Section, where he also studied playwriting and directing. He has since worked as an actor with some of Quebec's best-known directors. Notably, he also appeared in the production of Camus's *Caligula* at the Nouvelle Compagnie Théâtrale/Théâtre Denise-Pelletier and in his own play, *Alphonse*.

With Isabelle Leblanc, Mouawad co-founded the Théâtre Ô Parleur. The company first staged a "walking" production of *Macbeth* in Old Montreal in the wee hours of the morning and went on to co-produce the first plays in Mouawad's quartet of plays entitled "The Blood of Promises." From 2000–2004, he was artistic director of Montreal's Théâtre de Quat'Sous. He has written fifteen plays, many of which are about childhood, war, and exile, and a novel, *Visage retrouvé*, the story of an exiled child, which is reminiscent of Kafka's *The Metamorphosis*. In 2004, Mouawad published the essay, *Je suis le méchant!*, comprised of a series of ten interviews with director André Brassard. As a director, he has staged classics by Shakespeare, Sophocles, Euripides, Pirandello, Wedekind, and Chekhov, as well as contemporary plays by Jason Sherman (*Reading Hebron*) and Ahmed Ghazali. In 2007, Mouawad was appointed Artistic Director of French Theatre at the National Arts Centre in Ottawa. Since he took up this position, his projects have garnered broad critical acclaim.

In recognition of his body of work and his contribution to the arts, the French government appointed Mouawad Chevalier in the Ordre des Arts et des Lettres, and in 2004 he was awarded the *Grand Prix de la Francophonie*. In 2005, he turned down France's prestigious Molière Award in protest against French theatre directors' lack of interest in contemporary playwrights. In 2005, Mouawad was shortlisted for the Siminovitch Prize, and in 2006, the Quebec-based organization Artists for Peace named him Peace Artist of the Year. In 2009, Mouawad was appointed to the Order of Canada and *The Globe and Mail* selected him as runner-up for their Arts Person of the Year award. That same year, the Académie française awarded him the *Grand Prix du théâtre* for his accomplishments as a playwright. (Writers such as Jean Anouilh and Marguerite Duras have also won this prestigious prize.) Mouawad received the Governor General's Literary Award in 2000 for *Littoral* (translated by Shelley Tepperman as *Tideline*, 2002). The play, which follows the journey of a young Montreal man who attempts to bury his deceased father in his native, corpse-strewn Lebanon, went on to be performed in Beirut by Québécois actors in 2001. In 2004, Mouawad co-wrote the screenplay and directed the film version of *Littoral*.

Mouawad's other plays include *Journée de noces chez les cromagnons*, co-produced in English in Shelley Tepperman's translation, *Wedding Day at the Cro-Magnons*, by Toronto's Theatre Passe Murraille and the National Arts Centre in 1996; *Alphonse, ou, Les aventures extraordinaires de Pierre-Paul-René, un enfant doux, monocorde et qui ne s'étonne jamais de rien* (translated by Shelley Tepperman as *Alphonse, or, The Adventures of Pierre-Paul-René, a Gentle Boy with a One-note Voice Who Was Never Surprised by Anything*, 2002); *Rêves* (translated by Linda Gaboriau as *Dreams*, 2007); and *Assoiffés* (2007), which was nominated for a Governor General's Literary Award. *Forêts* (*Forests*)—the third part of the quartet that begins with *Littoral* (*Tideline*) and *Incendies* (*Scorched*)—toured France for six months in 2006, had its premiere in Montreal at Théâtre Espace Go in 2007, and went on to be performed in Ottawa at the National Arts Centre in 2008. In 2009, Mouawad remounted these three works at the Festival d'Avignon in France where he completed the quartet with the production of *Ciels* (*Skies*). In 2008, Mouawad premiered his one-man show, *Seuls*, in France before playing to sold-out houses at Théâtre d'Aujourd'hui in Montreal and the National Arts Centre in Ottawa.

Wajdi Mouawad is very much an *artiste engagé* and he frequently speaks out on controversial political and cultural issues. Like Judith Thompson, Mouawad has protested the federal government's cuts to arts funding by widely circulating a passionate letter to Prime Minister Stephen Harper in 2008.

Incendies was first presented at l'Hexagone Scène Nationale de Meylan in France in 2003, and later that same year at Théâtre de Quat'Sous during the Festival de théâtre des Amériques, with Mouawad directing. It won the Quebec Theatre Critics Association's 2004 Critics Choice Award. *Scorched*, the English-language translation by Linda Gaboriau, was commissioned by Ottawa's National Arts Centre English Theatre and premiered at Toronto's Tarragon Theatre in co-production with the NAC English Theatre in 2007. That production subsequently toured across Canada—from Montreal's Centaur, to Winnipeg's Manitoba Theatre Centre, and then to Edmonton's Citadel Theatre. Other productions include the 2009 productions at Sage Theatre in Calgary and the Wilma Theatre in Philadelphia.

The play follows the journey of a twin brother and sister who, in order to carry out their mother's last wishes, travel from Montreal to her birthplace in an unnamed, war-torn Middle Eastern country, where they are meant to find the father they thought long dead and a brother whose existence they were unaware of. The play moves back and forth over the past fifty years, sometimes existing in three timeframes simultaneously. In the course of their search for the truth about their origins, the twins learn about their mother's courageous involvement in the civil war and unearth the unsettling story of her tragic past.

Incendies was first presented in France at l'Hexagone Scène Nationale de Meylan, on March 14, 2003 and subsequently in Québec, at Théâtre de Quat'sous during the tenth edition of the Festival de théâtre des Amériques on May 23, 2003 with the following company:

NAWAL AT 40 AND 45	Annick Bergeron
NIHAD	Éric Bernier
ANTOINE DUCHARME	Gérald Gagnon
NAWAL AT 60 AND 65	Andrée Lachapelle
SAWDA	Marie-Claude Langlois
JEANNE	Isabelle Leblanc
SIMON	Reda Guerinik
NAWAL AT 14 AND 19	Isabelle Roy
HERMILE LEBEL	Richard Thériault

Directed by Wajdi Mouawad

• • •

Incendies was produced by Théâtre de Quat'Sous, in co-production with Théâtre Ô Parleur, Festival de théâtre des Amériques, l'Hexagone Scène Nationale de Meylan, Dôme Théâtre d'Alberville Scène Conventionnée, Théâtre Jean Lurçat Scène Nationale d'Aubusson, Festival des théâtres francophones en Limousin, Théâtre 71 Scène Nationale de Malakoff.

• • •

Scorched, the English-language adaptation of *Incendies*, was made possible through the assistance of the National Arts Centre (Ottawa) and with the financial support of the Government of Canada through the Interdepartmental Partnership with the Official Languages Communities (IPOLC), an initiative of the Department of Canadian Heritage.

• • •

Scorched was first presented in a staged reading at The Old Vic Theatre in London, as part of "4play Canada," a showcase event co-presented by the National Arts Centre (Ottawa) and the Canadian High Commission (London, UK). The reading was directed by Braham Murray, Artistic Director of the Royal Exchange Theatre, Manchester.

CHARACTERS

NAWAL
JANINE
SIMON
ALPHONSE LEBEL
ANTOINE
SAWDA
NIHAD

TRANSLATOR'S NOTE

For the benefit of readers who might wish to compare this translation with the original as published by Leméac/Actes Sud-Papier (2003), it is important to note that, at the playwright's request, this version of the translation is based on the script as it was revised by the author, for the new French edition published by Leméac/Actes Sud-Papiers in 2009. The translator would like to thank Lise Ann Johnson and Marti Maraden for their support and their determination to make this play available to English-speaking audiences, and Richard Rose and the wonderful cast who first brought the translation to life at the Tarragon Theatre in Toronto.

SCORCHED

NAWAL'S FIRE

1. Notary

Day. Summer. Notary's office.

ALPHONSE LEBEL   For sure, for sure, for sure, I'd rather watch birds in the sky. But you have to call a spade a spade: from here, instead of birds, you see cars and the shopping centre. When I was on the other side of the building, my office looked out over the highway. It wasn't the Taj Nepal, but I finally hung a sign in my window: *Alphonse Lebel, Notary.* At rush hour it was great publicity. Now I'm here on this side and I've got a view of the shopping centre. A shopping centre's not a gaggle of geese. Your mother's the one who taught me that geese live in gaggles. I'm sorry. I hate to mention your mother because of the tragedy that has struck, but we have to face the music. Life goes on, as they say. C'est la vie. Come in, come in, come in, you can't stay in the hallway. This is my new office. I'm just moving in. The other notaries have left. I'm all alone in this building. It's much nicer here because there's less noise, with the highway on the other side. I've lost my rush-hour advertising, but at least I can keep my window open and that's lucky, because I don't have air conditioning yet.

Right. Well…

For sure, it's not easy.

Come in, come in, come in! Don't stand there in the hallway, it's the hallway!

Even though I understand, I understand you might not want to come in.

I wouldn't come in.

Right. Well…

For sure, for sure, for sure, I would've preferred to meet you under other circumstances, but hell isn't paved with good circumstances, so these things are hard to foresee. Death can't be foreseen. You can't negotiate with death. Death breaks all promises. You think it will come later, but death comes when it pleases. I loved your mother. I'm telling you that, straight and narrow: I loved your mother. She often talked to me about the two of you. Actually, not often, but she did talk to me about you. A bit. Occasionally. Just like that. She'd say: the twins. The twin sister, the twin brother. You know how she was, she never said anything to anyone. I mean long before she stopped saying anything at all, she already said nothing and she didn't say anything about the two of you. That's how she was. When she died, it was raining. I don't know. I was really sad that it was raining. In her country it never rains, so a will, you can imagine all the bad weather in a will. It's not like birds, someone's will, for sure, it's different. It's strange and weird, but it's necessary. I mean it remains a necessary evil. I'm sorry.

He bursts into tears.

2. Last will and testament

A few minutes later.

Notary. Twin brother and sister.

ALPHONSE LEBEL   The Last Will and Testament of Madame Nawal Marwan. The witnesses who attended the reading of the will when it was registered are Monsieur Trinh Xiao Feng, owner of the Vietcong Burgers restaurant and Madame Suzanne Lamontagne, waitress at Vietcong Burgers.

That's the restaurant that used to be on the ground floor of the building. In those days, whenever I needed two witnesses, I'd go down to get Trinh Xiao Feng. And he'd come up with Suzanne. Trinh Xiao Feng's wife, Hui Huo Xiao Feng would take care of the restaurant. The restaurant's closed now. It's closed. Trinh died. Hui Huo Xiao Feng remarried, she married Réal Bouchard who was a clerk in this office, with my colleague, Notary Yvon Vachon. That's how life is. Anyway.

The opening of the will takes place in the presence of her two children: Janine Marwan and Simon Marwan, both twenty-two years of age and both born on the twentieth of August 1980 at the Saint-François Hospital in Ville Émard.... That's not far from here…

According to Madame Nawal Marwan's wishes and in keeping with her rights and the regulations, Notary Alphonse Lebel is named executor of her last will and testament…

I want you to know that that was your mother's decision. I was against it myself, I advised her against it, but she insisted. I could have refused, but I couldn't.

The notary opens the envelope.

The will is read.

All my assets are to be divided equally between the twins Janine and Simon Marwan, my offspring, flesh of my flesh. I leave my money to them in equal shares, and I want my furniture to be disposed of according to their wishes and mutual consent. If there is any dispute or disagreement, the executor of my estate will sell the furniture and divide the proceeds equally between the twin brother and sister. My clothing will be donated to the charity chosen by my executor.

Special bequests:

I leave my black fountain pen to my friend, Notary Alphonse Lebel.

I leave the khaki jacket with the number seventy-two on the back to Janine Marwan.

I leave the red notebook to Simon Marwan.

The notary takes out the three objects.

Burial:

To Notary Alphonse Lebel.

My notary and friend,

Take the twins with you

Bury me naked

Bury me without a coffin

No clothing, no covering

No prayers

Face to the ground.

Place me at the bottom of a hole,

Face first, against the world.

As a farewell gesture,

You will each throw

A pail of cold water

On my body.

Then you will fill the hole with earth and seal my grave.

Tombstone and epitaph:

To Notary Alphonse Lebel.

My notary and friend,

Let no stone be placed on my grave

Nor my name engraved anywhere.

No epitaph for those who don't keep their promises

And one promise was not kept.

No epitaph for those who keep the silence.

And silence was kept.

No stone

No name on the stone

No epitaph for an absent name on an absent stone.

No name.

To Janine and Simon, Simon and Janine.

Childhood is a knife stuck in the throat.

It can't be easily removed.

Janine,

Notary Lebel will give you an envelope.

This envelope is not for you.

It is for your father,

Your father and Simon's.
Find him and give him this envelope.

Simon,
Notary Lebel will give you an envelope.
This envelope is not for you.
It is for your brother.
Your brother and Janine's.
Find him and give him this envelope.

Once these envelopes have been delivered to their recipients
You will be given a letter
The silence will be broken
And then a stone can be placed on my grave
And my name engraved on the stone in the sun.

>   *Long silence.*

SIMON   She had to piss us off right to the very end! That bitch! That stupid bitch! Goddamn fucking cunt! Fucking bitch! She really had to piss us off right to the very end! For ages now, we've been thinking, the bitch is going to croak any day now, she'll finally stop fucking up our lives, the old pain in the ass! And then, bingo! She finally croaks! But, *surprise*! It's not over yet! Shit! We never expected this. Christ! She really set us up, calculated everything, the fucking whore! I'd like to kick her corpse! You bet we're going to bury her face down! You bet! We'll spit on her grave.

>   *Silence.*

At least I'm going to spit!

>   *Silence.*

She died, and just before she died she asked herself how she could fuck up our lives even more. She sat down and thought hard and she figured it out! She could write her will, her fucking will!

ALPHONSE LEBEL   She wrote it five years ago.

SIMON   I don't give a shit.

ALPHONSE LEBEL   Listen! She's dead. Your mother is dead. I mean she is someone who is dead. Someone none of us knew very well, but someone who was someone nevertheless. Someone who was young, who was an adult, who was old and who died! So there has to be an explanation in all that somewhere! You can't ignore that! I mean, the woman lived a whole life, for heaven's sake, and that has to count for something somehow.

SIMON   I'm not going to cry! I swear I'm not going to cry! She's dead! Who gives a shit, for Chrissake! Who gives a shit if she's dead. I don't owe that woman a thing. Not a single tear, nothing! People can say what they want. That I didn't cry over my mother's death! I'll say she wasn't my mother! That she was nothing! What makes you think we give a shit, eh? I'm not going to start pretending! Start crying! When did she ever cry over me? Or Janine? Never! Never! She didn't have a heart, her heart was a brick. You don't cry over a brick, you don't cry! No heart! A brick, goddammit, a brick! I don't want to think about her or hear about her again, ever!

ALPHONSE LEBEL   Yet she did express a wish concerning the two of you. Your names are in her last will and testament—

SIMON   Big deal! We're her children and you know more about her than we do! So what if our names are there. So what!

ALPHONSE LEBEL   The envelopes, the notebook, the money—

SIMON   I don't want her money, I don't want her notebook…. If she thinks she can touch me with her goddamn notebook! C'mon! What a joke! Her last wishes: "Go find your father and your brother!" Why didn't she find them herself if it was so fucking important?! Why didn't she worry more about us, the bitch, if she was so concerned about a son somewhere else? When she talks about us in her goddamn will, why doesn't she use the word *my children*? The word *son*, the word *daughter*! I mean, I'm not stupid! I'm not stupid! Why does she always say the twins? The twin sister, the twin brother, "the offspring of my flesh," like we were a pile of vomit, a pile of shit she had to get rid of! Why?!

ALPHONSE LEBEL   Listen. I understand!

SIMON   What can you understand, you dickhead?

ALPHONSE LEBEL   I can understand that hearing what you just heard can leave you stranded high and low, thinking what's going on, who are we and why not us! I understand, I mean I understand! It's not often we find out that the father we thought was dead is still alive and that we have a brother somewhere in this world!

SIMON   There's no father, no brother. It's all bullshit!

ALPHONSE LEBEL   Not in someone's will! Not things like that!

SIMON   You don't know her!

ALPHONSE LEBEL   I know her in a different way.

SIMON   Anyway, I don't feel like discussing this with you!

ALPHONSE LEBEL   You have to trust her.

SIMON   I don't feel like it—

ALPHONSE LEBEL   She had her reasons.

SIMON   I don't feel like discussing this with you. I don't feel like it. I've got a boxing match in ten days, that's all I care about. We'll bury her and that's it.

We'll go to a funeral home, we'll buy a coffin, we'll put her in the coffin, put the coffin in a hole, some earth in the hole, a stone on the earth and her name on the stone, and we'll get the hell out of there.

ALPHONSE LEBEL   That's impossible. Those are not your mother's last wishes and I will not allow you to go against her wishes.

SIMON   And who are you to go against us?

ALPHONSE LEBEL   I am, unfortunately, the executor of her will and I don't share your opinion of this woman.

SIMON   How can you take her seriously? C'mon! For years, she spent day after day at the courthouse, attending the trials of all sorts of perverts, sickos, and murderers, then, from one day to the next, she shuts up, never says another word! Never! For years! Five years without a word, that's a helluva long time! Not another word, not a sound, nothing ever comes out of her mouth again. A loose wire, a short circuit, she blows a fuse, whatever, and she invents a husband still alive, who's been dead for ages, and another son who never existed, the perfect fantasy of the child she wished she'd had, the child she could've loved, and now the goddamn bitch wants me to go find him! How can you talk about her last wishes—

ALPHONSE LEBEL   Calm down!

SIMON   How can you try to convince me that we're dealing with the last wishes of someone who hasn't lost her mind—

ALPHONSE LEBEL   Calm down!

SIMON   Jesus Christ! Goddamn sonofabitching fucking shit, shit, shit......

   Silence.

ALPHONSE LEBEL   For sure, for sure, for sure, but still, you have to admit it suits you to see things that way.... I don't know, it's none of my business... you're right... nobody understood why she stopped talking for such a long time and yes... yes... at first glance, it seems like an act of madness... but maybe not... I mean, maybe it was something else... I don't want to upset you but if it were an act of madness she wouldn't have spoken again. But the other day, the other night, you know that, you can't deny it, they called you, she spoke. And you can't tell me that was a coincidence, a mere fluke! Personally, I don't believe that! I mean, it was a present she was offering you! The most beautiful present she could give you! I mean that's important. The day and the hour of your birth she spoke again! And what does she say? She says: "Now that we're together, everything feels better. Now that we're together, everything feels better." I mean that's no ordinary sentence! She didn't say: "You know, I'd love to have a hot dog, all-dressed." Or : "Pass me the salt!" No! "Now that we're together, everything feels better." C'mon! The nurse heard her. He heard her. Why would he make that up? He couldn't have. Couldn't have made up something that true. You know it, I know it, we all know it, a sentence like that resembles her, like two peas in a pot. But okay, I agree with you. It's true. She shut up for years. I agree and I also agree, if things had stayed like that, I would've had my doubts too. I admit it. But still, we can't forget, I believe we have to take it into consideration. She acted rationally. "Now that we're together, everything feels better." You can't deny it. Deny your birthday! That's not the kind of thing you can deny. Now you're free to do what you want, that's for sure, for sure, for sure, you're free not to respect your mother's last wishes. Nothing obliges you to. But you can't ask the same of other people. Of me. Of your sister. The facts are there: your mother is asking each of us to do something for her, those are her wishes, and everyone can do what he wants. Even someone sentenced to death has a right to his last wishes. Why not your mother…

SIMON exits.

The envelopes are here. I'll keep them. Today you don't want to hear about them, but maybe later. Rome wasn't built in the middle of the day. Some things take time. You can call me when you're ready…

JANINE exits.

3. Graph theory, peripheral vision

Classroom where JANINE teaches. Overhead projector.

JANINE turns on the overhead projector.

Course begins.

JANINE There's no way of knowing today how many of you will pass the tests ahead of you. Mathematics as you have known them so far were all about finding strict and definitive answers to strict and definitively stated problems. The mathematics you will encounter in this introductory course on graph theory are totally different since we will be dealing with insoluble problems that will always lead to other problems, every bit as insoluble. People around you will insist that what you are wrestling with is useless. Your manner of speaking will change and, even more profoundly, so will your manner of remaining silent and of thinking. That is exactly what people will find the hardest to forgive. People will often criticize you for squandering your intelligence on absurd theoretical exercises, rather than devoting it to research for a cure for AIDS or a new cancer treatment. You won't be able to argue in your defence, since your arguments themselves will be of an absolutely exhausting theoretical complexity. Welcome to pure mathematics, in other words, to the world of solitude…. Introduction to graph theory.

Gym. SIMON with RALPH.

RALPH   You know why you lost your last fight, Simon? And you know why you lost the one before that?

SIMON   I wasn't in shape, that's why.

RALPH   You're never going to qualify if this keeps up. Put on your gloves.

JANINE   Let's take a simple polygon with five sides labelled A, B, C, D, and E. Let's call this polygon Polygon K. Now let's imagine that this polygon represents the floor plan of a house where a family lives. And one member of the family is posted in each corner of the house. For the time being, let's replace A, B, C, D, and E by the grandmother, the father, the mother, the son, and the daughter who live together in Polygon K. Now let's ask ourselves who, from his or her position, sees whom. The grandmother sees the father, the mother, and the daughter. The father sees the mother and the grandmother. The mother sees the grandmother, the father, the son, and the daughter. The son sees the mother and the sister. And the sister sees the brother, the mother, and the grandmother.

RALPH   You're not looking! You're blind! You don't see the footwork of the guy in front of you. You don't see his defence…. That's what we call a peripheral vision problem.

SIMON   Okay, okay!

JANINE   We call this application the theoretical application of the family living in Polygon K.

RALPH   Warm up!

JANINE   Now, let's remove the walls of the house and draw arcs between the members of the family who can see each other. The drawing this creates is called the visibility graph of Polygon K.

RALPH   There are three things you have to remember.

JANINE   So there are three parameters we'll be dealing with over the next three years: the theoretical application of polygons…

RALPH   You're the strongest!

JANINE   The visibility graphs of polygons…

RALPH   No pity for the guy you're facing!

JANINE   And finally, polygons and the nature of polygons.

RALPH   And if you win, you become a pro!

JANINE   The problem is as follows: for every simple polygon, I can easily draw its visibility graph and its theoretical application, as I have just demonstrated. Now, how, working from a theoretical application like this one, for instance, can I draw the visibility graph and the corresponding polygon? What is the shape of the house where the members of the family represented in this application live? Try to draw the polygon.

Gong. SIMON attacks immediately and punches into his trainer's hands.

RALPH   You're not there, you're not concentrating,

SIMON   My mother died!

RALPH   I know, but the best way to get over your mother's death is to win your next fight. So go in there and fight! You'll never succeed otherwise.

JANINE   You'll never succeed. All graph theory is essentially based on this problem, which remains for the time being impossible to solve. And it's this impossibility that is beautiful.

Gong. End of training session.

4. The hypothesis to be proven

Evening. Notary's office.

ALPHONSE LEBEL and the twin sister.

ALPHONSE LEBEL   For sure, for sure, for sure, there are times in life like this, where you're stuck between the devil and the Blue Danube. You have to act. Dive in. I'm glad you've come back. Glad for your mother's sake.

JANINE   Do you have the envelope?

ALPHONSE LEBEL   Here it is. This envelope isn't for you, it's for your father. Your mother wants you to find him and give it to him.

JANINE prepares to leave the office.

She also left you this khaki jacket with the number seventy-two on the back.

JANINE takes the jacket.

Do you believe your father is alive?

JANINE exits. Pause. JANINE returns.

JANINE   In mathematics, one plus one doesn't equal 1.9 or 2.2. It equals two. Whether you believe it or not, it equals two. Whether you're in a good mood or feeling miserable, one plus one equals two. We all belong to a polygon. I thought I knew my place in the polygon I belong to. I thought I was the point that only sees her brother Simon and her mother Nawal. Today, I found out that, from the position I hold, it is also possible for me to see my father; and I learned that there is another member of this polygon, another brother. The visibility graph I've always drawn is wrong. Where do I stand in the polygon? To find out, I have to prove a hypothesis. My father is dead. That is the hypothesis.

Everything leads us to believe this is true. But nothing proves it. I never saw his body or his grave. It is therefore possible, between one and infinity, that my father is still alive. Goodbye, Mr. Lebel.

JANINE exits.

NAWAL (age fourteen) is in the office.

ALPHONSE LEBEL walks out of his office and calls from the hallway.

ALPHONSE LEBEL   Janine!

NAWAL   *(calling)* Wahab!

ALPHONSE LEBEL   Janine! Janine!

>   *ALPHONSE LEBEL comes back into the office, takes out his cellphone and dials a number.*

NAWAL   *(calling)* Wahab!

WAHAB   *(in the distance)* Nawal!

NAWAL   *(calling)* Wahab!

WAHAB   *(in the distance)* Nawal!

ALPHONSE LEBEL   Hello, Janine? It's Notary Lebel. I just thought of something.

NAWAL   *(calling)* Wahab!

WAHAB   *(in the distance)* Nawal!

ALPHONSE LEBEL   Your mother met your father when she was very young.

NAWAL   *(calling)* Wahab!

ALPHONSE LEBEL   I just wanted to tell you, I don't know if you knew that.

WAHAB   *(in the distance)* Nawal!

5. Something is there

> *Dawn. A forest. A rock. White trees. NAWAL (age fourteen).*
>
> *WAHAB.*

NAWAL   Wahab! Listen to me. Don't say a word. No. Don't speak. If you say a word, a single word, you could kill me. You don't yet know the happiness that will be our downfall. Wahab, I feel like the minute I release the words about to come out of my mouth, you will die too. I'll stop talking, Wahab, so promise me you won't say anything, please, I'm tired, please, accept silence. Shhhh! Don't say anything. Don't say anything.

> *She falls silent.*

I called for you all night. I ran all night. I knew I'd find you at the rock where the white trees stand. I'm going to tell you. I wanted to shout it so the whole village would hear, so the trees would hear, so the night and the moon and the stars would hear. But I couldn't. I have to whisper it in your ear, Wahab, and afterwards I won't dare hold you in my arms, even if that's what I want most in the world, even if I'm sure I'll never feel complete if you remain outside me, and even if I was just a girl when I found you, and with you I finally fell into the arms of my real life, I'll never be able to ask anything of you again.

He kisses her.

I have a baby in my belly, Wahab! My belly is full of you. Isn't it amazing? It's magnificent and horrible, isn't it? It's an abyss, and it's like freedom to wild birds, isn't it? And there are no more words. Just the wind! I have a child in my belly. When I heard old Elhame tell me, an ocean exploded in my head. Seared.

WAHAB   Maybe Elhame is wrong.

NAWAL   Elhame is never wrong. I asked her. "Elhame, are you sure?" She laughed. She stroked my cheek. She told me she's the one who has delivered all the babies in the village for the last forty years. She took me out of my mother's belly and she took my mother out of her mother's belly. Elhame is never wrong. She promised she wouldn't tell anyone. "It's none of my business," she said, "but in two weeks at the most, you won't be able to hide it anymore."

WAHAB   We won't hide it.

NAWAL   They'll kill us. You first.

WAHAB   We'll explain to them.

NAWAL   Do you think that they'll listen to us? That they'll hear us?

WAHAB   What are you afraid of, Nawal?

NAWAL   Aren't you afraid? *(beat)* Put your hand here. What is it? I don't know if it's anger, I don't know if it's fear, I don't know if it's happiness. Where will we be, you and me, in fifty years?

WAHAB   Listen to me, Nawal. This night is a gift. It might be crazy for me to say that, but I have a heart and it is strong. It is patient. They will scream, and we will let them scream. They will curse and we will let them curse. It doesn't matter. After all that, after their screams and curses, you and I will remain, you and I and our child, yours and mine. Your face and my face in the same face. I feel like laughing. They will beat me, but I will always have a child in the back of my mind.

NAWAL   Now that we're together, everything feels better.

WAHAB   We will always be together. Go home, Nawal. Wait till they wake up. When they see you, at dawn, sitting there waiting for them, they will listen to you because they will sense that something important has happened. If you feel scared, remember that at that very moment, I'll be at my house, waiting for everyone to wake up. And I'll tell them, too. Dawn isn't very far away. Think of me like I'll think of you, and don't get lost in the fog. Don't forget: now that we're together, everything feels better.

WAHAB leaves.

6. Carnage

In NAWAL's house.

Mother and daughter (age fourteen).

JIHANE   This child has nothing to do with you, Nawal.

NAWAL   It's in my belly.

JIHANE   Forget your belly! This child has nothing to do with you. Nothing to do with your family. Nothing to do with your mother, nothing to do with your life.

NAWAL   I put my hand here and I can see his face.

JIHANE   It doesn't matter what you see. This child has nothing to do with you. It doesn't exist. It isn't there.

NAWAL   Elhame told me. She said: "You are expecting a baby."

JIHANE   Elhame isn't your mother.

NAWAL   She told me.

JIHANE   It doesn't matter what Elhame told you. This child does not exist.

NAWAL   And when it arrives?

JIHANE   It still won't exist.

NAWAL   I don't understand.

JIHANE   Dry your tears!

NAWAL   You're the one who's crying.

JIHANE   I'm not the one who's crying, your whole life is pouring down your cheeks! You've gone too far, Nawal, you've come back with your spoiled belly, and you stand here before me, in your child's body, and tell me: I am in love and I am carrying my love in my belly. You come back from the woods and you tell me I'm the one who's crying. Believe me, Nawal, this child does not exist. You're going to forget it.

NAWAL   A person can't forget her belly.

JIHANE   A person can forget.

NAWAL   I won't forget.

JIHANE   Then you will have to choose. Keep this child and this instant, this very instant, you will take off those clothes that don't belong to you and leave this house, leave your family, your village, your mountains, your sky, and your stars, and leave me...

NAWAL   Mother.

JIHANE   Leave me, naked, with your belly and the life it is carrying. Or stay and kneel down, Nawal, kneel down.

NAWAL   Mother.

JIHANE   Take off your clothes or kneel.

NAWAL kneels.

You will stay inside this house, the way this life lies hidden inside you. Elhame will come and take this baby from your belly. She will take it and give it to whoever she wants.

7. A knife stuck in the throat

NAWAL (age fifteen) with her grandmother, NAZIRA.

NAWAL   Now that we're together, everything feels better. Now that we're together, everything feels better. Now that we're together, everything feels better. Now that we're together, everything feels better. Now that we're together, everything feels better.

NAZIRA   Be patient, Nawal. You only have one more month to go.

NAWAL   I should have left, Grandmother, and not knelt, I should have given back my clothes, everything, and left the house, the village, everything.

NAZIRA   Poverty is to blame for all of this, Nawal. There's no beauty in our lives. No beauty. Just the anger of a hard and hurtful life. Signs of hatred on every street corner. No one to speak gently to things. You're right, Nawal, you lived the love you were meant to live, and the child you're going to have will be taken away from you. What is left for you? You can fight poverty, perhaps, or drown in it.

NAZIRA is no longer in the room. Someone is knocking on the window.

WAHAB'S VOICE   Nawal! Nawal, it's me.

NAWAL   Wahab!

WAHAB'S VOICE   Listen to me, Nawal. I don't have much time. At dawn, they're taking me away, far from here and far from you. I've just come back from the rock where the white trees stand. I said goodbye to the scene of my childhood, and my childhood is full of you, Nawal. Tonight, childhood is a knife they've stuck in my throat. Now I'll always have the taste of your blood in my mouth. I wanted to tell you that. I wanted to tell you that tonight, my heart is full of love, it's going to explode. Everyone keeps telling me I love you too much. But I don't know what that means, to love too much, I don't know what it means to be far from you, what it means not to have you with me. I will have to learn to live without you. Now I understand what you were trying to say when you asked: "Where will we be in fifty years?" I don't know. But wherever I am, you will be there. We dreamed of seeing the ocean together. Listen, Nawal, I'm telling you, listen, the day I see the ocean, the word ocean will explode in your head, it will explode and you will burst into tears because you will know that I'm thinking of you. No matter where I am, we will be together. There is nothing more beautiful than being together.

NAWAL   I hear you, Wahab.

WAHAB'S VOICE   Don't dry your tears, because I won't dry mine from now to dawn, and when you give birth to our child, tell him how much I love him, how much I love you. Tell him.

NAWAL   I'll tell him, I promise you I'll tell him. For you and for me, I'll tell him. I'll whisper in his ear: "No matter what happens, I will always love you." I'll tell him for you and for me. And I'll go back to the rock where the white trees stand and I'll say goodbye to childhood, too. And my childhood will be a knife stuck in my throat.

> *NAWAL is alone.*

8. A promise

> *Night. NAWAL is giving birth.*
>
> *NAZIRA, JIHANE, and ELHAME.*
>
> *ELHAME hands the baby to NAWAL (age fifteen).*

ELHAME   It's a boy.

NAWAL   No matter what happens, I will always love you! No matter what happens, I will always love you.

> *NAWAL slips a clown nose into the baby's swaddling clothes. They take the child away from her.*

ELHAME   I'm going south. I'll take the child with me.

NAZIRA   I feel like I'm a thousand years old. Days go by and months are gone. The sun rises and sets. The seasons go by. Nawal no longer speaks, she wanders about in silence. Her belly is gone and I feel the ancient call of the earth. Too much pain has been with me for too long. Take me to my bed. As winter ends, I hear death's footsteps in the rushing water of the streams.

NAZIRA is bedridden.

9. Reading, writing, counting, speaking

NAZIRA is dying.

NAZIRA Nawal!

NAWAL (age sixteen) comes running.

Take my hand, Nawal!

There are things we want to say at the moment of our death. Things we'd like to tell the people we have loved, who have loved us… to help them one last time… to tell them one last time… to prepare them for happiness…! A year ago, you gave birth to a child, and ever since, you've been walking around in a haze. Don't fall, Nawal, don't say yes. Say no. Refuse. Your love is gone, your child is gone. He turned one. Just a few days ago. Don't accept it, Nawal, never accept it. But if you're going to refuse, you have to know how to talk. So be courageous and work hard, sweet Nawal! Listen to what an old woman on her deathbed has to say to you: learn to read, learn to write, learn to count, learn to speak. Learn. It's your only hope if you don't want to turn out like us. Promise me you will.

NAWAL I promise you I will.

NAZIRA In two days, they will bury me. They'll put me in the ground, facing the sky, and everyone will throw a pail of water on me, but they won't write anything on the stone because no one knows how to write. When you know how to write, Nawal, come back and engrave my name on the stone: Nazira. Engrave my name because I have kept my promises. I'm leaving, Nawal. My time has come. We… our family, the women in our family… are caught in the web of anger. We have been for ages: I was angry at my mother, and your mother is angry at me, just as you are angry at your mother. And your legacy to your daughter will be anger too. We have to break the thread. So learn. Then leave. Take your youth and any possible happiness and leave the village. You are the bloom of this valley, Nawal. You are its sensuality and its smell. Take them with you and tear yourself away from here, the way we tear ourselves from our mother's womb. Learn to read, write, count, and speak. Learn to think. Nawal. Learn.

NAZIRA dies.

She is lifted from her bed.

She is lowered into a hole.

Everyone throws a pail of water on her body.

It is nighttime.

Everyone bows their head in silence.

A cellphone starts ringing.

10. Nawal's burial

Cemetery. Day.

ALPHONSE LEBEL, JANINE, and SIMON at a graveside.

ALPHONSE LEBEL answers the phone.

ALPHONSE LEBEL   Hello, Alphonse Lebel, Notary.

Yes, I called you. I've been trying to reach you for two hours! What's going on? Nothing. That's the problem. We were supposed to have three pails of water at the graveside, and they're not here. Yes, I'm the one who called for the pails of water.

What do you mean, "What's the problem, there's no problem." There's one big problem. I told you we requested three pails of water and they're not here. We're in the cemetery, where do you think we are, for crying out loud! How thick can you get? We're here for Nawal Marwan's burial.

Three pails of water!

Of course it was understood. Clearly understood. I came myself. I notified everyone: a special burial, we only need three pails of water. It didn't seem that complicated, I even asked the custodian: "Do you want us to bring our own pails of water?" He said "Of course not. We'll prepare them for you. You've got enough on your mind already." So I said fine. But here we are in the cemetery and there are no pails of water, and now we've got a lot more on our minds. I mean. This is a burial! Not a bowling party. Honestly! I mean, we're not difficult: no coffin, no tombstone, nothing. The bare minimum. Simple. We're making it very simple, we're only asking for three miserable pails of water, and the cemetery administration can't meet the challenge. Honestly!

What do you mean you're not used to requests for pails of water? We're not asking you to be used to it, we're asking for the pails of water. We're not asking you to reinvent the deal. That's right. Three. No. Not one, three. No, we can't take one and fill it three times. We want three pails of water filled once.

Yes, I'm sure.

Fine, what can I say? Make your calls.

He hangs up.

They'll make some calls.

SIMON   Why are you doing all this?

ALPHONSE LEBEL   All what?

SIMON   All this. The burial. The last wishes. Why are you the one doing all this?

ALPHONSE LEBEL   Because the woman in that hole, face to the ground, the woman I always called Madame Nawal, is my friend. My friend. I don't know if that means something to you, but I never realized how much it meant to me.

> *ALPHONSE LEBEL's cellphone rings.*
>
> *He answers.*

Hello, Alphonse Lebel, Notary.
Yes, so, what's happening?
They were prepared and placed in front of another grave.
Well, that was a mistake…. Nawal Marwan…. Your efficiency is overwhelming.

> *He hangs up.*
>
> *A man arrives with three pails of water.*
>
> *He sets them down.*
>
> *Each one picks up a pail. Empties it into the hole.*
>
> *NAWAL is buried and they leave without placing a gravestone.*

11. Silence

Day. On the stage of a theatre.

ANTOINE is there.

JANINE   Mr. Antoine Ducharme? Janine Marwan, I'm Nawal Marwan's daughter…

I went by the hospital and they told me that you stopped working as a nurse after my mother's death. That you're working in this theatre now. I've come to see you because I want to know exactly what she said…

ANTOINE   I can still hear your mother's voice ringing in my ears. "Now that we're together, everything feels better." Those were her exact words. I called you immediately.

JANINE   I know.

ANTOINE   She had been perfectly silent for five years. I'm really sorry.

JANINE   Thank you, anyway.

ANTOINE   What are you looking for?

JANINE   She always told us that our father died during the war in the country where she was born. I'm looking for proof of his death.

ANTOINE   I'm glad you've come, Janine. Ever since she died, I've wanted to call you, you and your brother. To tell you, to explain to you. But I hesitated. And here you are in this theatre. In the course of all those years spent at her bedside, I got dizzy listening to your mother's silence. One night, I woke up with a strange idea. Perhaps she speaks when I'm not there? Perhaps she talks to herself? I brought in a tape recorder. I hesitated. I had no right. If she talks to herself, that's her choice. So I promised myself I'd never listen to the tapes. Just record without ever knowing. Just record.

JANINE   Record what?

ANTOINE   Silence, her silence. At night, before leaving her, I'd start the recording. One side of a cassette lasts one hour. That was the best I could do. The next day, I'd turn the cassette over, and before leaving her, I'd start recording again. I recorded more than five hundred hours. All the cassettes are here. Take them. That's all I can do for you.

JANINE takes the box.

JANINE   Antoine, what did you do with her all that time?

ANTOINE   Nothing. I often just sat beside her. And talked to her. Sometimes I played some music. And I danced with her.

ANTOINE puts a cassette in the tape recorder. Music. JANINE exits.

CHILDHOOD ON FIRE

12. The name on the stone

NAWAL (age nineteen) at her grandmother's grave.

She is engraving NAZIRA's name on the stone in Arabic.

NAWAL *Noûn, Aleph, zaïn, yé, rra! Nazira.* Your name lights up your grave. I came into the village by the low road. My mother was standing there, in the middle of the street. She was waiting for me, I think. She must've expected something. Because of the date. We stared at each other like two strangers. The villagers gathered around. I said: "I've come back to engrave my grandmother's name on her tombstone." They laughed. "You know how to write now?" I said yes. They laughed. One man spit on me. He said: "You know how to write but you don't know how to defend yourself." I took a book out of my pocket. I hit him so hard, I bent the cover and he passed out. I went on my way. My mother watched me until I reached the fountain and turned, on my way up here to the cemetery to come to your grave. I've engraved your name, now I'm leaving. I'm going to find my son. I kept my promise to you, I'll keep my promise to him, the promise made the day of his birth: "No matter what happens, I will always love you." Thank you, Grandmother.

NAWAL exits.

13. Sawda

NAWAL (age nineteen) on a sun-parched road.

SAWDA is there.

SAWDA I saw you. I watched you from afar, I saw you engrave your grandmother's name on her gravestone. Then you stood up suddenly and ran off. Why?

NAWAL What about you, why did you follow me?

SAWDA I wanted to see you write. To see if it really existed. The rumour spread so fast this morning. You were back, after three years. In the camp, people were saying: "Nawal is back, she knows how to write, she knows how to read." Everyone was laughing. I ran to wait for you at the entrance to the village but you'd already arrived. I saw you hit the man with your book, I watched the book tremble in your hand, and I thought of all the words, all the letters, burning with the heat of the anger on your face. You left, and I followed you.

NAWAL What do you want?

SAWDA Teach me how to read and write.

NAWAL I don't know how.

SAWDA   Yes, you do. Don't lie. I saw you.

NAWAL   I'm leaving. I'm leaving the village. So I can't teach you.

SAWDA   I'll follow you. I know where you're going.

NAWAL   How could you know?

SAWDA   I knew Wahab. We're from the same camp. We came from the same village. He's a refugee from the South, like me. The night they took him away, he was shouting your name.

NAWAL   You want to find Wahab.

SAWDA   Don't be silly. I'm telling you, I know where you're going. It's not Wahab you want to find. It's your child. You see, I'm right. Take me with you and teach me how to read. I'll help you in exchange. I know how to travel and we'll be stronger together. Two women, side by side. Take me with you. If you're sad, I'll sing, if you feel weak, I'll help you, I'll carry you. There's nothing here for us. I get up in the morning and people say, "Sawda, there's the sky," but no one has anything to say about the sky. They say, "There's the wind," but no one has anything to say about the wind. People show me the world but the world is mute. And life goes by and everything is murky. I saw the letters you engraved and I thought: that is a woman's name. As if the stone had become transparent. One word and everything lights up.

NAWAL   What about your parents?

SAWDA   My parents never say anything to me. They never tell me anything. I ask them: "Why did we leave our country?" They say, "Forget that. What's the point. Don't think about it. There is no country. It's not important. We're alive and we eat every day. That's what matters." They say, "The war won't catch up with us." I answer, "Yes, it will. The earth is being devoured by a red wolf." My parents don't say anything. I tell them, "I remember, we fled in the middle of the night, men came and chased us from our house. They destroyed it." They tell me, "Learn to forget." I say, "Why was my father on his knees crying in front of our burning house? Who burned it down?" They answer, "None of that is true. You dreamt it, Sawda, you dreamt it." So I don't want to stay here. Wahab was shouting your name and it was a miracle in the middle of the night. If they took me away, no name would fill my throat. Not a single one. How can we love here? There is no love, no love. They always tell me, "Forget, Sawda, forget," so I will forget. I'll forget the village, the mountains and the camp and my mother's face and the despair in my father's eyes.

NAWAL   We can never forget, Sawda, believe me. Come with me anyway.

    They exit.

    JANINE is listening to her mother's silence.

14. Brother and Sister

SIMON is facing JANINE.

SIMON   The university is looking for you. Your colleagues are looking for you. Your students are looking for you. They keep calling me, everyone's calling me: "Janine has stopped coming to the university. We don't know where Janine is. The students don't know what to do." I've been looking for you, I've been calling you. You don't answer.

JANINE   What do you want, Simon? Why have you come to my house?

SIMON   Because everyone thinks you're dead.

JANINE   I'm fine. You can leave.

SIMON   No, you're not fine and I won't leave.

JANINE   Don't shout.

SIMON   You're starting to act like her.

JANINE   How I act is my own business, Simon.

SIMON   No. I'm sorry, but it's my business, too. I'm all you have left, and you're all I have left. And you're acting like her.

JANINE   I'm not doing anything.

SIMON   You've stopped talking. Like her. One day she comes home and she locks herself in her room. She sits there. One day. Two days. Three days. Doesn't eat. Or drink. She disappears. Once. Twice. Three times. Four times. Comes home. Refuses to talk. Sells her furniture. Your furniture's gone. Her phone rang, she wouldn't answer. Your phone rings, you won't answer. She locked herself in. You lock yourself in. You refuse to talk.

JANINE   Simon, come sit beside me. Listen. Listen for a bit.

JANINE gives SIMON one of her earphones and he presses it to his ear.
JANINE presses the other earphone to her ear. They both listen to the silence.

You can hear her breathing. You can hear her move.

SIMON   You're listening to silence!

JANINE   It's her silence.

NAWAL (age nineteen) is teaching SAWDA the Arabic alphabet.

NAWAL   *Aleph, bé, tâ, szâ, jîm, hâ, khâ…*

SAWDA   *Aleph, bé, tâ, szâ, jîm, hâ, khâ…*

NAWAL   *Dâl, dââl, rrâ, zâ, sîn, shîn, sâd, dââd…*

SIMON   You're going crazy, Janine.

JANINE   What do you know about me? About her? Nothing. You know nothing. How can we go on living now?

SIMON   How? You throw the tapes away. You go back to the university. You give your courses and you finish your Ph.D.

JANINE   I don't give a damn about my Ph.D.!

SIMON   You don't give a damn about anything!

JANINE   There's no point in trying to explain it, you wouldn't understand. One plus one equals two. You don't even understand that.

SIMON   I forgot, we have to talk to you in numbers! If your math professor told you you were going crazy, you might listen to him. But your brother—forget it! He's too dumb, too slow!

JANINE   I don't give a damn about my Ph.D. There's something in my mother's silence that I want to understand, something I need to understand.

SIMON   And I'm telling you there's nothing to understand!

JANINE   Fuck off!

SIMON   You fuck off!

JANINE   Leave me alone, Simon. We don't owe each other anything. I'm your sister, not your mother. You're my brother, not my father!

SIMON   It's all the same thing.

JANINE   No, it's not the same.

SIMON   Yes, it is!

JANINE   Leave me alone, Simon.

SIMON   The notary is expecting us in three days, we have to sign the papers. Are you going to come…? You're going to come, Janine…. Janine… answer me, are you going to come?

JANINE   Yes. Leave now.

> *SIMON leaves.*

> *NAWAL and SAWDA are walking side by side.*

SAWDA   *Aleph, bé, tâ, szâ, jîm, hâ, khâ, dâl, dââl, rrâ, zâ, sîn, shîn, sâd… tââ… oh, no…*

NAWAL   Start over.

> *JANINE is listening to her mother's silence.*

JANINE   Why didn't you say anything? Speak to me. Say something. You're alone. Antoine isn't with you. You know that he's recording you. You know that he won't listen to anything. You know that he'll give us the cassettes. You know. You've figured it all out. You know. So speak. Why won't you say something to me? Why won't you say something to me?

JANINE smashes her Walkman on the ground.

15. Alphabet

NAWAL (age nineteen) and SAWDA on a road in the sun.

SAWDA & NAWAL   *Aleph, bé, tâ, szâ, jîm, hâ, khâ, dâl, dââl, rrâ, zâ, sîn, shîn, sâd, dââd, tââ, zââ, ainn, rain, fa, Kââf, kaf, lâm, mime, noun, hah, lamaleph, wâw, ya.*

NAWAL   That's the alphabet. Twenty-nine sounds. Twenty-nine letters. Those are your weapons. Your bullets. You have to remember them. And how to put them together, to make words.

SAWDA   Look. We've reached the first village in the South. The village of Nabatiyé. The first orphanage is here. Let's go ask.

They pass JANINE.

JANINE is listening to silence.

16. Where to begin

JANINE walks onto the stage in the theatre.

Loud music.

JANINE   *(calling)* Antoine... Antoine... Antoine!

ANTOINE appears. The music is too loud for them to talk.

ANTOINE gestures for her to wait. The music stops.

ANTOINE   Sorry, we're doing sound checks for the show tonight.

JANINE   Help me, Antoine.

ANTOINE   What do you want me to do?

JANINE   I don't know where to begin.

ANTOINE   You have to begin at the beginning.

JANINE   There's no logic.

ANTOINE   When did you mother stop talking?

JANINE   In the summer of '97. In August. On the twentieth. The day of our birthday. Mine and Simon's. She came home and she refused to talk. Period.

ANTOINE   What happened that day?

JANINE   I don't know. At the time she was following some preliminary hearings at the International Criminal Tribunal.

ANTOINE   Why?

JANINE   They were related to the war in the country where she was born.

ANTOINE   And on that particular day?

JANINE   Nothing. I read and reread the minutes a hundred times, trying to understand.

ANTOINE   You never found anything else?

JANINE   Nothing. A little photograph. She'd already shown it to me. Her, when she was thirty-five, with one of her friends. Look.

> *She shows him the photo.*
>
> *ANTOINE studies the photo.*
>
> *NAWAL (age nineteen) and SAWDA in the deserted orphanage.*

SAWDA   There's no one here, Nawal. The orphanage is empty.

NAWAL   What happened?

SAWDA   I don't know.

NAWAL   Where are the children?

SAWDA   There are no more children here. Let's go to Kfar Rayat. That's where the biggest orphanage is.

> *ANTOINE keeps the photo.*

ANTOINE   Leave the photo with me. I'll have it blown up. I'll study it for you. I'm used to looking for little details. That's where we have to begin. I miss your mother. I can see her. Sitting there. In silence. No wild look in her eyes. No lost look. Lucid and piercing.

JANINE   What are you looking at, Mama, what are you looking at?

17. Orphanage in Kfar Rayat

> *NAWAL (age nineteen) and SAWDA in the orphanage in Kfar Rayat with a DOCTOR.*

NAWAL   There was no one in the orphanage in Nabatiyé. We came here. To Kfar Rayat.

THE DOCTOR   You shouldn't have. There are no children here either.

NAWAL   Why?

THE DOCTOR Because of the war.

SAWDA What war?

THE DOCTOR Who knows.... Brothers are shooting their brothers and fathers are shooting their fathers. A war. But what war? One day five hundred thousand refugees arrived from the other side of the border and said: "They've chased us off our land, let us live side by side." Some people from here said yes, some people from here said no, some people from here fled. Millions of destinies. And no one knows who is shooting whom or why. It's a war.

NAWAL And where are the children who were here?

THE DOCTOR Everything happened so fast. The refugees arrived. They took all the children away. Even the newborn babies. Everyone. They were angry.

SAWDA Why did the refugees take the children?

THE DOCTOR Out of revenge. Two days ago, the militia hanged three young refugees who strayed outside the camps. Why did the militia hang the three teenagers? Because two refugees from the camp had raped and killed a girl from the village of Kfar Samira. Why did they rape the girl? Because the militia had stoned a family of refugees. Why did the militia stone them? Because the refugees had set fire to a house near the hill where thyme grows. Why did the refugees set fire to the house? To take revenge on the militia who had destroyed a well they had drilled. Why did the militia destroy the well? Because the refugees had burned the crop near the river where the dogs run. Why did they burn the crop? There must be a reason, that's as far as my memory goes, I can't retrace it any further, but the story can go on forever, one thing leading to another, from anger to anger, from sadness to grief, from rape to murder, back to the beginning of time.

NAWAL Which way did they go?

THE DOCTOR They were headed south. To the camps. Now everyone is afraid. We're expecting retaliation.

NAWAL Did you know the children?

THE DOCTOR I was their doctor.

NAWAL I'm trying to find a child.

THE DOCTOR You'll never find him.

NAWAL I will find him. A boy of four. He arrived here a few days after his birth. Old Elhame delivered him from my belly and took him away.

THE DOCTOR And why did you give him to her?

NAWAL They took him away from me! I didn't give him away! They took him from me. Was he here?

THE DOCTOR   Elhame brought many children.

NAWAL   Yes, but she didn't bring many in the spring four years ago. A newborn boy. From the North. Do you have records?

THE DOCTOR   No more records.

NAWAL   A cleaning woman, a kitchen worker, someone who would remember. Remember having found the child beautiful. Having taken him from Elhame.

THE DOCTOR   I'm a doctor, not an administrator. I travel around to all the orphanages. I can't know everything. Go look in the camps, down south.

NAWAL   Where did the children sleep?

THE DOCTOR   In this ward.

NAWAL   Where are you? Where are you?

JANINE   Mama, what are you looking at?

NAWAL   Now that we're together, everything feels better.

JANINE   What did you mean by that?

NAWAL   Now that we're together, everything feels better.

JANINE   Now that we're together, everything feels better.

> *Night. Hospital. ANTOINE comes running in.*

ANTOINE   What? What? Nawal? Nawal!

SAWDA   Nawal!

ANTOINE   What did you say? Nawal!

> *ANTOINE picks a tape recorder up off the floor beside NAWAL (age sixty-four).*

NAWAL   If I could turn back the clock, he would still be in my arms…

SAWDA   Where are you going? Where are you going?

> *ANTOINE picks up the phone and dials a number.*

ANTOINE   Miss Janine Marwan…?

NAWAL   South.

ANTOINE   Antoine Ducharme, your mother's nurse.

SAWDA   Wait! Nawal! Wait!

ANTOINE   She just spoke. Nawal just spoke.

> *NAWAL exits.*

18. Photograph and southbound bus

ANTOINE and JANINE at the university. The photograph of NAWAL (age thirty-five) and SAWDA is projected on the wall.

ANTOINE   They're back in your mother's country. It's summertime, you can tell from the flowers behind them. Those are the wild herbs that bloom in June and July. The trees are parasol pines. They're found throughout the region. And there's something written on the burnt-out bus in the background, you see. I asked the grocer at the corner of my street, he comes from there, and he read: Refugees of Kfar Rayat.

JANINE   I've done research on the history of the hearings. One of the longest chapters concerns a prison built during the war in Kfar Rayat.

ANTOINE   Now look. You see that, just above her hand…

JANINE   What is it?

ANTOINE   The butt of a gun. Her friend has one too, you can see the outline under her blouse.

JANINE   What were they doing with guns?

ANTOINE   We can't tell from the photo. Maybe they were working as guards in the prison. What year was the prison built?

JANINE   1978. According to the tribunal records.

ANTOINE   Good. Now we know that your mother, towards the end of the '70s, was in the vicinity of the village of Kfar Rayat where a prison was built. She had a friend whose name we don't know and both of them carried guns.

   Silence.

Are you all right? Janine? Are you all right?

JANINE   No, I'm not all right.

ANTOINE   What are you afraid of?

JANINE   Of finding out.

ANTOINE   What are you going to do now?

JANINE   Buy an airplane ticket.

   NAWAL (age nineteen) is waiting for the bus. SAWDA is at her side.

SAWDA   I'm leaving with you.

NAWAL   No.

SAWDA   I can't leave you alone!

NAWAL   Are you sure there's a bus on this road?

SAWDA Yes, it's the one the refugees take back to the camps. You see that cloud of dust down there, that must be it. Nawal, the doctor said you should wait. He said there'll be trouble in the camps, because of the children who were kidnapped.

NAWAL So I have to be there!

SAWDA What difference can one day make?

NAWAL One day more to hold my child in my arms. I look up at the sun and I think he's looking at the same sun. A bird flies by, perhaps he sees the same bird. A cloud in the distance, and I think it's passing over him, that he's running to escape the rain. I think of him every minute and every minute is like a promise of my love for him. He turned four today. He knows how to walk, he knows how to talk and he must be afraid of the dark.

SAWDA And if you die, what's the point?

NAWAL If I die, it will be because he was already dead.

SAWDA Nawal, don't go today.

NAWAL Don't tell me what to do.

SAWDA You promised you'd teach me.

NAWAL We must go our separate ways now.

The bus arrives. NAWAL climbs aboard. The bus leaves. SAWDA is left standing at the roadside.

19. Lawns in the suburbs

ALPHONSE LEBEL's house.

In his backyard.

ALPHONSE, JANINE, and SIMON.

Noise of traffic and jackhammers close by.

ALPHONSE LEBEL Not every day is Sunday, for sure, but once in a while, it does you good. I get to the office and the landlord is there. Right away, I thought, watch out, there's some fishing going on here. He says, "Mr. Lebel, you can't go in, we're taking up the carpet and redoing the floors." I say, "You could have let me know, I have work to do, I'm expecting clients." He says, "You're always busy, what's the difference, today or tomorrow, you would've complained anyway." "I'm not complaining, I just would've liked to know," I say, "especially since I'm in a rush period." So then he looks at me and he says, "That's because you're not well-organized." Wait. Me, not well-organized. "You're the one who's not well-organized. You show up like a fly in the appointment, and you announce:

I'm going to redo your floors." "Whatever!" he says. So I said "Whatever!" back to him and I left. Good thing I was able to reach you.

Come out, come out, come out, it's nicer outside, it's too hot to stay in the house. Come out in the yard. I'll turn on the sprinklers to water the lawn. That'll cool us off.

> *ALPHONSE turns on the faucet to water his lawn. JANINE and SIMON join ALPHONSE. Sound of jackhammers.*

They're redoing the street. They'll be at it till winter. Come out, come out, come out. I'm happy to see you here in my home. It was my parents' house. There used to be fields as far as the eye could see. Today there's the Canadian Tire store and the hydro plant. It's better than a tar pit, for sure. That's what my father said just before he died: "Death is better than a tar pit." He died in his bedroom upstairs in this house. Here are the papers.

> *Sound of the jackhammers.*

They've changed the bus route, because of the construction work. Now the bus stop is right there, just the other side of the fence. All the buses on this line stop here and every time a bus stops, I think of your mother.... I ordered a pizza. We can share it. It comes with the special: soft drinks, fries, and a chocolate bar. I ordered all-dressed without the pepperoni because it's hard to digest. It's an Indian pizzeria, the pizzas are really good, I don't like to cook, so I order out.

SIMON   Okay, fine. Can we get this over with? I've got a fight tonight and I'm already late.

ALPHONSE LEBEL   Good idea. While we're waiting for the pizza, we can settle the paperwork.

JANINE   Why do you think of our mother every time a bus stops?

ALPHONSE LEBEL   Because of her phobia!

JANINE   What phobia?

ALPHONSE LEBEL   Her... bus phobia. Here are the papers and they're all in order. Didn't you know?

JANINE   No!

ALPHONSE LEBEL   She never took a bus.

JANINE   Did she tell you why?

ALPHONSE LEBEL   Yes. When she was young, she saw a bus full of civilians riddled with machine-gun fire, right in front of her. A horrible sight.

JANINE   How do you know that?

> *Sound of jackhammers.*

ALPHONSE LEBEL   She told me.

JANINE   Why did she tell you that?

ALPHONSE LEBEL   How do I know? Because I asked her!

> *ALPHONSE hands them the papers. JANINE and SIMON sign where he indicates.*

So these papers settle your mother's estate. Except for her last wishes. At least, in your case, Simon.

SIMON   Why in my case?

ALPHONSE LEBEL   Because you still haven't taken the envelope to be delivered to your brother.

> *SIMON glances at JANINE.*

JANINE   Yes, I've taken mine.

SIMON   I don't get it.

> *Sound of the jackhammers.*

JANINE   What don't you get?

SIMON   I don't get what you're up to.

JANINE   Nothing.

SIMON   Why didn't you tell me?

JANINE   Simon, it's hard enough as it is.

SIMON   What are you going to do, Janine? Run around everywhere shouting: "Papa, papa, where are you? I'm your daughter." This is no mathematical problem, for Chrissake. You won't find the solution. There is no solution. There's nothing left…

JANINE   I don't want to discuss this with you, Simon.

SIMON   …no father, no brother, just you and me.

JANINE   Exactly what did she say about the bus?

SIMON   What are you going to do? Fuck! Where are you going to start looking for him?

JANINE   What did she say?

SAWDA   *(screaming)* Nawal!

SIMON   Forget about the bus and answer me! Where are you going to find him?

> *Sound of jackhammers.*

JANINE   What did she tell you?

SAWDA   *(screaming)* Nawal!

ALPHONSE LEBEL   She told me she had just arrived in a town…

SAWDA   *(to JANINE)* Have you seen a girl named Nawal?

ALPHONSE LEBEL   Travelling on a bus…

SAWDA   *(screaming)* Nawal!

ALPHONSE LEBEL   Packed with people.

SAWDA   *(screaming)* Nawal!

ALPHONSE LEBEL   Some men came running up, they blocked the way of the bus, doused it with gasoline, and then some others arrived with machine guns and…

> *Long sequence of jackhammer noise that entirely drowns the sound of ALPHONSE LEBEL's voice. The sprinklers spray blood and flood everything. JANINE exits.*

NAWAL   *(screaming)* Sawda!

SIMON   Janine! Come back, Janine!

NAWAL   I was in the bus, Sawda, I was with them! When they doused us with gas, I screamed: "I'm not from the camp, I'm not one of the refugees from the camp, I'm one of you, I'm looking for my child, one of the children they kidnapped." So they let me off the bus, and then, then they opened fire, and in a flash, the bus went up in flames, it went up in flames with everyone inside, the old people, the children, the women, everyone! One woman tried to escape through a window, but the soldiers shot her, and she died there, straddling the window with her child in her arms in the middle of the blaze, her skin melted, her child's skin melted, everything melted and everyone burned to death. There is no time left, Sawda. Time is like a chicken with its head cut off, racing around madly, every which way. Blood is flowing from its decapitated neck, and we're drowning in blood, Sawda, drowning.

SIMON   *(on the phone)* Janine! You're all I've got left, Janine. I'm all you've got left. We have no choice. We have to forget. Call me back, Janine, call me back!

20. The very heart of the polygon

SIMON is dressing for his fight.

JANINE, with a backpack, is holding a cellphone.

JANINE   Simon, it's Janine. I'm at the airport, Simon. I'm calling to tell you that I'm leaving for her country. I'm going to try to find this father of ours, and if I find him, if he's still alive, I'll give him the envelope. I'm not doing it for her,

I'm doing it for myself. And for you. For the future. But first we have to find Mama, we have to discover her past, her life during all those years she hid from us. She blinded us. Now I'm afraid of going crazy. I have to hang up, Simon. I'm going to hang up and tumble headfirst into a world far from here, far from the strict geometry that has defined my life. I've learned to write and count, to read and speak. Now all that is of no use. The hole I'm about to tumble into, the hole I'm already slipping into, is that of her silence. Simon, are you crying? Are you crying?

SIMON's fight. SIMON is knocked out.

Where are you leading me, Mama? Where are you leading me?

NAWAL To the very heart of the polygon, Janine, to the very heart of the polygon.

JANINE places her earphones on her ears, slips a new cassette into the recorder, and starts to listen to her mother's silence again.

JANNAANE'S FIRE

21. The Hundred Years War

NAWAL (age forty) and SAWDA. A building in ruins. Two dead bodies lie on the floor.

SAWDA   Nawal!

NAWAL   They went to Abdelhammas's house too. They killed Zan, Mira, Abiel. At Madelwaad's, they searched the whole house and didn't find him so they slit everyone's throat. The whole family. And they burned his eldest daughter to death.

SAWDA   I've just been to Halam's. They were at his house too. They couldn't find him so they took his daughter and his wife away. No one knows where.

NAWAL   They killed everyone who contributed money to the newspaper. Everyone who worked at the newspaper. They burned the printing press. Burned the paper. Threw out the ink. And now look. They've killed Ekal and Faride. We're the ones they're searching for, Sawda, they're after us and if we stay here another hour, they'll find us and kill us too. So let's go to the camps.

SAWDA   We'll go to my cousin's house, we'll be a bit safer there.

NAWAL   Safer…

SAWDA   They even destroyed the homes of people who read the newspaper.

NAWAL   And it's not over yet. Believe me. I've thought it through. We are at the beginning of the hundred years war. At the beginning of the last war in the world. I'm telling you, Sawda, our generation is an "interesting" generation. Seen from above, it must be very instructive to see us struggling to name what is barbarous and what isn't. Yes. Very "interesting." A generation raised on shame. Really. At the crossroads. We think, this war will only end with the end of time. People don't realize, if we don't find a solution to these massacres immediately, we never will.

SAWDA   Which war are you talking about?

NAWAL   You know very well which war. The war pitting brother against brother, sister against sister. The war of angry civilians.

SAWDA   How long will it last?

NAWAL   I don't know.

SAWDA   The books don't say?

NAWAL   Books are always way behind the times, or way ahead. It's all so ridiculous. They've destroyed the newspaper, we'll start another one. It was called *The Morning Light*, we'll call the next one *The Rising Sun. (beat)* Words are horrible. We can't let them blind us. We have to do as our ancestors did in ancient times: try to read in the flight of birds the presages of things to come. Divination.

SAWDA   Divine what? Ekal is dead. All that's left is his camera. Shattered images. A broken life. What kind of a world is this where objects have more hope than we do?

> *Beat. SAWDA sings a song like a prayer.*

22. Abdessamad

> *JANINE is in NAWAL's native village.*

> *ABDESSAMAD is standing with her.*

JANINE   Are you Abdessamad Darazia? They told me to come see you because you know all the tales of the village.

ABDESSAMAD   The true and the false, too.

JANINE   Do you remember Nawal? *(showing him the photo of NAWAL (thirty-five) and SAWDA)* Her. She was born and grew up in this village.

ABDESSAMAD   There is Nawal who left with Sawda. But that's a legend.

JANINE   Who is Sawda?

ABDESSAMAD   A legend. They called her the girl who sings. A deep, sweet voice. She always sang at the right moment. A legend.

JANINE   And what about Nawal? Nawal Marwan.

ABDESSAMAD   Nawal and Sawda. A legend.

JANINE   And what does the legend say?

ABDESSAMAD   It says that one night they separated Nawal and Wahab.

JANINE   Who is Wahab?

ABDESSAMAD   A legend! They say if you linger too long in the woods, near the rock where the white trees stand, you'll hear their laughter.

JANINE   The rock where the white trees stand?

> *WAHAB and NAWAL (age fourteen) at the rock where the white trees stand. NAWAL is unwrapping a present.*

WAHAB   I brought you a present, Nawal.

NAWAL   A clown nose!

WAHAB   The same one we saw when the travelling circus came to town. Remember how hard you laughed! You kept saying, "His nose, his nose! Look at his nose!" I loved to hear you laugh like that. I went to their campsite, I almost got eaten alive by the lion, trampled on by the elephant, I had to negotiate with the tigers, I swallowed three snakes and I walked into the clown's tent. He was sleeping, his nose was on the table, I grabbed it and ran!

ABDESSAMAD   In the cemetery, the stone still stands where, according to the legend, Nawal engraved her grandmother's name. Letter by letter. The first epitaph in the cemetery. She'd learned to write. Then she left. Sawda went with her and the war began. It's never a good sign when the young people flee.

JANINE   Where is Kfar Rayat?

ABDESSAMAD   In hell.

JANINE   More specifically.

ABDESSAMAD   South of here. Near Nabatiyé. Follow the road.

ABDESSAMAD exits. JANINE makes a phone call.

JANINE   Hello, Simon, it's Janine. I'm calling from the village where Mama was born. Listen. Listen to the sound of the village.

She walks off holding her phone aloft.

23. Life is around the knife.

SAWDA and NAWAL (age forty) are leaving the village. Morning.

A MILITIAMAN appears.

MILITIAMAN   Who are you? Where are you coming from? The roads are closed to travellers.

NAWAL   We've come from Nabatiyé and we're on our way to Kfar Rayat.

MILITIAMAN   How do we know you're not the two women we've been looking for? Our entire company is looking for them, and the soldiers who've come from the South are looking for them, too. They know how to write and they're putting ideas into people's heads.

Silence.

You are those two women. One writes and the other sings.

Beat.

You see these shoes? I took them off the feet of a corpse last night. I killed the man who was wearing them in a one-on-one fight, looking him in the eye. He told me: "We're from the same country, the same blood," and I smashed his skull and stripped off his shoes. In the beginning, my hands shook. It's like everything else. The first time, you hesitate. You don't know how tough a skull can be. So you don't know how hard you have to hit. And you don't know where to stab your knife. You don't know. The worst isn't stabbing the knife, it's pulling it out, because all the muscles contract and hold on to the knife. The muscles know that's where life is. Around the knife. So you sharpen the blade and then there's no problem. The blade slips out as easily as it slips in. The first time is hard. Then it gets easier, like everything else.

The MILITIAMAN grabs NAWAL and holds a knife to her throat.

I'm going to slit your throat and we'll see if the one who knows how to sing has a pretty voice, and if the one who knows how to think still has any bright ideas.

SAWDA takes out a gun and fires one shot.

The MILITIAMAN falls.

SAWDA   Nawal, I'm afraid he's right. You heard what he said: "The first time is hard, then it gets easier."

NAWAL   You didn't kill him, you saved our lives.

SAWDA   Those are just words, nothing but words.

SAWDA fires another shot into the MILITIAMAN's body.

24. Kfar Rayat

JANINE in the Kfar Rayat prison. The guide is with her. She is taking photos.

GUIDE   This prison was turned into a museum in 2000, to revive the tourist trade. I used to be a guide up north, I did the Roman ruins. My speciality. Now I do the Kfar Rayat prison.

JANINE   *(showing him the picture of NAWAL and SAWDA)* Do you know these two women?

GUIDE   No, who are they?

JANINE   Maybe they worked here.

GUIDE   Then they fled at the end of the war with the torturer, Abou Tarek. This is the most famous cell in Kfar Rayat prison. Cell number seven. People make pilgrimages here. It was the cell of the woman who sings. She was a prisoner here for five years. When the others were being tortured, she'd sing—

JANINE   Was the woman who sings named Sawda?

GUIDE   No one knew her name. They just had serial numbers. The woman who sings was number seventy-two. It's a famous number around here.

JANINE   Did you say number seventy-two?!

GUIDE   Yes, why?

JANINE   Do you know anyone who worked here?

GUIDE   The janitor at the school. He was a guard here back then.

JANINE   How long ago was this prison built?

GUIDE   1978. The year of the massacres in the refugee camps of Kfar Riad and Kfar Matra. That's not far from here. The soldiers surrounded the camps and they sent in the militia. The militiamen killed everything in sight. They were crazy. Their leader had been assassinated. So they didn't fool around. A huge wound in the flank of the country.

JANINE exits.

25. Friendships

NAWAL (age forty) and SAWDA.

SAWDA   They entered the camps. With knives, grenades, machetes, axes, guns and acid. Their hands were not shaking. Everyone was fast asleep. They plunged their weapons into their sleep and they murdered the dreams of the men, women, and children who were sleeping in the great cradle of the night!

NAWAL   What are you going to do?

SAWDA   Leave me alone!

NAWAL   Where are you going?

SAWDA   I'm going into every house.

NAWAL   To do what?

SAWDA   I don't know.

NAWAL   Are you going to fire a bullet into every head?

SAWDA   An eye for an eye, a tooth for a tooth, that's what they say!

NAWAL   Not that way.

SAWDA   There's no other way! Now that death can be contemplated in cold blood, there's no other way!

NAWAL   So now you want to go into houses and kill men, women, and children!

SAWDA   They killed my parents, my cousins, my neighbours, my parents' distant friends! It's the same thing.

NAWAL   Yes, it's the same thing, Sawda, you're right, but think about it.

SAWDA   What's the point of thinking about it. Thinking about it can't bring anyone back to life.

NAWAL   Think about it, Sawda. You are a victim and you're going to kill everyone who crosses your path, and then you'll be the murderer. Then in turn, you'll be the victim again! You know how to sing, Sawda, you know how to sing!

SAWDA   I don't want to sing! I don't want to be consoled, Nawal. I don't want your ideas, your images, your words, your eyes, the time we spent side by side— I don't want all that to console me after everything I've seen and heard! They stormed into the camps like madmen. The first screams woke the others and soon everyone heard the fury of the militiamen! They began by throwing children against the walls, then they killed every man they could find. They slit the boys' throats and burned the girls alive. Everything was on fire, Nawal, everything was on fire, everything went up in flames. Blood was flowing through the streets. Screams filled throats and died, another life gone. One militiaman was preparing the death of three brothers. He lined them up against the wall. I was at their feet, hiding in the gutter. I could see their legs shaking. Three brothers. The militiamen pulled their mother by the hair, stood her in front of her sons and one of them shouted: "Choose, choose which one you want to save. Choose or I'll shoot all three of them. I'm going to count to three, and at three, I'm going to kill all three of them. Choose!" Listen to me, Nawal, I'm not making this up. I'm telling you the pain that fell at my feet. I could see her, through her sons' trembling legs. Unable to speak, unable to think, shaking her head, looking from one son to the next! With her heavy breasts and her body ravaged by having carried them, her three sons. And her entire body was shouting, "What was the point of bearing them, just to see their blood splattered against a wall?" And the militiaman kept shouting, "Choose! Choose!" Then she looked at him and said, as a last hope, "How dare you, look at me, I could be your mother." And he hit her. "Don't insult my mother! Choose!" Then she said a name, she said, "Nidal. Nidal!" And she collapsed and the militiaman shot the youngest two. He left the eldest son alive, trembling! He just left him there and walked away. The two bodies lay at his feet. The mother stood up and in the middle of the town in flames, weeping in its fumes, she began to wail that she had killed her sons. Dragging her heavy body, she kept screaming that she was her sons' assassin!

NAWAL   I understand, Sawda, but you can't just strike back blindly. Listen. Listen to what I'm saying: we have blood on our hands and in a situation like this, a mother's suffering is less important than the terrible machine that is crushing us. That woman's pain, your pain and mine, the pain of those who died that night is no longer a scandal, it is an accumulation, an accumulation too monstrous to be calculated. So you, Sawda—you who were reciting the alphabet a long time ago on the road to the sun, when we were travelling side by side to find my son born of a love story the likes of which is no longer told—you can't add to this monstrous accumulation of pain. You simply can't.

SAWDA   So what can we do? What can we do? Just fold our arms and wait? And tell ourselves this has nothing to do with us, let the idiots fight it out among themselves! Are we supposed to stick to our books and our alphabet where everything is so nice, so beautiful, so extraordinary, so interesting?! "Nice, beautiful, interesting, extraordinary." That's like spitting in the victims' faces. Words! What good are words if I don't know what I should do today? What can we do, Nawal?

NAWAL   I can't answer that question, Sawda. There are no values to guide us, so we have to rely on makeshift values... on what we know and what we feel. This is good, that is bad. But I know one thing: we don't like war, and we are forced to be part of it. We don't like unhappiness and we are drowning in it. You want to take revenge, burn down houses, make people feel what you feel so they'll understand, so they'll change, so the men who have done this will be transformed. You want to punish them so they'll understand. But this idiotic game feeds off the madness and the pain that are blinding you.

SAWDA   So we don't make a move, is that it?

NAWAL   Who are you trying to convince? Can't you see that there are men who can no longer be convinced? Men who can no longer be persuaded of anything? The guy who was shouting "Choose!" at that woman, forcing her to condemn her own children, do you think you can convince him that he made a mistake? What do you expect him to do? Tell you, "Oh, Miss Sawda, your argument is very interesting, I'm going to change my mind, my feelings, my blood, my world, my universe, my planet, and I'm going to apologize immediately." What do you think? That you're going to teach him something by spilling the blood of his wife and son? Do you think that from one day to the next, with the bodies of his loved ones lying at his feet, he's going to say, "This gives me food for thought, now I can see that the refugees deserve a home. I'll give them mine and we'll live in peace and harmony, all of us together!" Sawda, when they yanked my son from my body, tore him from my arms, from my life, I realized that I had a choice: either I lash out at the world or I do everything I can to find him. I think of him every day. He's twenty-five now, old enough to kill, old enough to die, old enough to love and to suffer. So what do you think I'm thinking when I tell you all that? I'm thinking of his probable death, of my ridiculous search, of the fact that I will be forever incomplete because he left my life and I will never see him standing before me. Don't think I can't feel that woman's pain. It's inside me like a poison. And I swear, Sawda, that I would be the first to grab the grenades, to grab dynamite, bombs, and anything that could do the most damage, I would wrap them around me, I would swallow them, and I would head into the midst of those stupid men and blow myself up with a joy you can't imagine. I swear I'd do it, because I have nothing left to lose and my hatred for those men is deep, so deep! I see my life in the faces of the men who are destroying our lives. I'm etched in every one of their wrinkles and it would be so easy to blow myself up so I could tear them to shreds, right to the marrow of their soul, do you hear me? But I made a promise... I promised an old woman I would learn to read, to write, and to speak, so I could escape poverty and hatred. And this promise is going to guide me. No matter what. Never let hatred be your guide, never, reach for the stars, always. A promise made to an old woman who wasn't beautiful or rich or anything special, but who helped me, who cared for me and who saved me.

SAWDA   So what can we do?

NAWAL   Let me tell you what we can do. But you have to hear me out. You have to promise me you won't argue. That you won't try to prevent anything.

SAWDA   What are you thinking of?

NAWAL   Promise!

SAWDA   I'm not sure.

NAWAL   Remember, a long time ago, you came to me and said: "Teach me to read and write." I said yes, and I kept my promise. Now, it's your turn to promise me. Promise.

SAWDA   I promise.

NAWAL   Listen. We're going to strike. But we're going to strike a single spot. Just one. And we're going to hurt. We won't touch a single man, woman, or child, except for one man. Just one. We'll get him. Maybe we'll kill him, maybe we won't, that doesn't matter, but we'll get him.

SAWDA   What are you thinking of?

NAWAL   I'm thinking of Chad.

SAWDA   The paramilitary leader. We'll never get to him.

NAWAL   The girl who teaches his children used to be my student. She's going to help me. I'm going to replace her for a week.

SAWDA   Why are you saying "I"?

NAWAL   Because I'm going alone.

SAWDA   And what will you do?

NAWAL   At first, nothing. I'll teach his daughters.

SAWDA   Then?

NAWAL   Then? The last day, just before leaving, I'll fire two shots at him, one for you, one for me. One for the refugees, one for the people from my country. One for his stupidity, one for the army that has invaded us. Two twin bullets. Not one, not three. Two.

SAWDA   And then what? How will you get away?

Silence.

I refuse. It's not up to you to do that.

NAWAL   Who is it up to, then? You, maybe?

SAWDA   Why not?

NAWAL   Why are we doing this? For revenge? No. Because we still want to love with passion. And in a situation like this, some people are bound to die and others not. Those who have already been passionately in love should die before those who have never loved. I have lived the love I was meant to live. I had the child I was meant to have. Then I had to learn, and I learned. Now all I have left is my death and I have chosen it and it will be mine. You have to go hide at Chamseddine's house.

SAWDA   Chamseddine is as violent as the rest of them.

NAWAL   You have no choice. Don't betray me, Sawda. You have to live for me, and go on singing for me.

SAWDA   How can I go on living without you?

NAWAL   And how can I go on living without you? Remember the poem we learned a long time ago, when we were still young. When I still thought I would find my son. *(They recite the poem "Al Atlal" in Arabic.)* Recite it every time you miss me, and when your courage fails, you can recite the alphabet. And when my courage fails, I'll sing. I'll sing, Sawda, the way you taught me to. And my voice will be your voice and your voice will be my voice. That's how we can stay together. There is nothing more beautiful than being together.

26. The khaki jacket

JANINE and the school JANITOR.

THE JANITOR   I'm a school janitor.

JANINE   I know, but before…. When the prison was still a prison.

THE JANITOR   You have outstayed your welcome.

JANINE takes out the khaki jacket. The man grabs it from her.

JANINE   There's a number printed on the back. Number seventy-two…

THE JANITOR   The woman who sings.

JANINE   *(handing him the photo)* Is that her?

THE JANITOR   *(studying the photo)* No, that is.

JANINE   No! That's her!

THE JANITOR   I saw that woman for more than five years. She was always in her cell. The woman who sings. I was one of the few people to see her face.

JANINE   Please. Are you sure that this woman, the one with the long hair who's smiling, is the woman who sings?

THE JANITOR   That is the woman I knew in her cell.

JANINE   And who is this?

THE JANITOR   I don't know her.

JANINE   Sawda. She is the woman who sings! Everyone told me that.

THE JANITOR   Well, they lied to you. The woman who sings is this one.

JANINE   Nawal? Nawal Marwan?

THE JANITOR   No one ever spoke her name. She was simply the woman who sings. Number seventy-two. Cell number seven. The one who assassinated the paramilitary leader. Two bullets. The whole country quaked. They sent her to Kfar Rayat. All her friends were captured and killed. One of them reached the café where the militia hung out and she blew herself up. Only the woman who sings survived. Abou Tarek handled her. The nights when Abou Tarek raped her, we couldn't tell their voices apart.

JANINE   Oh, I see, she was raped!

THE JANITOR   It was very common around here. And inevitably, she got pregnant.

JANINE   What?!

THE JANITOR   That was common, too.

JANINE   Of course, she got pregnant…!

THE JANITOR   The night she gave birth, the whole prison fell silent. She gave birth all alone, crouching in a corner of her cell. We could hear her screams and her screams were like a curse on us all. When it was over, I entered the cell. Everything was dark. She had put the child in a pail and covered it with a towel. I was the one who always took the babies to the river. It was winter. I took the pail, I didn't dare look in it, and I went out. The night was clear and cold. Pitch black. No moon. The river was frozen. I went to the ditch and I left the pail there and started back. But I could hear the child crying and I could hear the song of the woman who sings. So I stopped and thought, and my conscience was as cold and dark as the night. Their voices were like banks of snow in my soul. So I went back, I took the pail and I walked and walked, until I ran into a peasant who was returning with his flock to the village higher up, near Kisserwan. He saw me, he saw my grief, he gave me some water and I gave him the pail. I told him, "This is the child of the woman who sings." And I left. Later on people found out. And they forgave me. They left me alone. And today I work in this school. Everything worked out.

Long pause.

JANINE   So she was raped by Abou Tarek.

THE JANITOR   Yes.

JANINE   She got pregnant and she had the child in prison.

THE JANITOR   Yes.

JANINE   And you took the child and instead of killing it, like all the others, you gave it to a peasant? Is that right?

THE JANITOR   Yes, that's right.

JANINE   Where is Kisserwan?

THE JANITOR   A little farther west. Overlooking the sea. Ask for the man who raised the child of the woman who sings. They'll know him. My name is Fahim. I threw a lot of children into the river, but I didn't throw that one. His crying touched me. If you find him, tell him my name, Fahim.

JANINE puts on the jacket.

JANINE   Why didn't you tell us? We would have loved you for it. Been so proud of you. Defended you. Why didn't you ever tell us, Mama? Why did I never hear you sing?

27. Telephones

JANINE is in a phone booth.

SIMON is at the gym.

The following two speeches overlap.

JANINE   Listen, Simon, listen! I don't give a damn! I don't give a damn about your boxing match! Shut up! Listen to me! She was in jail. She was tortured! She was raped! Do you hear me! Raped! Do you hear what I'm saying? And our brother is the child she had in jail. No! Fuck, Simon, I'm halfway round the world, in the middle of nowhere, there's a sea and two oceans between us, so shut up and listen to me…! No, you're not going to call me back, you're going to see the notary, you're going to ask him for the red notebook and you're going to see what's in it. Period.

SIMON   No! No! I'm not interested in that. My boxing match! That's all I care about! I'm not interested in knowing who she was! No, I'm not interested! I know who I am today, and that's enough for me. Now, you listen to me! Come home! Come home, fuck, right away! Come home, Janine…! Hello? Hello…? Fuck! Don't you have the number of your goddamn phone booth so I can call you?

She hangs up.

28. The real names

JANINE at the peasant's house.

JANINE   A shepherd directed me to you. He said: "Go up to the pink house and you'll find an old man. His name is Abdelmalak, but you can call him Malak. He will take you in." So here I am.

MALAK   Who sent you to the shepherd?

JANINE   Fahim, the janitor at the school in Kfar Rayat.

MALAK   And who told you about Fahim?

JANINE   The guide in the Kfar Rayat prison.

MALAK   Mansour. That's his name. Why did you go to see Mansour?

JANINE   Abdessamad, a refugee who lives in a village up north, directed me to the Kfar Rayat prison.

MALAK   And who sent you to see Abdessamad?

JANINE   At this rate, we'll go back to the day of my birth.

MALAK   Perhaps. Then we'll find a beautiful love story. You see that tree over there, it's a walnut tree. It was planted the day I was born. It's a hundred years old. Time is a strange beast, isn't it? So?

JANINE   Abdessamad lives in the village where my mother was born.

MALAK   And what was your mother's name?

JANINE   Nawal Marwan.

MALAK   And what's your name?

JANINE   Janine Marwan.

MALAK   So what do you want from me? Who do you want me to direct you to now?

JANINE   To the child that Fahim gave you one day, on behalf of my mother.

MALAK   But I don't know your mother.

JANINE   You don't know Nawal Marwan?

MALAK   The name doesn't mean anything to me.

JANINE   What about the woman who sings?

MALAK   Why are you talking about the woman who sings? Do you know her? Has she come back?

JANINE   The woman who sings is dead. Nawal Marwan is her name. Nawal Marwan is the woman who sings. And she is my mother.

The old man takes JANINE into his arms.

MALAK   Jannaane!

NAWAL (age forty-five) is there, facing MALAK, who stands holding two babies in his arms.

The word spread around the country that you had been released.

NAWAL   What do you want from me?

MALAK   I want to give back your children. I cared for them as if they were my own!

NAWAL   So keep them!

MALAK   No, they are yours. Take them. You don't realize what they will be for you. It took many miracles for them to be alive today, and many miracles for you to be alive. Three survivors. Three miracles looking at each other. Not often you see that. I gave them each a name. The boy's name is Sarwane and the girl is Jannaane. Sarwane and Jannaane. Take them and remember me.

MALAK gives the children to NAWAL.

JANINE   No! No, that can't be us. That's not true. My name is Janine and my brother is Simon.

MALAK   Jannaane and Sarwane.

JANINE   No! We were born in the hospital. We have our birth certificates! And we were born in the summer, not in the winter, and the child born in Kfar Rayat was born in the winter because the river was frozen, Fahim told me, that's why he couldn't throw the pail into the deep water.

MALAK   Fahim is mistaken.

JANINE   Fahim isn't mistaken. He saw her every day! He took the child, he took the pail, the child was in the pail, and there was only one child, not two, not two!

MALAK   Fahim didn't look carefully.

JANINE   My father is dead, he gave his life for this country, and he wasn't a torturer, he loved my mother and my mother loved him!

MALAK   Is that what she told you? Why not, children need bedtime stories to help them fall asleep. I warned you, the question-and-answer game can easily lead back to the birth of things, and it's led us back to the secret of your birth. Now you listen to me: Fahim hands me the pail and he goes running off. I lift up the cloth covering the child, and what do I see, two babies, two newborn babies, red with anger, pressed against each other, clinging to each other with all the fervour of the beginning of their lives. I took the two of you and I fed you and named you. Jannaane and Sarwane. And here you are. You've come back to me after your mother's death, and I can see, from the tears running down your cheeks, that I wasn't so wrong. The offspring of the woman who sings were born of rape and horror, but they will restore the lost cries of the children thrown into the river.

29. Nawal speaks

SIMON opens the red notebook.

NAWAL (age sixty) is testifying before the tribunal.

NAWAL Madam President, ladies and gentlemen of the tribunal. I wish to make my testimony standing, my eyes wide open, because I was often forced to keep them closed. I will make my testimony facing my torturer. Abou Tarek. I speak your name for the last time in my life. I say it so you know that I recognize you. So you can entertain no doubt about that. There are many dead who, if they arose from their bed of pain, would also recognize you, recognize the horror of your smile. Many of your men feared you, although they were nightmares, too. How can a nightmare fear a nightmare? The kind and just men who come after us might be able to solve this enigma. I recognize you, but you might not recognize me, despite my conviction that you can place me perfectly since your job as a torturer required an excellent memory for family names and given names, for dates, and places, and events. Nevertheless, let me remind you of my face, because my face was what you cared least about. You remember much more clearly my skin, my smell, the most intimate details of my body, which you treated as a territory to be massacred, bit by bit. There are ghosts speaking to you through me. Remember. Perhaps my name will mean nothing to you, because all the women were nothing but whores to you. You used to say, whore number forty-five, whore number sixty-three. That gave you a certain style and elegance, a know-how, a weight, an authority. And the women, one after another, felt fear and hatred awake inside them. Perhaps my name will mean nothing to you, perhaps my whore number will mean nothing, but there's one thing you haven't forgotten, something that still rings in your ears despite all your efforts to prevent it from drowning your heart, one thing will certainly burst the dike that allows you to forget: the woman who sings. Now do you remember? You know the truth of your anger towards me, when you hanged me by the feet, when the water and the electrical current… the shards under my fingernails… the gun loaded with blanks against my temple…. The gunshots and death that are part of torture, and the urine on my body, yours, in my mouth, on my sex, and your sex in my sex, once, twice, three times, so often that time was shattered. My belly growing big with you, your ghastly torture in my belly, and left alone, all alone, you insisted that I be alone to give birth. Two children. Twins. You made it impossible for me to love the children. Because of you, I struggled to raise them in grief and in silence. How could I tell them about you, tell them about their father, tell them the truth, which, in this case, was a green fruit that could never ripen? So bitter. Bitter is the spoken truth. Time will pass, but you will not escape the justice that escapes us all: these children we gave birth to, you and I, are alive, they are beautiful, intelligent, sensitive, bearing their own share of victories and defeats, already seeking to give meaning to their lives, their existence…. I promise you that sooner or later they will come and stand before you, in your cell, and you will be alone with them, just as I was alone with them, and like me, you will lose all sense of being alive. A rock would feel more alive than you. I speak from experience. I also promise that when they stand before you, they will both know who you are. You and I come from the same land, the same language, the same history, and each land, each language, each history is responsible for its people, and each people is responsible for their traitors and their heroes. Responsible for their executioners and their victims, for their victories and their defeats. In this sense, I am responsible for you, and you are responsible for me. We didn't like war or violence, but we went to war and were violent. Now all that is left is our possible dignity. We've failed at everything, but perhaps that's one thing we still can save: dignity. Speaking to you as I am today bears witness to the promise I kept for a woman who once made me understand the importance of rising above poverty: "Learn to read, to speak, to write, to count, learn to think."

SIMON *(reading from the red notebook)* My testimony is the result of this effort. To remain silent about your acts would make me an accomplice to your crimes.

SIMON closes the notebook.

30. Red wolves

SIMON and ALPHONSE LEBEL.

ALPHONSE LEBEL What do you want to do?

SIMON I don't know what I want to do. A brother…. What's the point?

ALPHONSE LEBEL To know—

SIMON I don't want to know.

ALPHONSE LEBEL Then for Janine. She can't go on living if she doesn't know.

SIMON But I'll never be able to find him!

ALPHONSE LEBEL Of course you'll be able to find him! You're a boxer!

SIMON An amateur boxer. I've never fought a professional fight.

ALPHONSE LEBEL I'll help you, we'll go get our passports together, I'll go with you, I won't leave you alone. We'll find your brother! I'm sure of it. Maybe what you learn will help you live, will help you fight, and win, and become a professional. I believe in that kind of thing… it's all in the cosmos. You have to have faith.

SIMON   Do you have the envelope for my brother?

ALPHONSE LEBEL   Of course! You can count on me, I swear, you can count on me. We're beginning to see the train at the end of the tunnel.

> *ALPHONSE exits. NAWAL (age sixty-five) is with SIMON.*

NAWAL   Why are you crying, Simon?

SIMON   It feels like a wolf… it's coming closer. He's red. And there's blood on his jaws.

NAWAL   Come now.

SIMON   Where are you taking me, Mama?

NAWAL   I need your fists to break the silence. Sarwane is your real name. Jannaane is your sister's real name. Nawal is your mother's real name. Abou Tarek is your father's name. Now you must discover your brother's name.

SIMON   My brother!

NAWAL   Your blood brother.

> *SIMON is left alone.*

SARWANE'S FIRE

31. The man who plays

A young man on the roof of an apartment building.

Alone. Walkman (1980s model) on his ears.

Using a telescopic rifle in lieu of a guitar, he passionately plays the first bars of "The Logical Song" by Supertramp.

NIHAD is wielding the "guitar" and shouting the instrumental opening at the top of his lungs.

When the lyrics begin, his rifle becomes a microphone. His English is approximate. He sings the first verse.

Suddenly, something in the distance attracts his attention.

He raises his rifle, quickly takes aim, while continuing to sing.

He fires one shot, reloads immediately,

Shoots again while changing position. Shoots again, reloads, freezes, and shoots again.

NIHAD hastily grabs a camera. He aims it in the same direction, focuses, and takes a picture.

He begins singing again.

Suddenly he stops. He falls to the ground. He grabs his rifle and takes aim at something close by.

He leaps to his feet and fires one shot. He runs towards the place he shot at.

He has dropped his Walkman, which goes on playing.

NIHAD comes back, dragging a wounded man by the hair. He throws him on the ground. (The assumption is that NIHAD and the man are speaking in French. NIHAD's French is fluent, while his English is broken.)

THE MAN   No! No! I don't want to die!

NIHAD   "I don't want to die!" "I don't want to die!" That's the dumbest sentence I know!

THE MAN   Please, let me go! I'm not from around here. I'm a photographer.

NIHAD   Photographer?

THE MAN   Yes... a war photographer.

NIHAD   Did you take my picture?

THE MAN   I wanted a shot of a sniper... I saw you shoot... I came up here.... But I can give you the film...

NIHAD   I'm a photographer, too. My name is Nihad. War photographer. Look.
I took these.

> *NIHAD shows him photo after photo.*

THE MAN   Very nice…

NIHAD   No, it's not nice. People usually think it's shots of people sleeping. They're
not sleeping, they're dead. And I'm the one who killed them! I swear.

THE MAN   I believe you.

> *Searching through the photographer's bag, NIHAD takes out an automatic
> camera equipped with a trigger cord. He looks through the viewfinder and
> fires off some shots of the man. He takes some heavy adhesive tape and tapes
> the camera to the end of his rifle.*

What are you doing?

> *The camera is well-secured.*

> *NIHAD attaches the trigger cord to the trigger of his gun.*

> *He looks through the viewfinder and aims at the man.*

Don't kill me! I could be your father, I'm the same age as your mother…

> *NIHAD shoots. The camera goes off at the same time. We see the photo of the
> man at the moment when the bullet hits him. NIHAD performs for the dead
> man. He imitates an interview on a US talk show in his broken English.*

NIHAD   Kirk, I very habby to be here at *Star TV Show*…
Thank you to you, Nihad. So Nihad, wath is your nesxt song?
My nesxt song will be love song.
Love song!
Yes, love song, Kirk.
This something new on you career, Nihad.
You know, I wrote this song when it was war. War on my country. Yes, one day
a woman that I love die. Yes.
Shooting by a sniper. I feel big crash in my hart. My hart colasp. Yes, I cry. And
I write this song.
It will be pleasure to heare you love song, Nihad.
No problem, Kirk.

> *NIHAD stands up again, takes his pose, using his rifle as a mic.*

> *He adjusts his earphones, turns on his Walkman.*

One, two, one, two, three, four!

> *He sings out the thirty-two drumbeats of "Roxanne" by the Police, shouting
> "Da, na, na, na, na…" then he sings the song, twisting the words.*

32. Desert

ALPHONSE LEBEL and SIMON in the middle of the desert.

SIMON   There's nothing in that direction.

ALPHONSE LEBEL   But the militiaman told us to go that way.

SIMON   He could've told us to pound sand, too.

ALPHONSE LEBEL   Why would he have done that?

SIMON   Why not?

ALPHONSE LEBEL   He was very helpful. He told us to go find a man named Chamseddine, the spiritual leader of the resistance movement in the South. He told us to head that way, so we'll head that way.

SIMON   And if someone tells you to shoot yourself…

ALPHONSE LEBEL   Why would anyone tell me to do that?

SIMON   Great, so now what do we do?

ALPHONSE LEBEL   What do you want to do?

SIMON   Let's open the envelope I'm supposed to give my brother! And stop playing hide-and-go-seek.

ALPHONSE LEBEL   That's out of the question!

SIMON   What prevents me from doing it?

ALPHONSE LEBEL   Listen to me, young man, because I won't repeat it from now to Bloomsday. That envelope isn't yours. It belongs to your brother.

SIMON   Oh yeah, so what?

ALPHONSE LEBEL   Look me in the bright of the eyes! Doing that would be like raping someone!

SIMON   Well, that makes sense. I have a precedent. My father was a rapist!

ALPHONSE LEBEL   That's not what I meant.

SIMON   Okay. Fine! We won't open the goddamn envelope! But fuck! We'll never find him!

ALPHONSE LEBEL   Mr. Chamseddine?

SIMON   No, my brother.

ALPHONSE LEBEL   Why not?

SIMON   Because he's dead! I mean, for Chrissake! At the orphanage, they said in those days the militiamen kidnapped the kids to blow them up in the camps. So he's dead. We went to look in the camps, and they told us about the 1978 massacres. So again, he must be dead. We went anyway to see a militiaman who came from the same orphanage and he told us he can't remember much, except for one guy like him, who had no mother, no father, who took off one day and he figures he must've died. So if I know how to count, he died blowing up like a bomb, he died with his throat slit, and he disappeared and died. That's a lot of deaths. So I think we can forget Sheik Chamseddine.

ALPHONSE LEBEL   For sure, for sure, for sure! But if we want to get to the bottom of it, the militiaman told us to go see Mr. Chamseddine who was the spiritual leader of the resistance during the war against the army that invaded the South. He must have contacts. Those people are way up in the hierarchy. Those political types know the business. They know everything. I mean, why not? Your brother might still be alive, I mean, we can't know for sure. We found out his name, that's a start. Nihad Harmanni.

SIMON   Nihad Harmanni.

ALPHONSE LEBEL   Harmanni, right, and there are as many Harmannis as there are Tremblays in the phone book, but still, we're pretty close to finding him. Mr. Chamseddine will tell us.

SIMON   And where are we going to find Mr. Chamseddine?

ALPHONSE LEBEL   I don't know… in that direction.

SIMON   There's nothing but desert in that direction.

ALPHONSE LEBEL   That's right! Exactly! The perfect hiding place! Those people have to hide! I mean, Mr. Chamseddine, I bet he's not a member of the local video club, and he doesn't call and have them deliver Hawaiian pizzas! No, he's in hiding! Maybe he's watching us right now, so let's get a move on, and sooner or later he'll show up and ask us what we're doing on his land!

SIMON   What movie are you in?

ALPHONSE LEBEL   Please, Simon! Sarwane! Let's give it a try and maybe we'll find your brother! You never know. Maybe your brother's a notary like me. We can chat about notarized minutes and deeds. Or maybe a greengrocer, a restaurant owner, I don't know, take Trinh Xiao Feng, he was a general in the Vietnamese army, and he ended up selling hamburgers on Curé-Labelle Boulevard, and Hui Huo Xiao Feng got married again with Réal Bouchard! I mean, you never know! Maybe your brother is married to a rich American from San Diego and they have eight kids, and that makes you an uncle eight times over! Who knows. Let's get going!

They continue on their way.

33. A sniper's principles

NIHAD, with the camera attached to the end of his rifle, is shooting.

A first photo of a man on the run appears.

NIHAD takes another step, shoots again.

A photo of the same man, mortally wounded, appears.

NIHAD   You know, Kirk, sniper job is fantastic job.
Excellent, Nihad, can you tell us about this?
Yeah! It is very artistic job.
Because good sniper don't shoot just any way, no, no!
I have lot of principles, Kirk!
First, when you shoot, you have to kill, immediate, for not make suffering the person.
Sure!
Second, you shoot all person. Fair and same with everyone.
For me, Kirk, my gun is like my life.
You know, Kirk,
Every bullet I put in gun
Is like a poetry.
And I shoot a poetry to the people, and it is precision of my poetry that kill people and that's why my photos is fantastic.
And tell me, Nihad, you shoot everybody.
No, Kirk, no everybody…
I suppose you don't kill children.
Yes, yes, I kill children. No problem. It like pigeon, you know.
So?
I don't shoot woman like Elizabeth Taylor. Elizabeth Taylor is good actress. I like very much and I don't want kill Elizabeth Taylor. So, when I see woman like her, I no shoot her…
You don't shoot Elizabeth Taylor.
No, Kirk, sure not!
Thank you, Nihad.
Welcome, Kirk.

NIHAD stands up, aims his gun, and fires again.

34. Chamseddine

SIMON and ALPHONSE LEBEL facing CHAMSEDDINE.

NAWAL (age forty-five).

ALPHONSE LEBEL   Talk about searching! We searched! Here, there, and everywhere! Mr. Chamseddine is here, Mr. Chamseddine is there, no answer. You're as famous as Shakespeare's Skylock, but you're not easy to find.

CHAMSEDDINE   Are you Sarwane?

SIMON   I am.

CHAMSEDDINE   I've been waiting for you. When I heard that your sister was in the region a while ago, I thought: "If Jannaane doesn't come to see me, Sarwane will." When I heard that the son of the woman who sings was looking for me, I knew that she had died.

NAWAL   The next time you hear about me, I will have left this world.

SIMON   I'm looking for the son she had before us. They said you could help me.

CHAMSEDDINE   I can't.

SIMON   They told me you know everyone.

CHAMSEDDINE   I don't know him.

SIMON   His name was Nihad Harmanni.

CHAMSEDDINE   Why are you talking about Nihad Harmanni?

SIMON   One of the militiamen knew him as a child. They joined the militia together, then he lost track of him. He told us: "Chamseddine must've caught him and killed him." He told us you flayed every militiaman and every foreign soldier your men caught.

CHAMSEDDINE   Did he tell you that Nihad Harmanni was the son of the woman who sings, the one born of her relationship with Wahab who no one ever laid eyes on?

SIMON   No. He didn't know anything about that. Never heard of the woman who sings. He simply said that Nihad Harmanni passed through these parts.

CHAMSEDDINE   So how can you say that he is the son of the woman who sings?

ALPHONSE LEBEL   If I may say so, I think I can explain. Alphonse Lebel, notary and executor of the estate of the woman who sings. Now, Mr. Chamseddine, I can tell it to you the way it is: all the details add up.

CHAMSEDDINE   Speak!

ALPHONSE LEBEL   A real puzzle! First we went to Madame Marwan's native village. That led us to Kfar Rayat. There, we followed some leads based on the arrival dates of several boys in the orphanage. Toni Moubarak, but it's not him, he was reunited with his parents after the war, an unpleasant character and not at all helpful. Toufic Hallabi, but it's not him either, he makes great shish taouk up north, near the Roman ruins, he doesn't come from these parts, his parents died, it was his sister who placed him in the orphanage in Kfar Rayat. We followed two other bad leads and we finally found a more serious one. This lead led us to the Harmanni family who have since passed away. The grocer told us about their adopted son. Told us his name. I went to see a colleague, Notary Halabi, very nice man who handled the Harmanni family affairs. He recorded that Roger and Souhayla Harmanni, unable to have children of their own, had adopted, on their way through Kfar Rayat, a boy they named Nihad. The child's age and the date of his arrival at the orphanage coincided perfectly with what we know about Madame Nawal. And most important of all, this boy was the only one of our candidates brought to the orphanage by the midwife from Madame Nawal's village. A certain Elhame Abdallâh. With all that, Mr. Chamseddine, we were pretty sure we were right.

CHAMSEDDINE   If the woman who sings chose to trust you, you must be noble and worthy. But step outside. Leave us alone.

ALPHONSE LEBEL exits.

Sarwane, stay with me. And listen to me. Listen carefully.

35. The voice of ancient times.

ALPHONSE LEBEL and JANINE.

ALPHONSE LEBEL   He still hasn't said a word. He stayed with Chamseddine and when he came out, Janine, your brother had the same look in his eyes as your mother. He didn't say a thing all day. Or the next day. Or the day after that. He wouldn't leave the hotel. I knew you were in Kfar Rayat. I didn't want to disturb your solitude, but Simon refuses to speak, Janine, and I'm afraid. Maybe we pushed too hard to discover the truth.

JANINE and SIMON sit facing each other.

SIMON   Janine, Janine.

JANINE   Simon!

SIMON   You always told me that one plus one equals two. Is that true?

JANINE   Yes. It's true…

SIMON   You didn't lie to me?

JANINE   No! One plus one equals two!

SIMON   It can never be one?

JANINE   What did you find, Simon?

SIMON   Answer me! Can one plus one equal one?

JANINE   Yes.

SIMON   How?

JANINE   Simon.

SIMON   Explain it to me!

JANINE   Fuck! This is no time for math, tell me what you found out!

SIMON   Explain how one plus one can equal one! You always said I didn't understand anything. So, now's your chance. Explain!

JANINE   Okay! There's a strange hypothesis in math. A hypothesis that's never been proven. You can give me a figure, any figure. If it's an even number, you divide it by two. If it's uneven, you multiply it by three and you add one. You do the same thing with the figure you get. This theory posits that no matter what number you start with, you'll always end up with one. Give me a figure.

SIMON   Seven.

JANINE   Okay. Seven is uneven. You multiply it by three and add one, that makes—

SIMON   Twenty-two.

JANINE   Twenty-two is even, you divide by two.

SIMON   Eleven.

JANINE   Eleven is uneven, you multiply by three, you add one—

SIMON   Thirty-four.

JANINE   Thirty-four is even. You divide by two, seventeen. Seventeen is uneven, you multiply by three you add one, fifty-two. Fifty-two is even, you divide by two, twenty-six. Twenty-six is even, you divide by two, thirteen. Thirteen is uneven. You multiply by three and add one, forty. Forty is even. You divide by two, twenty. You divide by two, ten. Ten is even, you divide by two, five. Five is uneven, you multiply by three and add one, sixteen. Sixteen is even, you divide by two, eight, you divide by two, four, you divide by two, two, you divide by two, one. No matter what number you start with, you always end up with…. No!

SIMON   You've stopped talking. The way I stopped talking when I understood. I was in Chamseddine's tent, and in that tent I saw silence come and drown everything. Alphonse Lebel had stepped outside. Chamseddine came over to me.

CHAMSEDDINE   Sarwane, it's not mere chance that has led you to me. Your mother's spirit is here. And the spirit of Sawda. The friendship of women like a star in the sky. One day a man approached me. He was young and proud. Try to imagine him. Can you see him? He is your brother, Nihad. He was searching for the meaning of his life. I told him to fight for me. He accepted. He learned how to use guns. A great marksman. Deadly. One day, he left. "Where are you going?" I asked him.

NIHAD   I'm headed north.

CHAMSEDDINE   And what about our cause? Fighting for the people here, the refugees? The meaning of your life?

NIHAD   No cause. No meaning!

CHAMSEDDINE   And he left. I tried to help him. I had him watched. That's when I realized he was looking for his mother. He searched for years, and never found her. He started to laugh at nothing. No more cause. No more meaning. He became a sniper. He collected photographs. Nihad Harmanni. A real reputation as an artist. He could be heard singing. A killing machine. Then the foreign army invaded the country. They came all the way north. One morning, they caught him. He had killed seven of their marksmen. He'd shot them in the eye. The bullet in their scopes. They didn't kill him. They kept him and trained him. They gave him work.

SIMON   What work?

CHAMSEDDINE   In a prison they had just built, in the South, in Kfar Rayat. They were looking for a man to take charge of the interrogations.

SIMON   So he worked with my father, Abou Tarek?

CHAMSEDDINE   No. Your brother didn't work with your father. Your brother is your father. He changed his name. He forgot Nihad and became Abou Tarek. He searched for his mother, he found her, but he didn't recognize her. She searched for her son, she found him and didn't recognize him. He didn't kill her, because she sang and he liked her voice. Yes, that's right. The earth stops turning, Sarwane. Abou Tarek tortured your mother, and your mother was tortured by her son and the son raped his mother. The son is the father of his brother and his sister. Can you hear my voice, Sarwane? It sounds like the voice of centuries past. But, no, Sarwane, it is the voice of today. The stars fell silent inside me, the second you pronounced the name of Nihad Harmanni. And I can see that the stars have now fallen silent inside you, Sarwane. The silence of the stars, and your mother's silence. Inside you.

NIHAD Harmanni, known as Abou Tarek, at his trial.

NIHAD   I don't contest anything that has been said at my trial over these past years. The people who claimed I tortured them—I did torture them. And the people I am accused of having killed—I did kill them. In fact, I would like to thank them all, because they made it possible for me to take some very beautiful photographs. The men I hit, and the women I raped, their faces were always more moving after the blow and after the rape. But essentially, what I want to say is that my trial has been tedious, boring beyond words. Not enough music. So I'm going to sing you a song. I say that because dignity has to be preserved.

I'm not the one who said that, it was a woman, the one everyone called the woman who sings. Yesterday she came and stood before me and spoke of dignity. Of saving what is left of our dignity. I thought about it and I realized she was right about something. This trial has been such a bore! No beat, no sense of showbiz. That's where I find my dignity. And always have. I was born with it. The people who watched me grow up always said this object was a sign of my origins, of my dignity, since, according to the story they tell, it was given to me by my mother. A little red nose. A little clown nose. What does it mean? My personal dignity is a funny face left by the woman who gave birth to me. This funny face has never left me. So let me wear it now and sing you one of my songs, to save dignity from the horror of boredom.

He puts on the clown nose. He sings.

NAWAL (age fifteen) gives birth to NIHAD.

NAWAL (age forty-five) gives birth to JANINE and SIMON.

NAWAL (age sixty) recognizes her son.

JANINE, SIMON, and NIHAD are all together.

36. Letter to the father

JANINE gives the envelope to NIHAD. NIHAD opens the envelope. NAWAL (age sixty-five) reads.

NAWAL   I am trembling as I write to you.
I would like to drill these words into your ruthless heart.
I push down on my pencil and I engrave every letter
Remembering the names of all those who died at your hands.
My letter will not surprise you.
Its only purpose is to tell you: Look:
Your daughter and your son are facing you.
The children we had together are standing before you.
What will you say to them? Will you sing them a song?
They know who you are.
Jannaane and Sarwane.
The daughter and the son of the torturer, children born of horror.
Look at them.
This letter was delivered by your daughter.
Through her, I want to tell you that you are still alive.
Soon you will stop talking.
I know this.
Silence awaits everyone in the face of truth.

The woman who sings.
Whore number seventy-two.

Cell number seven.
In the Kfar Rayat Prison.

> *NIHAD finishes reading the letter. He looks at JANINE and SIMON. He tears up the letter.*

37. Letter to the son

> *SIMON hands his envelope to NIHAD, who opens it.*

NAWAL   I looked for you everywhere.
Here, there, and everywhere.
I searched for you in the rain.
I searched for you in the sun.
In the forest
In the valleys
On the mountaintops
In the darkest of cities
In the darkest of streets
I searched for you in the south
In the north
In the east
In the west
I searched for you while digging in the earth to bury my friends
I searched for you while looking at the sky
I searched for you amidst a flock of birds
For you were a bird.
And what is more beautiful than a bird,
The fiery flight of a bird in the sunlight?
What is more alone than a bird,
Than a bird alone amidst the storm clouds,
Winging its strange destiny to the end of day?
For an instant, you were horror.
For an instant, you have become happiness.
Horror and happiness.
The silence in my throat.
Do you doubt?
Let me tell you.
You stood up
And you took out that little clown nose.
And my memory exploded.
Don't be afraid.
Don't catch cold.
These are ancient words that come from my deepest memories.
Words I often whispered to you.

In my cell,
I told you about your father.
I told you about his face,
I told you about the promise I made the day of your birth:
No matter what happens, I will always love you.
No matter what happens, I will always love you.
Without realizing that in that very instant, you and I were sharing our defeat.
Because I hated you with all my being.
But where there is love, there can be no hatred.
And to preserve love, I blindly chose not to speak.
A she-wolf always defends her young.
You are facing Janine and Simon.
Your sister and your brother
And since you are a child of love
They are the brother and sister of love.
Listen
I am writing this letter in the cool evening air.
This letter will tell you that the woman who sings was your mother
Perhaps you too will stop talking.
So be patient.
I am speaking to the son, I am not speaking to the torturer.
Be patient.
Beyond silence,
There is the happiness of being together.
Nothing is more beautiful than being together.
For those were your father's last words.

Your mother.

> *NIHAD finishes reading the letter. He stands.*
>
> *JANINE and SIMON stand and face him.*
>
> *JANINE tears up every page in her notebook.*

38. Letter to the twins

ALPHONSE LEBEL is holding the third envelope, addressed to the twins.

ALPHONSE LEBEL   The sky is overcast. It's going to rain, for sure, for sure, for sure. Shouldn't we go home? Mind you, I understand how you feel. If I were you, I wouldn't go home. This is a beautiful park.... In her will, your mother left a letter to be given to the two of you, if you fulfilled her wishes. And you have more than fulfilled them. It's going to rain. In her country, it never rains. We'll stay here. It will cool us off. Here's the letter.

> *SIMON opens the letter.*

NAWAL   Simon,
   Are you crying?
   If you are crying, don't dry your tears
   For I don't dry mine.
   Childhood is a knife stuck in the throat
   And you managed to remove it.
   Now you must learn to swallow your saliva again.
   Sometimes that is a very courageous act.
   Swallowing your saliva.
   Now, history must be reconstructed.
   History is in ruins.
   Gently
   Console every shred
   Gently
   Cure every moment
   Gently
   Rock every image.

   Janine,
   Are you smiling?
   If you are smiling, don't stifle your laughter.
   For I don't stifle mine.
   It's the laughter of rage
   That of women walking side by side
   I would have named you Sawda
   But this name remains, in its spelling
   In every one of its letters,
   An open wound in my heart.
   Smile, Janine, smile
   We
   Our family
   The women in our family are trapped in anger.
   I was angry at my mother
   Just as you are angry with me
   And just as my mother was angry with her mother.
   We have to break the thread.

   Janine, Simon,
   Where does your story begin?
   At your birth?
   Then it begins in horror.
   At your father's birth?
   Then it is a beautiful love story.
   But if we go back farther,
   Perhaps we will discover that this love story
   Has roots in violence and rape,

And that in turn,
The brute and the rapist
Had his origin in love.
So,
When they ask you to tell your story,
Tell them that your story
Goes back to the day when a young girl
went back to her native village to engrave her grandmother's name
Nazira on her gravestone.
That is where the story begins.
Janine, Simon,
Why didn't I tell you?
There are truths that can only be revealed when they have been discovered.
You opened the envelope, you broke the silence
Engrave my name on the stone
And place the stone on my grave.

Your mother.

SIMON   Janine, let me hear her silence.

> *JANINE and SIMON listen to their mother's silence.*
>
> *Torrential rain.*
>
> *The end.*

Man Out of Joint

by Sharon Pollock

Sharon Pollock

Born Mary Sharon Chalmers in Fredericton in 1936, playwright, actor, director, teacher, and theatre administrator Sharon Pollock attended school in Quebec's Eastern Townships and then the University of New Brunswick. Pollock left before graduating to marry Ross Pollock, a Toronto insurance broker, in 1954. When the couple separated, Pollock and her five children returned to Fredericton. She did various jobs at Fredericton's Playhouse Theatre, where she met the actor Michael Ball. She moved with him to Calgary, where she continues to live, in 1966.

Pollock worked as an actor for a number of years before she began writing plays, which she was inspired to write, in part, because she was frustrated with the dearth of Canadian voices and stories on stage. She then produced a number of radio plays before writing for the stage. Her first effort (which she wrote while pregnant with her sixth child), *A Compulsory Option*, won the 1971 Alberta Playwriting Competition and was performed in 1972 by Vancouver's New Play Centre. In 1980, she received the "Nellie" ACTRA award for Best Radio Drama (*Sweet Land of Liberty*, 1979), about an American Vietnam War veteran who seeks refuge from his bellicose father in Alberta. Pollock has also produced several television scripts; in 1981, she won the Golden Sheaf Award for the television film *The Person's Case*.

In 1973, Theatre Calgary premiered *Walsh*, Pollock's second full-length play, which revealed the Canadian government's callous treatment of the Sioux Nation between 1877 and 1881. Other history plays, such as *The Komagata Maru Incident* (1976), about the government's refusal to allow Sikh immigrants onto Canadian soil, and her prison drama, *One Tiger to a Hill* (1980), produced in most major theatre centres in Canada, have earned her a reputation as a playwright of conscience. Subsequent works, such as *Generations* (1980), *Blood Relations* (1980), and *Doc* (1984), are less concerned with social issues and more with domestic conflict. *Blood Relations*, about Lizzie Borden, the acquitted axe murderer, won the Governor General's Literary Award; Pollock played the role of Miss Lizzie in Theatre Calgary's 1981 production of the play. Another historical murder case, *Whiskey Six Cadenza* (1983), was shortlisted for the Governor General's Literary Award, and her next play, *Doc*, earned her a second Governor General's Literary Award. Loosely based on Pollock's own family background, *Doc* is brutally honest and painfully telling. Pollock has also received several international awards: the Canada-Australia Prize in 1987 and the Japan Foundation Award in 1995. In 1999, she received the Harry and Martha Cohen Award for her contribution to Theatre Calgary. Pollock also holds four honorary doctorates from the University of New Brunswick, the University of Alberta, Queen's University, and the University of Calgary.

In 1992, Pollock founded the Garry Theatre in Calgary, where she wrote and directed *Saucy Jack* (1993), which tells the story of Jack the Ripper from a woman's perspective, and *Death in the Family* (1993), in which she performed a major role. In 1993, *Fair Liberty's Call*, which examines the history of the United Empire Loyalists migration to the Maritimes after the American War of Independence, premiered at the Stratford Festival. Three of Pollock's lays—*Moving Pictures* (1999), *End Dream* (2000), which she directed, and *Angel's Trumpet* (2001), about the fraught relationship between F. Scott and Zelda Fitzgerald, received premier productions at Calgary's Theatre Junction. These works focus on women struggling to pursue their artistic talents and ambitions within male-dominated environments. In 2005, Pollock played the role of early filmmaker Nell Shipman in *Moving Pictures* at the University of Alberta's Studio Theatre.

Pollock continues to perform on stage. In 2008, she acted in Downstage Theatre's production of Judith Thompson's *Habitat*. Pollock also continues to write politically provocative plays. In 2007, Calgary's Downstage Theatre premiered *Man Out of Joint*, and in 2009, *Kabloona Talk*, a courtroom drama commissioned by Stuck in a Snowbank Theatre about two Inuit charged with murdering two Oblate priests, won the Gwen Pharis Ringwood Award for Drama at the Alberta Literary Awards. Currently, Pollock is working on a play about American journalist, writer, correspondent, and activist Agnes Smedley, best known for her supportive reporting on the Chinese Revolution.

Pollock has taught playwriting at the University of Alberta, run the Playwrights' Colony at the Banff Centre from 1977–1980, and been appointed playwright-in-residence at Calgary's Alberta Theatre Projects from 1977–1979 and at the National Arts Centre from 1981–1982. She was artistic director at Theatre Calgary in 1984, and then at Theatre New Brunswick from 1988–1990. In 1998, she was elected president of the Alberta Playwrights Network.

Since 2006, Pollock has served as dramaturge and artistic consultant with the Atlantic Ballet Company of Canada, and in 2008, she travelled to Pristina, Kosovo, to work with young theatre artists; at that time, she also initiated with Jeton Neziraj, Artistic Director of the Kosovo National Theatre, an ongoing process of collaboration. The playwright also gained a large following for her weekly reviews of Calgary theatre productions for CBC Radio's *Homestretch*, titled "Pollock on Plays."

Man Out of Joint draws attention to the torture and abuse of detainees at Guantanamo Bay, and specifically to Omar Khadr, the fifteen-year-old Canadian citizen captured in Afghanistan and charged with murdering an American army medic in 2002. (As of 2010, Khadr is still imprisoned at Guantanamo Bay.) Interspersed with the prisoner stories are those about Joel Gianelli, a Canadian lawyer increasingly concerned with inconsistencies in reports about 9/11, and his client, Ed Leland, a character based on Delmart Vreeland, who appears to have accurately predicted the attacks on the World Trade Centre. Pollock's extensive research led her to the Center for Constitutional Rights's (CCR) report on the treatment of the Guantanamo Bay prisoners, and to the lawyer for the Toronto terror suspects, Rocco Galati (Gianelli), counsel for the Toronto terror suspects who defended Vreeland (Leland) on a fraud charge. But Pollock also reminds us that abuses of power are not limited to specific times/places/nationalities, because Gianelli is haunted by stories of his Italian father's internment in Canada during the Second World War. As Pollock stated in an interview with Jeff Kubik, "The play is about how we ordinary folk are at the mercy of power and war mongers, and that this happens over and over again.... I wish I believed it would become an irrelevant thing."

Note

Detainee abuse verified by the Center for Constitutional Rights (CCR), a non-profit legal and educational organization dedicated to protecting and advancing the rights guaranteed by the US Constitution and international law.

Report on Torture and Cruel, Inhuman and Degrading Treatment of Prisoners at Guantanamo Bay, Cuba, a CCR publication.

Man Out of Joint was first produced by The Downstage Performance Society in Calgary, Alberta, on May 10, 2007, with the following company:

JOEL GIANELLI	Robert Hay
JOE	Tim Culbert
SUZANNE SANDERSON	Carrie Schiffler
ERIN O'CASEY	Jill Belland
ED LELAND	Joel Cochrane
DOMINIC GIANELLI	Iain Dunbar
K.	Ron Gregory
SOLDIER #1	Aaron Coates
SOLDIER #2	Julie Mortensen
NECHLA	Sam Hageahmad
MAHJOUB	Ian Capell
MIRBATI	Col Cseke
AHMAD	Nima Fard
HAMAD	Howard Wright

Directed and produced by Simon Mallett
Set designed by Anton deGroot
Lighting designed by David R. Smith
Costumes designed by Andrea Shanks-Sunderland
Sound designed by Simon Mallett
Stage managed by Ruby Dawn Eustaquio
Rehearsal stage managed by Katt Boulet

Characters

JOEL GIANELLI, a lawyer
JOE, Joel
SUZANNE SANDERSON, Joel's wife
ERIN O'CASEY, Joel's law partner
DOMINIC GIANELLI, Joel's father, Italian, mid-80s
ED LELAND, a prisoner in Don Jail
K., sometimes heard as a voice-over with power and formality
SOLDIER #1, a male (Pete)
SOLDIER #2, a female (Lolly)
MOHAMMED NECHLA, a detainee
BAKAT AHMAD, a detainee
ABDEL HAMAD, a detainee
AL MIRBATI, a detainee
MOHAMMAD MAHJOUB, a detainee

Staging Notes

A forward slash (/) indicates the following line is tighter than an interruption.

Joe's dialogue (in a smaller font) is a soft murmur and not acknowledged by the other characters.

Stage directions reflect thoughts of the playwright and are not meant as absolute directives to a production.

Multiple dimensions of time and space are layered in the world of the play. Joe is always present, essentially motionless in his chair. He is aware in subtle ways of what is going on in front, or around him. He may, in subtle ways, react to what transpires.

Dominic, Joel's father, died several years ago.

Suzanne, Dominic, Erin, and Ed, when not directly involved in a scene, are always present, perhaps in shadows or "out of focus," although they remain engaged by what transpires and may subtly react to it. It's possible Dominic might roll, light, and smoke a cigarette as he watches. Suzanne might have a drink; Erin might study a file. The characters don't have to "enter" a scene to engage verbally in it. They can "throw" a comment in from the sidelines. There may be a desk and chair on stage. There may be a number of high black stools randomly placed around the periphery. Characters may sit/perch/lean on them at times, place a drink or files on them, etc. There are more stools than characters. On one of them is a package of documents and papers.

MAN OUT OF JOINT

Blackout.

K. *(voice-over)* Honour Bound to Defend Freedom!

Sound: a loud cacophony of disorienting music and sound.

Strobe light will reveal in the background a shuffling line of hooded men in orange jumpsuits, shackled hands and feet linked to a waist chain, herded by two soldiers. There is a cyc behind the men on which is projected a grid work of horizontal and vertical bars, like a cage magnified. At times words or documents will be projected onto or over the cage-like grid. The pages of the documents roll; they are not intended to be read, they are background to the action. At the opening a sign with the words "Honour Bound" is projected onto the grid on the cyc.

The hooded detainees will each be placed in his "cell"—a barred square of light on the floor.

The strobe also reveals two straight-backed chairs some distance apart. In front of each chair and embedded in the floor is a metal eyebolt. JOEL is sitting in the stage-right chair; JOE in the stage-left chair. The two are dressed in identical boxer shorts and undershirts, JOE's well-worn and not so clean. JOE himself is worn looking, somewhat dishevelled. Although JOE's hands are not "short shackled" to the eyebolt in the floor, the position in which he holds them suggests they are. Draped over the back of JOEL's chair are a dress shirt, tie, vest, suit jacket; shoes and socks on the floor behind the chair. Over the back of JOE's chair (or near it) are pants and a suit jacket (no dress shirt or tie) identical to JOEL's but they are dusty, dirty, and ragged. Hidden under the jacket is a kaffiyeh-style scarf. Scuffed, heavy, well-worn boots are under the chair. JOE's chair is in a "cell" of barred light similar to that of the detainees.

Sound and strobe light out.

The grid and image of the sign are faintly visible.

(voice-over) We claim the right to pick up individuals in every corner of the world, on suspicion they are affiliated with a terrorist organization.

Sound and strobe resume.

The soldiers cage a number of the detainees. One is pulled forward onto his knees. His hood removed and blinding goggles placed over his eyes, soundproof earphones over ears, thermal mitts taped over his hands, a deodorizing mask over nose and mouth.

Sound and strobe out.

The grid and image of the sign are faintly visible.

(voice-over) We claim the right to subject them to indefinite detention without judicial review.

Sound and strobe resume.

SOLDIER #2 writes a number with a thick black mark-it pen on a detainee's forehead. He's jerked to his feet and led away by SOLDIER #2, the other remains. His demeanour is more casual than military. The casualness is grounded in the possession of absolute power and control.

Sound and strobe out.

The grid and image of the sign are faintly visible.

(voice-over) Our decision to strip detainees of the protection of the Geneva Convention has laid the foundation for a prison beyond the law.

A brief blast of sound.

(voice-over) This place is a place beyond the law.

A brief blast of sound.

(voice-over) In this place, we are the law.

The sign on the cyc slowly bleeds out. The lighting effect bars of JOE's "cell" are slowly dissolving.

The grid image on the cyc remains. The detainees and soldiers may be seen as silhouettes in front of it.

I

JOE and JOEL's positions in their chairs are similar. They are still.

In the shadows upstage the detainees may shift slightly within their cells, extend a hand through the "bars," react minimally to heat or cold as K. emerges from the shadows. Who is K. speaking to? Neither JOE nor JOEL, and to both JOE and JOEL. K.'s focus is on neither man.

K.   You said, something? *(silence)* An objection, perhaps? *(silence)* No objection. *(silence)*

Quiet now… it is quiet most of the time—but…. Not all of the time. Actually not most of the time, but some of the time. Quiet. A bit of the time. Hardly ever…. Hardly. Ever. *(pause)* Acoustic bombardment? *(pause)* It works. Over time. *(pause)* The senses, you know. Sight. Sound. Touch. Are you cold? …Cold…. Hot. Heat. Yes? …Nothing? …What are you thinking? Warm? Warmer? Hot? Quite hot. Burning hot. Searing cold. Hot cold hot cold hot cold and so on and so on and so…. On. Prolonged extremes of temperature—did you say something? …No? …Continuing then. Post-sensory deprivation. No objection?

Lighting effect on SUZANNE in isolation.

SUZANNE   Joel!

K.   Touch /

SUZANNE   Joel! /

K.   Touch brings /

SUZANNE   Are you up /

K.   Touch brings results.

> *JOEL begins dressing in shirt, tie, vest, suit, socks, shoes during the following dialogue. When he removes the last item of clothing from the chair back (his suit jacket), chains with wrist and ankle cuffs are revealed. They dangle over the back of the chair. JOEL is oblivious of them.*

> *JOEL is not paying any particular attention to SUZANNE. She's calling to him from "downstairs." He is "upstairs." SUZANNE is isolated literally and metaphorically from JOEL.*

SUZANNE   What are you doing, are you up yet, Joel?

JOEL   Getting dressed.

SUZANNE   You in court today?

K.   Short /

SUZANNE   Joel?

K.   short shackled.

SUZANNE   What did you say /

JOEL   Nothing /

K.   Short shackled brings results /

SUZANNE   What?

JOEL   Nothing.

> *A detainee stirs in his cell, growing agitated, like a tiger in a zoo pacing in too small a cage. SOLDIER #1 is not particularly alert.*

SUZANNE   For Christ's sake come to the top of the stairs.

K.   Variations are effective.

SUZANNE   I'm taking your car. Had to cab it last night. Too much Merlot, and don't tell me that's no news to you and I don't want to talk about it. Call Erin to pick you up.

Can you hear me?

JOE   yea

K.   Good.

K. walks off; the detainee is increasingly agitated, the others are aware and SOLDIER #2 enters quickly.

SUZANNE   What're you doing anyway?

SOLDIER #2   *(to SOLDIER #1)* Asshole.

She confronts the agitated detainee, knees him in the groin, and as he bends over in pain, cracks him on the back of the head. She joins SOLDIER #1.

JOEL   Nothing.

SUZANNE   If this is supposed to make me feel guilty it's not working.

JOEL   What would.

SOLDIER #2 clips SOLDIER #1 on the back of the head.

SOLDIER #1   Fuck.

They continue their "guard" duty.

SUZANNE   My car's in the civic parkade. Level four—or—maybe six or seven. I don't know, it was late, I can't remember, look around you'll find it. Pick it up if you need it. I'm taking yours. All right?

JOEL   All right.

SUZANNE   Call Erin.

DOMINIC   *(Dressed in rough woolen pants, suspenders, boots, his clothes a little baggy. A period look to him. Age (or else death) has shrunk him. He speaks to JOEL.)* Why she call you that?

JOE   papa

SUZANNE   Joel!

DOMINIC   I'm asking why she call you that. *(JOEL is ignoring DOMINIC.)*

JOE   wh'

DOMINIC   Why that name, eh? …Speak up.

JOE   no

DOMINIC   Nothing? You want a smack? I give you a good smack.

JOEL Yeah you would, Papa.

DOMINIC Your name is Joseph.

JOEL Not a kid anymore, Papa.

DOMINIC So what's she call you? I don't hear Joseph. Name good enough for your grandpa, good enough for you.

JOEL I know.

DOMINIC Could be Joe. Nothing wrong with Joey. Your sister calls you that. Sonny when you were baby, thank God your mother's dead.

JOEL Yeah thank God.

JOE   yea

DOMINIC So stop with this Joel shit. You tell her. It's Joey…. Maybe Joe. Could be Joe now. Or Joseph. A good name for a lawyer. Joseph Gianelli…. Sounds good for a lawyer, eh? …Eh?

JOE   yea

JOEL Yeah.

DOMINIC What about family, Joey?

JOEL Family.

DOMINIC You see your sister on Sunday? …Eh? …Sister for dinner, eh Joey?

JOE   no

DOMINIC No. She don't like your sister. And then the boy, eh. She take even that away.

JOEL Don't think it.

JOE   no

DOMINIC What is he now, what would he be? *(silence)* Joey!

JOEL Four.

JOE   woul' be

DOMINIC Would be four. You still got the dog?

JOEL No.

DOMINIC She put him down, eh?

JOE   no

DOMINIC Eh!

JOEL A friend.

DOMINIC   A friend?

JOEL   Yeah, she took the dog. A friend took the dog.

DOMINIC   Should have shot him.

JOEL   Not the dog's fault.

DOMINIC   No? Whose fault then. Say it.

JOEL   Was my dog. She never liked the dog, I should have /

DOMINIC   The boy liked the dog, loved that dog.

JOEL   I know.

DOMINIC   So whose fault was it then?

JOE   her

DOMINIC   The boy,

JOE   no

DOMINIC   you should have called him Dominic.

JOEL   Maybe.

DOMINIC   Dominic! My name, his grampa's name, and you, you got your grampa's name.

JOEL   I know.

DOMINIC   But not for her son, no eh.

JOEL   My son too.

DOMINIC   Then why not Dominic?

JOEL   Makes no difference now.

DOMINIC   Your grampa, he was Joseph, and you are Joseph, I am Dominic and the boy, he should be Dominic!

JOEL   Should have.

DOMINIC   Heritage.

JOEL   Get over it.

DOMINIC   Family name!

JOEL   I know.

DOMINIC   Joseph Dominic Gianelli!

JOEL   Spencer.

DOMINIC   She don't even take your name. "Suzanne Sanderson"—what's wrong with Gianelli? You got a problem there. That one, I tell you right from the start, her nose is in the air so far I wonder she don't drown when it rains. Don't I tell you that from the start?

JOEL   You did.

JOE   wate'

JOEL   Drown when it rains, that's right.

DOMINIC   I tell you because I love you. You're my son. A man wants a son. A son with his name, it's a natural thing.

JOEL   Ah-huh.

DOMINIC   Close to one year now.

JOE   yea

JOEL   One year.

DOMINIC   You think /

JOEL   No /

DOMINIC   maybeee /

JOEL   No /

DOMINIC   You think… maybeee /

ERIN   *(from the periphery)* Joel?

DOMINIC   try again?

ERIN   Can you do me a favour?

DOMINIC   It's her.

JOEL   No way, she's just a friend.

DOMINIC   A good friend, Joey.

ERIN   I'm double-booked.

DOMINIC   You hear that before, eh Joey?

ERIN   Are you clear, can you handle it?

DOMINIC   You look tired she said.

JOE   said

DOMINIC   Then she hand you that Leland fellow.

JOEL   I think he's dead.

JOE   yea

DOMINIC   Are you gonna tell her?

JOE   don'

ERIN   *(approaching him)* Are you all right?

JOEL   I'm fine.

DOMINIC   She should know.

JOE   don'

ERIN   You look tired.

DOMINIC   Like before, she said same thing.

ERIN   You take on too much.

DOMINIC   Tell her.

JOEL   I will /

ERIN   Will what?

> *A detainee has collapsed on the floor. SOLDIER #2 is forcing him to his feet. JOE's head slumps forward. He appears to have lost consciousness.*

SOLDIER #2   Up! Up!

JOEL   *(to ERIN)* You remember Ed Leland.

SOLDIER #2   Motherfucker.

ERIN   Oh yeah. Real well.

SOLDIER #1   Yes, sir. *(as SOLDIER #2 turns control over to #1 and exits)*

JOEL   The intern finally got off his ass and came though with that research assignment.

ERIN   Why research Leland for Chrissake, it's been five years.

JOEL   Why not.

ERIN   Waste of time.

JOEL   Project for the intern.

ERIN   Make-work project. Leland's credibility went out the window when he jumped bail in '02.

JOEL   Maybe he got a phone call.

ERIN   Sure and maybe he flew the coop.

JOEL   There was a time you weren't so dismissive of phone calls.

ERIN   Well I was younger then.

JOEL   You were wiser then.

ERIN   So let's stop the back and forth, you're dying to tell me something—no, let me guess. The package Leland sent way back when. You opened it.

JOEL   Not yet.

ERIN   It's been nearly five years, Joel, the suspense is killing me.

JOEL   You think I should open it?

ERIN   I think you should shred it, or burn it. Get rid of it.

JOEL   After I read it?

ERIN   Before. And if anyone asks, you never received it.

JOEL   Maybe.

ERIN   No maybes about it, just get rid of it.

JOEL   About Leland /

ERIN   Forget Leland.

JOEL   No, listen. The intern found a little news item. Dated October 2004, Michigan paper. He was picked up with outstanding warrants in four states.

ERIN   And isn't that a big surprise.

JOEL   So the intern checked. No record of him in the US federal system, no record of him in any of the four states, no record as prisoner, parolee, or discharged.

ERIN   So they're late with data entry.

JOEL   It's 2007, Erin. Is that what you mean by late?

ERIN   It means drop it.

JOEL   It means he's dead.

ERIN   It means you're taking on too many of these terrorist detainee cases /

JOEL   It means he's dead, Erin /

ERIN . It means you should forget Guantanamo North, it means you should leave Omar Khadr and Gitmo to the Yankees, it means ever since Spencie died your marriage is going to shit, and I'm telling you this because I'm a friend of yours and I care. *(pause)*

JOEL   How's the dog?

ERIN   The dog is fine, how's your wife?

JOEL   I'll ask her.

ERIN   Goddamn it, do you hear a thing I say to you?

Following dialogue between ERIN, JOEL continues as GOVERNMENT OF CANADA BILL C-36, THE ANTI-TERRORISM ACT fades up on the cyc. It starts to scroll and quickens, scrolling too quickly to be read. The detainees murmur in the background of the principal dialogue, an ebbing and flowing, foreign words faintly audible; only emotion (anguish, anger, childish frustration, madness) as opposed to meaning can be deciphered.

JOE is speaking too, part of that background murmur of voices. JOE's mumbled dialogue is a bit incoherent and provided here, although his words aren't really comprehensible in performance and stop by scene II.

JOE   judge examine—in private—security, criminal intelligence—hear evidence—absence of applicant—and counsel—without disclosing to—not be admissible under Canadian law—base decision on that evidence—

JOEL and ERIN's dialogue builds in volume and can be heard simultaneously with and drowning out the blur of other voices. It's an unnatural and transitional moment in time and space.

JOEL   It was you turned Leland over to me.

ERIN   I know, I know!!

DOMINIC   I tell you, remember!

JOEL   You should have known I wouldn't let go!

ERIN   I should've known!

DOMINIC   Never forget!

ERIN   You're right!

II

Transitional interval ends. Murmuring of other voices stops with ERIN's previous line. C-36 scrolls, SOLDIER #1 exits, reappears with SOLDIER #2. On a stretcher is the detainee. They deposit him in a "cell" of barred light.

Simultaneously with the scrolling and this action is the following dialogue:

ERIN   But I'm double-booked.

DOMINIC   Remember /

ERIN   Are you clear

DOMINIC   how it started

ERIN   can you handle it?

DOMINIC   before.

JOEL   Yeah.

ERIN   Are you all right?

JOEL   Suzanne's exhausted and the baby's got colic. Makes for a long night.

ERIN   Well you look tired

DOMINIC   Tired.

ERIN   you take on too much.

JOEL   So you're asking me to do what?

ERIN   Well this is just a bitty thing, some screwball, name of Edward Leland, over at Don Jail, it won't take a minute.

JOEL   Then why don't you /

ERIN   Told you, I'm double-booked.

JOEL   I don't know why I do it.

ERIN   Do what?

JOEL   Cover your ass. Gimme the file.

ED   *(in prison garb, unlike the detainees)* You're not gonna believe this.

JOEL   *(to ED)* Try me.

ERIN   And Joel /

ED   I gotta be careful.

JOEL   Careful is good.

ERIN   Ignore his bullshit.

ED   So where's the other one, the first one I saw, the ah—leggy lawyer.

JOEL   In court.

ED   Yeah?

JOEL   Another case.

ED   Higher priority?

JOEL   Could be.

ED   Yuh think so?

JOEL   Well what we've got here is a request from the States for extradition.

ED   Yeah that's what she told me.

JOEL   It says credit-card fraud.

ED   Bullshit.

JOE   bullshi

JOEL   I'll need a bit more than that.

ED   What did the other one say?

JOEL   About what?

ED   My case maybe?

JOEL   Look, our time's kind of short /

ED   Yeah well I'm a suspicious kind of guy.

JOEL   If you'd rather /

ED   It's real simple so listen up. I go back to the States I am dead. Clear enough? There's no credit-card fraud, it's all bullshit and I can prove it.

JOEL   Ah-huh.

ED   No ah-huhs. That petty criminal stuff, it's a cover.

JOEL   Ah-huh.

ED   I'm tellin' yuh somethin' now shut the fuck up and listen.

JOEL   Have to say it's not the best start to a client-lawyer relationship.

ED   This thing's major, yuh gotta take me serious and you gotta listen.

JOEL   So what've you got?

ED   I know this sounds crazy

JOE   craz

ED   and that's workin' against me but… nothin' ventured, "eh"? …What would yuh say if I told yuh—okay—listen up— Told yuh I was workin' for ah—let's say 'merican Naval Intelligence.

JOEL   Is that what you're telling me?

ED   That's what I'm tellin' yuh.

ERIN   He's a nutbar!

ED   Stay with me here!

JOE   her'

ED   And if you wanna know why I'm a dead man walking, yuh ask to see the note I passed to these fuckhead guards in August. Course nobody got around to readin' it till after the Big Event.

JOEL   *(to ERIN)* I saw the note /

ERIN A con man /

JOEL I got a copy /

ERIN par excellence /

ED So it's refugee status in Canada, yuh read the note and yuh go for it!

JOEL I read it and so did you.

ERIN Did not.

ED Refugee status, you got it?

JOEL Why didn't you tell me?

ERIN Tell you what? That the guy's a nutbar? I was double-booked and you'd have blown me off.

JOEL Why don't I believe you?

ERIN Because you never accept what anybody says is how anything is.

DOMINIC Good.

JOEL Erin, the note is stamped. The guards stamped it on receipt. End of August 2001.

ERIN God you make me mad. You concentrate on those civil-liberty cases and /

JOEL That's my practice /

SUZANNE Work /

ERIN constitutional rights /

JOEL and yours too /

SUZANNE always work /

ERIN unpopular defendants /

JOEL difficult cases yes /

SUZANNE never home /

ERIN That's an understatement!

JOEL What the hell is wrong with you!

SUZANNE We need to talk

JOE   no

ERIN You're getting a reputation, Joel.

JOEL So we should throw these "unpopular defendants" to the wall, is that it?

ERIN That's not what I'm saying.

JOEL   So what are you saying?

SUZANNE   Maybe later?

ERIN   You're starting to see prosecutorial—or judicial malfeasance everywhere you look.

JOEL   If you're so concerned about that why the hell did you throw this one at me!

ERIN   Because /

JOEL   Why?

ERIN   Just because…

JOEL   Because why?

ERIN   I don't know, I should have passed it on to a junior, I should have /

JOEL   Why are we talking this shit? You read the note, I know that, so come on, come clean.

ERIN   All right I read it!

JOEL   And?

ERIN   And if there's the remotest chance this guy is who he says he is—and I find that hard to believe /

JOEL   But not impossible /

ERIN   Nothing's impossible /

JOEL   We can check it out.

ERIN   Oh yeah. That'll work.

JOEL   There'll be something somewhere.

ERIN   If there is it'll be expunged, redacted. But you'll be targeted and I'll be targeted.

JOEL   When did that start to concern you?

ERIN   I'm saying things have changed since 9/11 and I just don't think we want our names on a list.

JOEL   That's not like you.

ERIN   Yeah, well proximity to you has given me a touch of paranoia.

JOEL   Isn't paranoia an unreasonable fear?

JOE   reasob'

ERIN   That's what I keep telling myself. Followed by better safe than sorry.

JOEL   I don't believe you.

ERIN   I've worked too bloody hard to place everything I've achieved in jeopardy.

JOEL   Are you talking about the condo or the new car?

ERIN   That's a low blow, Joel.

JOEL   Sorry, but the man is a client. Let's look at the facts.

ERIN   The facts are ridiculous.

JOEL   Hang on. The note was sealed and stamped end of August, that we know. September eleventh the towers and Pentagon are hit. On September fourteenth the note's opened and read. Mr. Leland appears to have predicted the attacks.

ERIN   Appears to have.

JOEL   He lists the targets hit plus the White House and a couple of others, also the notation, "Let one happen, stop the rest."

ERIN   And what's that supposed to mean?

JOEL   Furthermore he claims he accessed this knowledge while working for American Naval Intelligence /

ERIN   Who must be harder up for agents than anyone thought /

JOEL   and the US government had prior knowledge of 9/11.

ERIN   Please don't tell me you believe that.

JOEL   So what do you think?

ERIN   I think Leland is setting you up for membership in the Flat Earth Society.

JOEL   Doesn't matter if he is or he isn't, we can't leave this off the table.

ERIN   There is no "me" in "we."

JOEL   Me we, sure there is.

ERIN   Uh-uh.

JOEL   We've got to check him out.

ERIN   I'm going.

JOEL   Not yet.

ERIN   I've got to.

JOEL   You're not really running out on me are you?

ERIN   Not running, but I am walking.

JOEL   Erin.

ERIN   I should never've passed it on to you. I don't know what I was thinking. I'm sorry.

JOEL   For what?

ERIN   I just didn't want to totally abandon him, you know, just in case—he's—not a nutbar. Which he is.

JOEL   Are you leaving something out here?

ERIN   ...Sort of.

JOEL   Sort of.

ERIN   I got a phone call, Joel.

JOE   Jo'

JOEL   So?

ERIN   After my meeting with Leland, I got a phone call.

JOEL   Not the first threat the firm's ever gotten, won't be the last.

ERIN   Yeah? Well this one was different.

JOEL   How different?

ERIN   Very scary different.

JOEL   How the hell different can threatening phone calls be? Anyway you know there's security out front. Who was it phoning?

ERIN   Not the kind of call where they leave their name.

JOEL   Which suggests there's something to Leland.

ERIN   Which suggests moving Leland to the "untouchable" file.

ED   *(to JOEL)* So whadda yuh got?

JOEL   I've never been able to find that file.

ERIN   Then create one. Please.

JOEL   You know I won't do that.

> *Dialogue continues as background silhouettes SOLDIER #2 nudging SOLDIER #1, then slipping off her helmet, undoing a hair clip. She approaches a detainee, assaults him sexually, ends with a squeeze to the testicles. The detainee makes an audible sound, which can be heard in the following scene when that action occurs. A series of flashes go off during SOLDIER #2's activity as SOLDIER #1 snaps photos.*

ED   I said whadda you got?

JOEL   The Navy never heard of you.

JOE   no

ED   What the fuck did yuh think they were gonna say? I mean "welcome home buddy"? Yuh read my note?

JOEL   I did.

ED   And?

JOEL   And what?

ED   And are yuh another dumbfuck like the rest of the assholes here?

JOEL   So you gave a list of targets prior to the attack, but no specific target date, no 9/11 plain and clear.

ED   When they disappear me will yuh believe me then? Is that what it's gonna take?

JOEL   I'm not saying I don't believe you. I'm commenting on the note.

ED   So yuh believe me.

JOEL   My legal opinion is that your note won't result in preventing your extradition on these fraud charges.

ED   Alleged fraud charges.

JOEL   Alleged fraud /

ED   Right.

JOEL   But the note alone won't sustain a claim for refugee status either. In fact I don't know what we have in hand that will.

ED   I'm countin' on you, man. Jesus Christ, I got no one else.

JOEL   And what I'm telling you is the note alone /

ED   I got that! *(pause)* Okay…. You ah—yuh need some more. I got that.

JOEL   I need more.

ED   I got that. *(pause)*

JOEL   The information in the note /

ED   the information yeah /

JOEL   you came into possession of this information /

ED   possession of it, yeah, I did /

JOEL   How?

ED   How? Yeah, well I was… shit… okay…. Okay, I was ah, workin' as a courier for O.N.I.

JOEL   O.N.I.?

ED Yeah Naval Intelligence, yuh know, like I said /

JOEL Yeah like you said /

ED and I go to Russia yuh see and I…

JOEL And you what in Russia?

ED and I ah… I meet this guy, this Canadian guy, see, with the—with ah, the embassy as it turns out—and maybe this is what yuh need, yeah, prove I know what I'm talkin' about—I pick up a pouch there, yeah a pouch, and things kinda get fucked up.

JOEL What things and how fucked?

ED I'm not gonna get into that! But I read some stuff I shouldn't have. I opened the pouch, yeah, and I read the material contained therein.

JOEL "The material contained therein"?

ED Yeah, all the material contained, therein, and then I get picked up in Canada on this warrant shit. But ah, but here's the kicker.

JOEL The kicker, eh.

ED This guy, name's Bastien, a good guy, I liked him, the embassy guy in Moscow you know.

JOEL Riiight, the embassy guy /

ED In Moscow and the Mounties come in here a coupla months ago and they tell me he's dead!

JOE   thin' he's

JOEL He's dead?

ED Yeah yuh got a hearin' problem? First name Luc, maybe Marc, he's dead, yeah this guy is dead.

JOEL Ah-huh.

ED Yuh can check it out.

JOEL Oh I will.

ED I liked the guy, well not that fuckin' much but—anyways he's dead—but that's not all.

JOEL Ah-huh.

ED Ah-huh?

JOEL And your story is?

ED   The "story" is I get my orders, I go to Russia, September 2000, I meet this ah, Bastien, Marc, or Luc, whatever. We do our thing, I bugger off but things ah, get hinky.

JOEL   Exactly what way hinky, you're not prepared to say.

JOE   don' sa'

ED   If this refugee thing goes tits up I need somethin' left to deal with! *(pause)* All right. So. What's important here is Bastien dies but I dunno it. I don't know he's dead.

JOEL   Ah-huh.

ED   Don't do that.

JOEL   Do what?

ED   Ah-huh.

JOEL   Ah-huh?

ED   Yeah you're pissin' me off.

JOEL   I'm sorry /

ED   I'm tryin' to build a little trust here.

JOEL   And I appreciate that.

ED   At some risk to myself I might add.

JOEL   I understand that.

ED   And to you. Do you understand that? *(pause)*

JOEL   I'm guessing you don't want ah-huh.

ED   It registers negative.

JOEL   "It registers negative"?

ED   I'm asking you do you understand the risk to yourself!—and I'm looking for something in the way of "firmly affirmative."

JOEL   Yes. How's that?

ED   So long as you get it.

JOEL   I get it.

ED   Remember it then.

DOMINIC   'Member it.

JOEL   So where were we?

ED   I find out my Moscow contact's dead. Why the fuck don't you listen?

JOEL   I am. So what happens next?

ED   So I'm picked up here, the States wants me back. I try to talk to someone—like pissin' in the wind, it all comes back. Then I hear via Mountie chit-chat that Bastien's dead. I left Moscow end of December 2000—he dies right after that. Natural causes they say.

JOEL   Which has to do with what?

ED   Natural causes my ass! He was murdered, they fuckin' well killed him!

JOEL   "They" being?

ED   Who the fuck you think? I send my note out! Nobody reads it! The towers come down, Pentagon is hit, and flight 93 is taken out 'fore it hits the White House—or Three Mile Island, which if you want to know what I think was actually the target.

JOEL   So you find out Bastien's dead, you send the note regarding 9/11 out, and you ask for refugee status.

ED   And I sit on my ass prayin' for a positive resolution of my problems and there you sit doin' fuck all!

JOEL   You've given me some specifics, I'll check them out.

ED   Do I gotta draw a diagram? Just get an autopsy! On Bastien! That'll prove it!

> *During the following dialogue various reactions to conditions ripple through the detainees: e.g., rocking back and forth; curled into a fetus-like ball, pacing, appealing, smiling in conversation with no one, and SOLDIER #1 pulls a collection of photos from a pocket. The two soldiers look through the pictures, ignoring the detainees. One of the detainees lies still and spread-eagled on the floor.*

ERIN   Forget it.

ED   Jesus Christ do I have to tell you everything!

ERIN   You don't have to open this can of worms.

ED   Your fuckin' government's in bed with the Americans—

ERIN   Just leave it!

ED   and I'm not the only one that's gettin' screwed!

DOMINIC   You are small, boy, and I tell you remember.

K.   *(voice-over)* Individuals exposed to isolation develop a predictable set of symptoms including bewilderment, anxiety, frustration, dejection, boredom, obsessive thoughts or ruminations, depression, hallucinations, infantile regression, induced schizophrenia; all aids to interrogation.

JOEL *(is not speaking to either ED or ERIN)* Canadian coroner's report. Marc Bastien. Deceased. Cause of death, poison——

ED *(not speaking to ERIN or JOEL)* Yes!

JOEL Manner of death, probable homicide.

ED Nothin' probable about it.

JOEL Speculation: Marc Bastien, a member of the Canadian embassy staff in Moscow, was slipped a concentrated anti-schizophrenic drug when drinking with an unknown individual in one of the city's bars.

ED One for the road.

JOEL It doesn't say on what basis they make this assumption.

ED They knew it.

JOEL Maybe they knew it.

JOE   kne'

ED What you need to ask yourself is how the hell did I know it.

> *During the following dialogue the spread-eagled detainee slowly brings himself to his knees, to his feet, to the tips of his toes, unfolding and extending his body as tall, as elongated as possible. His head suddenly jerks to an awkward angle, his arms hang loosely, he may sway slightly. The soldiers ignore any attempt by any detainee to attract their attention. When they notice the detainee who has hanged himself, one will lift him, the other "cut" him down, put him on the stretcher, carry him out. The other detainees are still during this, aware that something ominous has occurred, unsure what. This all happens as dialogue continues. The soldiers interchange of dialogue comes up when they notice the detainee. Can't be determined exactly where that will be, so guesstimate insertion.*

JOEL Who are you, Leland?

ED Let's say I'm an ex-con workin' for O.N.I. Does that help?

JOEL It's not a matter of helping.

ED So I'm a Naval Intelligence Officer with a cover.

JOEL Well, they've rescinded they never heard of you. Now they say you served four months, discharged in the late '80s.

ED So why doncha look up the Washington number, you give the switchboard a call and ask for me. Can we get back to the situation at hand?

JOEL If you want.

ED If you want? What the fuck kinda lawyer talk is that? Yeah I want.

SUZANNE   When?

JOEL   *(looking through papers)* Later.

SUZANNE   When later?

JOEL   Much later.

SUZANNE   How much later?

JOEL   I dunno.

JOE   dunno

SUZANNE   Later than much later?

JOEL   Maybe.

SUZANNE   Would that be… sometime tomorrow?

JOEL   Maybe.

SUZANNE   After work tonight, do you know what I'm thinking of doing?

JOEL   Yup.

SUZANNE   Going home, running a warm bath, lighting a few candles…. Are you listening?

JOEL   Ah-huh.

SUZANNE   And slitting my wrists in the bathtub.

JOEL   Right.

SUZANNE   On the other hand…

JOEL   Ah-huh.

SUZANNE   I might just slip a little arsenic into your Starbucks'.

     Pause. JOEL looks at her.

JOEL   Did you say something?

SUZANNE   Did I?

JOEL   I dunno, did you?

SUZANNE   Not really. Would you like some coffee?

JOEL   Look at this, Erin.

SOLDIER #2   Oh shit.

ERIN   No. No. No. Not looking.

JOEL   It's over a thousand pages.

SOLDIER #1   'Nother one.

ERIN   I don't want to see it.

JOEL   I asked for his Naval records.

ERIN   I want nothing to do with it.

JOEL   Four months service and over a thousand pages?

ED   What did I tell you?

JOEL   And they goofed big time, look at this.

ERIN   Why the hell did I turn Leland over to you?

JOEL   Just look.

ERIN   I should have known better.

JOEL   Redacted pages, lots of them—

ERIN   Isn't that what I told you?

JOE   yea

JOEL   But not this one! Read it.

ERIN   So it's his annual medical, so what.

JOEL   Check the date.

ERIN   1990?—it's blurred, '91, '92, what do I care?

JOEL   And O.N.I. says he was discharged in '88 after four month's service. Over a thousand pages for four month's service—

ERIN   Shit.

JOEL   and in error they've included his medical records for 1992!

ERIN   Let me see that.

> *JOE slowly rocks back and forth.*

K.   *(voice-over)* Based on official statements in 2003 there have been 350 cases of self-harm and 120 cases of hanging gestures. Reliable figures for 2006 are "unavailable." It is our intention to keep it that way.

ERIN   Fuck.

ED   Call Washington /

JOEL   I got the O.N.I. switchboard /

ERIN   Joel /

ED   Lieutenant Edward Leland!

ERIN   I begged you to /

JOEL I was connected to /

ERIN to keep me clear of this /

ED You were connected to who /

JOEL I was connected to the office of /

ED My office /

JOEL Lieutenant Edward Leland /

ERIN I refuse to listen to any of this /

JOEL I got his voice mail for Chrissake! *(pause)*

ERIN There's an explanation for all of it.

JOEL I'm afraid there is.

ERIN He had to have jail access to the Internet.

ED Shouldn't my lawyer be here? Shouldn't he be accompanyin' me to court?

ERIN He hacked into the system, something like that.

JOEL He had no Internet access prior to my Washington call.

ED I'm findin' all this just a little irregular.

JOEL I think Leland's genuine, Erin.

ERIN That's a thought we can't afford to have, Joel.

ED I need to speak to my lawyer. Gianelli, Joel Gianelli.

ERIN Who is it? *(no phone is present and no one mimes a phone)*

JOEL It's Leland. He's out. Been released.

ERIN That can't be.

ED Fuckin' irregular, man. They haul me into court, no lawyer, no nothin'.

ERIN Did you get notice of a hearing?

JOEL No notice.

ED They gimme bail. My lawyer not present and they gimme bail. My "mother" has put up bail—what the fuck, eh?

ERIN How did that happen?

ED Never look a gift horse in the mouth—

ERIN Where is he now?

ED On sober second thought I get to thinkin' maybe this is no gift horse, could be an equine of the Trojan persuasion.

JOEL Where are you now?

ED I get to thinkin' this when the judge announces to the world at large where I'll be livin' while I'm out, as in "confined to that address."

JOEL Where are you now?

ED I'm a fuckin' sittin' duck.

JOE   ru'

JOEL Where are you?

ED In a buildin' dedicated to transportation—

JOE   ru'

ED and in about fifteen minutes I'm gonna take advantage of what it has to offer.

JOE   ru'

JOEL Don't do that.

JOE   don'

ED Just wanted to say thanks.

JOEL This refugee status /

DOMINIC Don't trust it.

ED Are you kiddin' me, man? Not a chance.

> *ED scribbles a note, slips it into the package of documents on a stool and seals it during the following.*

JOEL Leland /

ED Call me Ed.

JOEL Ed /

ED You think your phone's clean?

JOEL 'Course my phone's /

ED If I send you a package, keep it close.

JOEL Ed /

ED Need to go, Joel. *(tosses the package to JOEL)*

> *Sound of a click. "QUESTIONS SURROUNDING 9/11 (www.whatreally happened.com)" bleed up on the cyc. They roll fairly quickly, are not intended to be read. They might begin with:*
> *"Did Delbert Vreeland warn Canadian Intelligence in August 2001 about possible terrorist attacks on New York and the Pentagon?*
> *Did he place the warning in an envelope while in prison in Toronto, Canada?*

> *Where did he get his information?*
> *Whom did he give the envelope to?*
> *Why was he placed in jail?"*

> *And then revert to SOLDIER #1 on the site.*

> *Dialogue and action continues in the foreground.*

That's it. *(casually checks his surroundings, and as he moves away he slowly whistles a childhood rhyme such as "Pop Goes the Weasel" or "London Bridge is Falling Down")*

ERIN   Reception's got a package for you.

JOEL   Ah-huh.

ERIN   Courier dropped it off.

JOEL   Got it.

JOE   ge' it

ERIN   That it?

JOEL   *(glances at a package)* Yeah it is.

> *As ED is moving away he staggers slightly, he stops whistling, seems a little unsteady on his feet, ends up with his back against a wall. He slowly slides down the wall. He sits somewhat sprawled, his head dropped forward. He remains in this position.*

> *The questions are continuing to scroll as dialogue continues.*

ERIN   *(picking it up)* Pretty hefty.

JOEL   Yeah it is.

ERIN   And the sender is— *(turning it to read the sender)*

JOEL   *(taking it from her, replacing it on the desk)* No one… in particular.

ERIN   Aren't you going to open it?

SUZANNE   I couldn't move! I wanted to move, oh God, yes! I wanted… I couldn't… I couldn't do… anything

ERIN   No?

JOE   no

DOMINIC   No /

SUZANNE   Spence turned and he smiled, and he… he tripped… and—

JOE   he fell.

III

The questions are continuing to scroll and dialogue continues as SOLDIER #2 walks off, returns with a sheet containing their orders, confers with SOLDIER #1. They will place a detainee in "Long Time Standing": forced to stand, handcuffed, feet shackled to an eyebolt in the floor for excess of forty hours. They will move to place a second detainee in "Cold Cell": for extended periods of time the detainee stands naked in a cell kept near ten degrees centigrade and is intermittently doused with cold water. This happens in the background as the following continues.

K. *(voice-over)* Enhanced interrogation techniques include waterboarding with the detainee bound to an inclined board, feet raised, head slightly below the feet, cellophane or wet towel wrapped over face, water poured over head to simulate drowning and stimulate fear—

JOE   int' wate'

K. *(voice-over)*   —there are variations, some report immersion of the head in water

JOE   drown

SUZANNE   What's the point of coming home when you bring work home?

JOE   home

SUZANNE   You may as well be at work… I said you may as well be at work!

JOEL   *(at papers)* I am at work.

SUZANNE   But you're at home!

JOEL   I know.

SUZANNE   But you're working! You're working at home! What's the point of coming home if you're just going to work at home!

JOEL   I don't know.

SUZANNE   What do you mean you don't know? Of course you know! Are you trying to drive me crazy?

JOEL   Would you rather I didn't?

SUZANNE   Didn't what?

JOEL   Come home.

SUZANNE   No!—I'd rather…. Nothing, forget it.

JOEL   If only, eh.

SUZANNE   Don't. *(Pause. JOEL returns to flipping through a file. SUZANNE watches him.)*

DOMINIC They come in the night. That's the way that they do it.

JOE   th' way

DOMINIC The house is dark. The children are sleeping. Everything quiet. Then, the loud bang, the banging on the door, it is loud, loud loud. I yell to Papa and then the shouting. Men's voices shouting very loudly as if it were yesterday.

SUZANNE What's that about?

JOEL Omar Khadr.

SUZANNE Who?

DOMINIC I tell you when you are little—

JOE   tel' me

JOEL Just a case.

SUZANNE I never would have guessed /

DOMINIC I tell you over and over what it is that they do, I am always telling you never forget /

SUZANNE So /

DOMINIC That's your defence, memory!

SUZANNE So what's this one about?

JOEL You really want to know?

SUZANNE I asked.

JOEL The Canadian boy in Guantanamo.

SUZANNE Why?

JOE   wh'

JOEL Why what?

SUZANNE Does anyone in this house ever listen to anyone?

JOEL There's only the two of us.

SUZANNE Do you think I don't know that? I know it!

JOEL I'm sorry.

SUZANNE Are you?

> At some point the questions roll into a list of names of the detainees and their country of origin held at Guantanamo. For example, Abdulbakar Mohammed, Libyan; Mahmood Ahmad, Saudi; Mullah Dadullah, Afghan. There are several hundred names, which will eventually bleed out behind the grid.

JOEL   Look, I'm just trying to review his case file from the American lawyer, is that what you want to know?

SUZANNE   I asked why.

JOEL   Because I'm going to Cuba, I told you that didn't I?

SUZANNE   I don't remember /

JOE   membe'

JOEL   Or weren't listening?

SUZANNE   I mean why, Joel /

JOE   Jo'

DOMINIC   You are a small boy but I tell you never forget /

SUZANNE   They're not nice people and I wish you wouldn't! /

> *JOEL ignores her.*

DOMINIC   Maria is crying, what a pair of lungs she had. Only three years old and that was the last I saw of her. They throw us in the truck. I hear Anna, you never knew my sister Anna, your aunt Anna? Oh the language that was coming out of her mouth. Words that I never knew that she knew.

SUZANNE   Talk to me, Joel.

DOMINIC   She was fourteen, Sophia eleven, Gina seven, and Maria was three when they took us away /

SUZANNE   Talk to me!

DOMINIC   Before they lock us in the back I see Anna. I can still see her. She is in the doorway of the house we had then, and the hall light is behind her. She is standing there with her arm round Mama and she is yelling. She is asking. Demanding even, demanding to know what is happening.

SUZANNE   Joel?

DOMINIC   We don't find out why until later. Male. Age sixteen and over. Enemy aliens.

JOE   yea

DOMINIC   I am sixteen. Our name is Gianelli. Italian. That is the proof of it. All that they need.

JOEL   What is it?

SUZANNE   It's... it's nothing.

DOMINIC "Defence of Canada Regulations," that is how they can do it. The Ottawa man, the big one. June 1940. Before he opens his mouth, we are citizens. He speaks a few words. He closes his mouth. Now we are enemy alien.

JOE yea

DOMINIC A few words and some paper is all that it takes.

SUZANNE Joel.

JOEL Now what do you want?

SUZANNE We need to talk.

JOEL What about?

SUZANNE Us.

JOEL Not now.

DOMINIC Handcuffed. Locked up. "Interned." No lawyer or trial. A few more words and some paper: "Custody of Alien Property." Papa's savings are frozen. The house is sold. Mama and the sisters register and report. What we worked for is lost.

JOE los'

DOMINIC We are just dirty wops. Anna leaves school. She goes on the street. It is necessary, Anna said, and it breaks Mama's heart but the money is needed. Government gives twelve dollars a month, from this—food for four sisters and Mama, rent on the flat, medicine for Maria too late to save her… for this my sister Anna is whoring. She is going on fifteen at the time. Her birthday comes in the fall.

SUZANNE Please.

JOEL I've got to get through this.

JOE throu' it

DOMINIC She stops coming round to the flat when Papa and I are released. Disappears. Maybe is best, Papa says. Anna knows the shame of it all.

SUZANNE Is it more important than us?

JOEL Possibly.

SUZANNE Do you really believe that?

JOE 'lieve it

JOEL Maybe.

SUZANNE What're you reading that's "possibly" more important than us?

JOEL *(reads from the file)* "Long Time Standing."

SUZANNE   *(smiles finding the term a bit funny)* "Long Time Standing"?

JOEL   Do you know what that is?

SUZANNE   A Japanese print of a crane on one leg?

JOEL   *(reads)* "Enhanced Interrogation Techniques. Number four: Long Time Standing: Forced to stand, handcuffed, feet shackled to an eyebolt in the floor for an excess of forty hours. Exhaustion and sleep deprivation is effective in yielding results."

SUZANNE   I think I prefer my Japanese print.

JOEL   Do you.

SUZANNE   Yes I do. Does that make me a bad person? Because I don't care to dwell on the kind of thing that you're reading?

JOEL   Number five, "The Cold Cell," does that peak your interest?

SUZANNE   I care about us.

JOEL   "For extended periods of time the detainee stands naked and is intermittently doused with cold water in a cell kept near ten degrees centigrade."

SUZANNE   That's the Americans, not us.

JOEL   No we'd never be party to a thing like that would we. What about this kid I'm hoping to see, this Canadian boy they're holding?

DOMINIC   No Italian internee ever charged, Joey.

SUZANNE   First of all, he's not Canadian, he's Muslim.

JOEL   Toronto born, Canadian.

DOMINIC   'Member that.

SUZANNE   But he was a soldier, he was killing people.

JOEL   Accused of, and only fifteen, under the care and influence of his father /

SUZANNE   I don't want to talk about this /

JOEL   and in a compound under attack by American soldiers.

SUZANNE   Oh for Chrissake.

JOEL   Do you feel that justifies his being held at Guantanamo Bay for the last five years and subjected to unspeakable abuse sanctioned by the president of the United States?

SUZANNE   I don't feel anything.

JOEL   Really?

SUZANNE   All right I feel something but—but it's not our problem. This *(she and he)* is our problem.

JOEL   But you have heard of Guantanamo North, our mini Guantanamo /

SUZANNE   Joel /

JOEL   where detainees are held indefinitely under security certificates /

SUZANNE   you and me /

JOEL   men, Muslim men /

SUZANNE   All right! /

JOEL   threatened with deportation to countries who torture /

SUZANNE   So take it to court /

JOEL   no access to evidence against them, no judicial review of proceedings against them /

SUZANNE   I don't want to talk about it /

JOEL   who've been held for five and six years without trial /

SUZANNE   Get off that hobby horse! /

DOMINIC   Enemy alien! /

JOEL   You call it a hobby horse? /

DOMINIC   Gianelli! Italian! That is the proof of it! /

SUZANNE   Our problem is you and me!

DOMINIC   All that they need! /

SUZANNE   You And Me. /

DOMINIC   Memory! That's your defence /

JOEL   What's the matter, does my client list embarrass you with the ladies who lunch?

SUZANNE   I don't get out to lunch. I'm in the office over lunch, I work damn hard and I'm proud of it. And yes I am embarrassed when I pick up the paper and read or see Mohammed this, Omar that, Abdul or Ali Baba with his lawyer Joel Gianelli.

JOEL   Those are not their names.

SUZANNE   Whatever their names, it doesn't matter.

JOE   matte'

JOEL   It's not even my name.

SUZANNE   Don't be stupid.

JOEL   My name is Joseph.

DOMINIC   Or Sonny.

JOEL   Or Joe.

SUZANNE   You're not a Joseph or Joe.

JOEL   What's wrong with Joe?

SUZANNE   Nothing's wrong with Joe. It's just not how I think of you.

JOEL   Try.

SUZANNE   No I'm not trying. How did we get on to this?

JOEL   You and me. You wanted to talk about you and me, what's wrong with Joe?

SUZANNE   I don't know.

JOEL   Then call me Joe. Or Joseph. Or Sonny.

SUZANNE   I'm not calling you Sonny.

JOEL   Why not?

SUZANNE   Sonny Gianelli?

JOEL   I like it.

SUZANNE   You're being funny.

JOEL   I'm serious.

SUZANNE   No you're not.

JOEL   Yes I am.

SUZANNE   You are not.

JOEL   What is wrong with Sonny Gianelli?

SUZANNE   Well if you don't mind people thinking you're a mafia hood.

JOEL   My father called me Sonny. I wasn't a mafia hood. Neither was he.

JOE   Jo'

JOEL   How about Joe, Joey Gianelli?

SUZANNE   It's Joel. Don't you remember when we first met?

JOEL   No.

SUZANNE   Yes you do. It was the bar thing for what's his name, and there were drinks at some restaurant and we always said it was fate when our eyes locked across the room, you remember now don't you?

JOEL   No.

JOE   membe'

SUZANNE   You do so, we've talked about it hundreds of times.

JOEL   Not that I recall.

SUZANNE   You're making me angry. We were introduced and I swear I heard "Joel" and it was months before you corrected me. By then it was too late.

JOEL   You heard a name you preferred.

SUZANNE   Preference had nothing to do with it, I heard Joel, I called you Joel, you answered to Joel and now you are Joel. You put it on your business cards for Chrissake.

JOEL   To appease you.

SUZANNE   Oh don't give me that! Even Erin calls you Joel!

JOEL   Now she does, yes, but before it was Joe. Because of you it's now Joel.

SUZANNE   That's right, everything's my fault isn't it.

JOE   Spenc'

JOEL   You prefer Suzanne Sanderson to Suzanne Gianelli?

SUZANNE   That's a professional thing.

JOEL   Is it?

SUZANNE   Can we just stop going on about names—what's in a name anyway?

JOEL   Good question, what is in a name?

SUZANNE   I don't want to talk about names! I want to talk about us! What's happening to us!

JOEL   You don't know what's happened?

SUZANNE   Why can't we start over?

> JOEL *returns to his files.*

You could…. Joel?

DOMINIC   Once I am walking. Walking along with you. Before we move west. I am—oh I don't know, you are maybe three, three years old then, and I am taking you for a haircut.

SUZANNE   You could dump all of this. People get the wrong impression and you know that it's dangerous. Even Erin says so.

JOEL   Does she?

SUZANNE   Not in so many words but I get what she means.

DOMINIC   I am taking the two of us for a little trim /

SUZANNE   You don't have to take on these kinds of cases or people!

JOEL   Mohammed and Omar and who was the other you mentioned, Ali Baba, is that who you mean?

SUZANNE   Whoever.

DOMINIC   A haircut you know.

SUZANNE   I mean why do you do it, why?

DOMINIC   Right along Spadina there. We are going along and I see, I see a woman there. On the sidewalk. A woman. She is in a bad way, she— *(pause)* This woman—well, I see her and I think not so good for a little boy to see someone like that, in such a bad way. Asking for a bit of change, you know, some money. And I think, maybe, offering something in return, but— People move away, around her, and she is angry and demanding… demanding, and maybe, maybe something is not right in her head. You know. This is not good for a little boy to see and I… I pick you up, I hold you at my shoulder looking, that way, the other way, and I think to hurry past and… and… she steps in front, she… she, yes, she is angry and she starts to speak, yell even, and… and she stops… I am looking into her eyes, she is looking into mine…. We say nothing. After what seems a very long time, she turns her head slightly and looks at the small boy I hold. You are facing over my shoulder, and you turn your head. You look at her. Into her eyes. I may have said "Anna." I may not have said, Anna. She, she turned and left us standing there. I did not call out "Anna." I did not go after her. The two of us went on. To get our hair cut, on Spadina.

SUZANNE   Please listen to me.

DOMINIC   Do you remember that woman?

SUZANNE   You could join Daddy's firm.

DOMINIC   You were about three, I was holding you up at my shoulder.

SUZANNE   You know he wants you, he'd love to have you, and it would be a fresh start. A fresh start for us, we could do it. Why don't you say yes?

JOEL   Joseph Gianelli.

JOE   Spenc'

SUZANNE   Why do you go on about that?

JOEL   Doesn't Daddy already have an Italian-Canadian?

SUZANNE   Don't be such a bastard, Joel.

JOEL Along with one Jew, one woman, plus one Asian-Canadian, specific ethnicity unknown, and a gaggle of just plain folks like himself in the firm?

SUZANNE Not true and not fair to Daddy and I'm really trying here. Why can't you meet me halfway? (*JOEL, after a moment, closes the file. His gaze rests on SUZANNE.*)

SUZANNE …What is it?

JOEL Nothing.

SUZANNE Why is it always "nothing"?

JOEL I was thinking.

SUZANNE About what?

JOEL Waterboarding.

SUZANNE Waterboarding?

JOEL It's an interrogation technique, number six.

SUZANNE That's not what you're thinking.

JOEL Listed as an "enhanced" interrogation technique.

SUZANNE Why do you do that?

JOEL Do what?

SUZANNE Bring it up. Why do you have to bring it up.

JOEL Bring what up? Waterboarding? Bring that up?

SUZANNE Do you think we'll ever get past this?

JOEL Past what?

SUZANNE Please don't do that.

JOEL Do what?

SUZANNE You know what I mean.

JOEL Oohhh, you mean Spencer? Get past Spencie? Is that what you mean by "get past it"?

SUZANNE I mean… get over it, be able to go on? You and me.

JOEL Go on without Spencie.

SUZANNE Yes.

JOEL Because Spence isn't with us anymore.

SUZANNE No.

JOEL   No…. Why isn't Spence with us? *(pause)*
No. I don't think I can get "past it" or "over it" or—what was the other? "Able to go on"? *(pause)*
How are you able to go on? I'd be interested in knowing.

SUZANNE   Is that a real question, or are you just trying to hurt me?

JOEL   So the "question" hurts you? You've gotten over the "event" itself have you?

SUZANNE   How can you ask me that? I'm sorry. I should have done this and done that and this and the other, I should have done something, I know that. But I didn't. I just—I froze and I'm sorry. It's been nearly a year.

JOEL   Three hundred and thirty-one days.

SUZANNE   I know that! And I'm sorry I'm sorry I'm sorry. I've wept myself dry and sorrow is embedded in every particle of my being, but we can't go back! Nothing can change! He's gone. Spence is gone and I cannot spend the rest of my—I will not spend the rest of my life saying I'm sorry. I Am Sorry. But I can't… I just can't do it anymore. If I do, it'll kill me. And every day you… I'm sorry. There. I'm sorry. That's it. The last time I'll say it. I'm sorry!

JOEL   You're sorry.

SUZANNE   I Am Sorry. Do you ever doubt that? *(pause)* Can you not just accept that? …And let us move on? *(pause)* The real question is…. The question is, do we move on together, or don't we?

JOEL   Don't we.

SUZANNE   Do we?

JOEL   *(back to his papers, reading to himself, ignoring her)* …A boy.

SUZANNE   It wasn't my dog! It was your stupid dog!

JOEL   Ten years old.

SUZANNE   Why weren't you walking the dog!

JOEL   Rumoured youngest "enemy combatant" held at Guantanamo.

SUZANNE   The damn dog wasn't my dog!

JOEL   Four women held at Guantanamo.

SUZANNE   Why was I walking the dog!?

JOEL   Or thought to be held.

SUZANNE   Why?! You tell me why! Why was I walking the dog!

JOEL   You were not walking the dog! You were standing! Standing and talking! Talking to your friend! Someone called Brandy or Randy or Sandy or some stupid fucking name with an unlikely spelling, and while you were standing there, chatting—about Holt Renfrew sales or some goddamn thing, the dog went down to the river, dogs do that you know—or didn't you know, or were you unable to guess? No, you were talking. And Spencie goes after the dog. He was three. That's what kids do, they follow the dog, what the fuck were you thinking? And when you see him standing there on the bank of the river, what do you do? You scream like a banshee, you scare Spencie to d—and he turns and he trips and he falls. Into the water, not—a fucking disaster, if maybe, you'd run, maybe you'd—jumped—into the water—maybe you'd grabbed him— maybe you'd, you'd saved him—maybe you'd done some fucking thing instead of standing there like a statue, like a, like a—if you'd done something, anything, done anything except stand there and watch. Watch while the river took Spencie away. You stupid… nothing. Just—nothing.

JOE's head is down. He may be or is quietly weeping.

SUZANNE   I—

JOEL   Don't talk to me. *(She moves slightly as if to touch him.)* Don't.

ED   *(lifts his head)* If I send you a package, keep it close.

ERIN   What is it?

JOEL   *(to ERIN)* Someone's in my office at night.

ERIN   We pay people for that.

JOEL   Going through files.

ERIN   They're called cleaners, they empty your garbage, dust, that sort of thing.

JOEL   Papers been moved, material on the men held at Guantanamo North /

ERIN   It's called the Kingston Immigration Holding Centre /

JOEL   On a hunger strike over seventy-five days /

ERIN   Joel /

JOEL   over six years without being charged /

ERIN   Joel! /

JOEL   no access to evidence no /

ERIN   No one is going through your files! *(pause)*

JOEL   You think not?

ERIN   I think not.

SUZANNE   I'm sorry.

ED   Keep it close.

DOMINIC   Memory.

JOEL   I want you to do something for me.

ERIN   You mean talk to Suzanne?

JOEL   Why that?

ERIN   Well, I hear…

JOEL   You hear what?

ERIN   Oh for Chrissake Joel, she called and—I dunno.

JOEL   Why do you call me that?

ERIN   Call you what?

JOEL   Joel.

ERIN   It's your name, could that be the reason?

JOEL   It's not my name.

ERIN   Then you should change the nameplate on your desk, the firm's letterhead, your business cards, and let accounting know for your cheques, what's wrong with you?

JOEL   How did this happen?

ERIN   I don't know, memory loss from a blow to the head, what the hell're you talking about?

JOEL   Wasn't I Joe when we met, didn't you call me Joe?

ERIN   Yeah, but you changed it, eh? Suze called you Joel, I thought you liked Joel.

JOEL   Did I like Joel? …I must have.

ERIN   Well thank God that's settled—have you thought of seeing anyone?

JOEL   I've got clearance for Cuba.

ERIN   A medical someone?

JOEL   How long have we known each other?

ERIN   You should talk to someone.

JOEL   I'm talking to you, how long?

ERIN   I don't know, since law school, why do you ask?

JOEL   I come from Little Italy and you come from the 'hood.

ERIN   And I ain't goin' back.

SUZANNE   I went on the Internet. I looked up how you do it. You can find anything on the Internet. So for a while, afterwards, after Spence died, I would go to those sites. I had the pills. It wasn't hard getting the pills. And the plastic.

A green garbage bag. It didn't seem as if it was that hard to do. Once you'd made up your mind. I'd made up my mind. I didn't think I'd find Spence, or see him again or, or anything like that. I just felt I couldn't go on. I didn't want to go on. But—when I had everything, when I knew what to do, when the time came to do it… I found that I did want to go on. So I have. I am. Going on.

JOEL   I have to get going.

SUZANNE   Do you care about that?

JOEL   About what?

SUZANNE   About my killing myself because of what happened to Spence.

JOEL   But you didn't.

SUZANNE   No I didn't. I made a decision. Not to. But if I had done it, do you think that would've made everything right?

JOEL   Do you?

ERIN   So what do you want me to do?

SUZANNE   I'm sorry.

> SOLDIERS #1 and #2 are short-shackling a detainee, dragging another across his cell, forcing him to stand, checking the cells during the following dialogue. A low, barely audible sound from the detainees under the dialogue.

JOEL   Look after this. (*package from ED*)

ERIN   What is it?

JOEL   Some documentation.

ERIN   Looks familiar.

JOEL   Well it's not.

ERIN   Isn't it?

JOEL   No it isn't, keep it safe somewhere, not at the office.

ERIN   Is this the package from Leland?

JOEL   No.

ERIN   Joel.

JOEL   What.

ERIN   Is so.

JOEL   So why did you ask?

ERIN   To see what you'd say.

JOEL   Well now you know. It's nothing. It's some papers. You don't know what it is.

ERIN   Do you?

JOEL   No.

ERIN   It is probably nothing.

JOEL   That's right. It's nothing.

A sudden punctuation of loud noise from the detainees. The sound isn't too long and is cut off as suddenly as it burst out.

IV

An image of the "bounty" pamphlet comes up overlaying the grid on the cyc. It sits there for some time and can be read.

PSYCHOLOGICAL OPERATIONS (PsyOp)
Leaflet No. TF11-RP 09-01
Help the anti-Taliban forces rid Afghanistan
of murderers and terrorists
you can receive millions of dollars for helping the anti-Taliban forces catch
Al-Qaeda and Taliban murderers.
This is enough to take care of your family,
your village, and your tribe for the rest of your life
and pay for livestock and doctors and school books
and housing for all of your people.

Starting partway through K.'s speech (at X) there is a faint murmur of voices that gradually grows in volume, a battle between K. and the increasing roar of multiple voices. Once K. gives up speaking, the detainees' voices and their words can be made out (starting with NECHLA: "Name? My name"). They tumble over each other and grow in volume. The soldiers move amongst them, attempting to control them, to shut them up. JOEL is present and hears the words of K., of the detainees, and the soldiers.

K.   The 2006 Military Commissions Act states an unlawful enemy combatant is an individual engaged in hostilities against the United States. The president may name as an unlawful enemy combatant any individual who acts in a manner the president deems hostile to the United States. An unlawful enemy combatant can be incarcerated indefinitely without charge. No alien enemy unlawful combatant subject to trial by military commission may invoke the Geneva Convention as a source of rights at his trial. The president has the authority to determine the meaning and application of the Geneva Conventions concerning whether or not a detainee has been tortured. No foreign or international law shall be used by any US court of law to interpret breaches of the Geneva Convention.

(X) This is a war that has no geographic or temporal borders! We claim the right to pick up alleged enemy combatants in every corner of the world, on suspicion they are affiliated with a terrorist organization, and to subject them to indefinite detention without judicial review!! We will determine what and who we detain and once that is determined there is no appeal!!!

NECHLA   Name? My name /

HAMAD   Name /

AHMAD   Name is /

HAMAD   Abdel Hamad /

MIRBATI   My name /

NECHLA   Mohammed Nechla /

MAHJOAB   Name is /

AHMAD   Bakar Ahmad /

NECHLA   I am social worker /

MAHJOAB   Mohammad Mahjoab /

AHMAD   Picked up in border village /

MIRBATI   Al Mirbati /

AHMAD   They say Taliban /

MIRBATI   Turned in for bounty /

HAMAD   I am hospital administrator /

NECHLA   Red Crescent Society /

HAMAD   In July 2002 I wake /

MAHJOAB   My boys are screaming /

NECHLA   United Arab Emirates, fall 2001/

MIRBATI   middle of night

AHMAD   guns in my face

HAMAD   World Assembly of Muslim Youth hospital /

MAHJOAB   They are age three and seven /

AHMAD   Sold for bounty /

MAHJOAB   They say I plan /

The soldiers have restrained MAHJOAB.

NECHLA   Attack on embassy /

HAMAD   Taken into custody /

AHMAD   Sold for bounty /

MIRBATI   Three months /

NECHLA   Allegations found without substance by Bosnian Supreme Court /

AHMAD   With document of freedom /

MIRBATI   Beaten at Bagram /

The soldiers restrain MIRBATI.

NECHLA   I am taken to yard for release, free /

HAMAD   Free /

AHMAD   Free /

NECHLA   But /

HAMAD   But in yard /

AHMAD   They say I am free but /

The soldiers restrain AHMAD.

K.   No.

JOEL   But I understood /

K.   Permission denied.

JOEL   But I have the papers right here /

K.   No access.

JOEL   But his legal team has requested /

K.   Permission denied.

NECHLA   But in the yard I am sold to American soldiers.
Why?—I do not know.
Forced down on ground.
Goggles on eyes, mask on mouth, coverings on ears.
Wrists shackled.
Pain from wrist restraints.
Hands. Numb.
Arms. Numb. Taken to plane.

SOLDIER #2   Goddamnit, you sit!

SOLDIER #1   So I'm going by one of the interview cells and I glance in that slit there and there's a detainee on the floor. Fetal position shackled to the floor eyebolt in there. I dunno how long he's been there but there's shit and piss all around him and the AC unit's off so it's 'bout a hundred in there, and here's the funny part. Somehow the son of a bitch has managed to pull out damn near all 'is hair. He's surrounded by all these clumps of hair. Now how the hell do yuh suppose he did that? Managin' to yank out your hair when yuh're all shackled up like that? Big clumps of hair. Shit and piss. It was disgustin' man, I tell yuh.

SOLDIER #2   We got some wusses here. And they're wearin' uniforms. I'm not naming names. I don't do that. But they know who they are…. And so do we.

SOLDIER #1   Yuh're referrin' to who?

NECHLA   Time?
Six hours, many hours.
I don't know.

SOLDIER #1   Who?

NECHLA   Plane lands.
Maybe Turkey
Barking, loud barking.

JOEL   Omar Khadr?

SOLDIER #2   Here's the thing. Military's done a lot for me and I got a future now. I never had no future. I had nobody and nothin'. That's right. Nobody and nothin'. Poor white trash, I don't mind sayin' that 'cause that's not who I am today. I'm proud of who I am today. Grew up in a fuckin' trailer full of empties and dog shit. I escaped. Smartest thing I ever did. I joined the military. I left all that crap behind. That nothingness.

NECHLA   Why dogs barking so close?

SOLDIER #2   Now I got family, I got a place, I found my place. I got a home. The military is my family, the military is my home /

NECHLA   Why? /

SOLDIER #2   I got brothers and sisters in the military who support me and I support them. I get orders /

NECHLA   Maybe they bite /

SOLDIER #2   I follow orders, I know what I'm to do and I do it.

NECHLA   Or kill /

SOLDIER #2   I'm like a machine /

NECHLA   Another plane /

SOLDIER #2   The military counts on me and I can count on it. I'm proud of who I am /

NECHLA   Long cold flight in plane /

SOLDIER #2   I'm proud of what I have become /

SOLDIER #1   No Delta Block duty for me, eh. There's double D's there. Delusional Detainees. Kind of a joke—double D's.

SOLDIER #2   I'm proud of what I can be /

SOLDIER #1   Hear 'em talkin' like kids. Little kids, their voices all kinda… talkin' or singin'. Loud. Like a song yuh know, like a kid's song in this little kid's voice all high and… same song over and over. Or talkin' like—Mother Goose rhymes or songs, if they got Mother Goose, I dunno, somethin' like that. All Delta Block's on a suicide watch. Twenty-four hour suicide watch. Hear 'em knocking their heads 'gainst the walls and the doors, and then…. Yeah. Yeah, I don't really like pullin' that duty. Remember that, will yuh?

SOLDIER #2   Shut the fuck up, soldier.

K.   Extreme sensory deprivation and sensory overload cause personality disintegration resulting in compliance. In most cases leading to positive interrogation results. And that is the point, is it not?

NECHLA   Are you listening?

AHMAD   Mustfa Ait Idir asks to speak with an officer after guards refuse to turn down fans making detainees very cold.

SOLDIER #1   Big mistake, buster.

MAHJOAB   Guards come in the night, say it is to search cell. He sits on the floor, hands shackled behind. Guards grab him, pick him up. We hear them curse him, say horrible things about family.

MIRBATI   Bunk three-foot high steel shelf /

AHMAD   Guards bang head and body on bunk /

HAMAD   throw him on floor, pound him /

MIRBATI   bang head and body on floor /

AHMAD   bang head on toilet unit in cell /

HAMAD   Solitary confinement after beating.

MAHJOAB   Much bruising much hurt /

AHMAD   Officer comes to look /

HAMAD   But medical /

MIRBATI   no /

AHMAD   no /

HAMAD   no medical man /

MIRBATI   not bother

K.   It's a matter of interpretation. One man's persuasion is another man's torture. Here we have perfected an interrogation paradigm with the assistance of qualified military psychologists. Tools include manipulation of sensory receptors, of cultural and sexual sensitivities, of individual fears and phobia, plus self-inflicted pain.

JOEL   Omar Khadr, Canadian citizen!

NECHLA   No feeling in arms or hands.
Given what? An apple?
Two days now, yes?
Plane lands—dragged to—bus, I think bus.
All covered, how can I know?

SOLDIER #1   Back and forth, back and forth, that's about it.

NECHLA   Soldiers screaming,
I don't know—maybe English.
Dragged out. Dogs.
Barking, hot breath of dogs is close.
Why are dogs so close if not to bite, maybe kill me?
Are you listening? Are you there?

SOLDIER #1   Sometimes yuh look and yuh see 'em. Them that's not rockin', they're pacin', like us, back and forth, back and forth, like somethin' that's caged. Hell they are caged. We're caged. We're pacin', they're pacin', we're all prisoners here.

SOLDIER #2   You say what?

SOLDIER #1   What?

SOLDIER #2   What did yuh say?

SOLDIER #1   Nothin', I didn't say nothin'.

NECHLA   Gravel. I feel gravel.
Forced down, legs straight, ankles shackled, waist shackled, wrists still shackled.
Yelling. Punch—another punch.

MIRBATI   I yell at the guard who is yelling at me. Bad mistake. The IRF enters cell, throw me to the floor, hold legs, choke me, soldier, a large man in riot gear jumps on my back, I am unconscious. The vertebrae in my back? This is permanent injury.

K.   Result of a degenerative disease.

NECHLA   Hit!
Hit!

MIRBATI   Later I ask soldier why do you do this? He tells me. Because he is
Christian.

JOEL   Omar Khadr, age fifteen, apprehended at Ab Khail by Special Forces, 2002.

NECHLA   Dizzy.
Too dizzy. *(He falls forward.)*

SOLDIER #1   Up! Up!

NECHLA   Up. *(He sits up and falls forward.)*

SOLDIER #2   Encourage him, soldier!

NECHLA   Punch blow,
Sun. Heat.

AHMAD   I write "have a nice day" on a polystyrene cup /

SOLDIER #2   Malicious damage to US government property /

SOLDIER #1   Solitary confinement /

NECHLA   –Difficulty
…breathing… mask.
Suffocating
…drowning… in heat

HAMAD   under fluorescent lights /

MAHJOAB   twenty-four hours /

MIRBATI   over three years /

NECHLA   drowning in sun
breathe
try to breathe

JOEL   Omar Khadr

NECHLA   Help. Help me!

JOEL   Incurs shrapnel wounds to the head and the eye /

NECHLA   Help! /

JOEL   at the bombing and strafing of the Ab Khail compound

NECHLA   Hand pulls mask out.
It snaps back
Stinging my face.

JOEL   Name is /

K.   No names here /

NECHLA   I cry out /

JOEL   Omar Khadr /

K.   Number 17379

NECHLA   Help me! /

SOLDIER #1   When I get outta here! /

AIIMAD   Hear me! /

SOLDIER #1   It'll be all right! /

HAMAD   You listening! /

MAHJOAB   I am here! /

SOLDIER #1   Yuh can forget things /

MIRBATI   Here /

SOLDIER #1   Forget! /

NECHLA   Hear me /

SOLDIER #1   Put 'em behind yuh! /

HAMAD   We are here!

SOLDIER #1   Kinda!… kinda funny though. The sleep thing is a big thing here. Like you keep 'em awake. One guy, every hour like, I go in, have 'im line up shoes, soap, brush, in a different order 'longside of 'is cage. Then you git tired of that, make 'im stand, search the cell. You git tired of that, boots, butt, smash, git 'im off the floor, on their feet. Longest no sleep time? Thirteen days that I know of. Hear some guy went fifty days sleep deprivation, dunno if it counts though 'cause they say most days he got four hours 'tween seven and 'leven in the mornin'. But here's the funny thing. I got trouble sleepin'. That's funny eh? I got trouble sleepin'. Lotta trouble sleepin'. But it'll be okay when I get back. Sort itself out then. Sleep like a baby then, you bet your ass I will!

Image of Omar Khadr comes up on cyc behind grid.

JOEL   They say Omar Khadr threw a grenade /

MIRBATI   I am long time standing /

JOEL   killing Special Forces Sergeant Christopher Speer,

AHMAD   I am naked in cold cell /

JOEL   he was subsequently shot three times /

NECHLA   I am finding white powder in my food /

JOEL   splitting his chest /

HAMAD   I am short-shackled to the floor /

JOEL   taken to Bagram for interrogation

MAHJOAB   I am tied to the board and drowning /

JOEL   pain medication withheld to induce co-operation

SOLDIER #1   First thing I see's a pool of blood on the floor. Then I look up and see 'im hangin' by 'is neck, yeah, by 'is neck from the top of the mesh metal that tops the cell. He's got this gash on the inside of 'is right arm, and he's bleedin' on the floor. He's engagin' in some "asymmetrical warfare," another hangin' gesture.

SOLDIER #2   Gimme the paperwork

NECHLA   No food /

SOLDIER #1   the paperwork /

NECHLA   Refuse food /

SOLDIER #1   Lolly winks at me *(SOLDIER #2).*

SOLDIER #2   No names /

SOLDIER #1   She says he slipped and fell /

SOLDIER #2   You stupid fuck!

SOLDIER #1   She's a gung-ho bitch but what the hell /

NECHLA   No food /

SOLDIER #1   we get along—leastwise I'm tryin'.

JOEL   Omar Khadr at Bagram, hands tied to a door frame, bag over his head, attack dogs at his chest.

SOLDIER #2   I don't wanna hear that shit /

SOLDIER #1   It's all shit!

JOEL   Transported to Guantanamo.

SOLDIER #2   Whatchesay?

NECHLA   No, nothing /

SOLDIER #1   Nothing /

K.   What we do here has two components. First: complete denial of physical comfort and space-time orientation. Second: removal of the inner comfort of identity.

SOLDIER #1   We got funny words for things, like a, "Yuh got a reservation" yuh say to the detainee, I mean, I mean yuh say to the illegal enemy combatant, reservation means yuh're goin' to interrogation. And when yuh're movin' someone every thirty minutes, keep 'em from sleepin'? Well he's a "frequent flyer." And this is Gitmo and if someone's getting IRF'ed, well then he's gettin' worked over by the Immediate Reaction Force.

SOLDIER #2   You're there, you're together, you get talkin' /

SOLDIER #1   Shorthand yuh know. Gettin' IRF'ed. Kinda funny /

SOLDIER #2   But I don't wanna listen 'cause I don't wanna hear it /

JOEL   Khadr's initial Gitmo reservation: short-shackled in a fetal position to the floor eyebolt; after one half-hour arms to legs shackled behind back; several hours later by wrists to ankles behind back in a kneeling position. He defecates and urinates. He is drenched with pine-oil solvent, then dragged by his feet through pine oil, defecation, and urine, a human mop.

SOLDIER #2   Soldier can't sleep he says. What the fuck do I care?

JOEL   He has no change of clothing or shower for two days.

SOLDIER #2   Don't be tellin' me that. He says he gets this dream. He's lookin' in the cage and he sees this guy's face in the corner of the cage. That's all he can see, just the face. It's black in there, and it's really just the eyes he sees. First of all the fuckin' lights are always on, it's never black in there so what's he talkin' about? But—it's just a dream, so I suppose—anyway, these eyes are beggin' like, pleadin' and full of pain and a lot of stuff he goes on about but can't really explain or find words for, thank God for that—anyway—these eyes, or whoever these eyes are, start to scream and scream and, he wakes up and it's him screamin'. It's not the eyes screamin', it's him.

NECHLA   No food /

SOLDIER #2   Now you tell me /

JOEL   Omar loses the sight in his left eye /

SOLDIER #2   What the fuck am I supposed to do with that /

JOEL   Omar's cell is kept cold /

SOLDIER #2   I got no problem sleepin' /

JOEL   Khadr, a frequent flyer, randomly beaten, short-shackled, confined in isolation, undertakes a hunger strike with two hundred others.

NECHLA   We refuse food.
Wrists. Ankles to waist. Restrained.
The man who is the medical man stands there.
He is watching.

The feeding tube drips blood and bile from the one who is before me.
By force of will I catch the eye of the medical man. He looks down examining
the fingernails on one hand. The tube is forcibly inserted by the riot guards.
I am restrained.
Food. Into the tube.
To—preserve life.
I am an educated man.
I am, amused.
I think, how ironic.
I think, these are foolish men.
I think.
Someday, I will act.

JOEL   Omar Khadr throws up blood, collapses on his return to his cell, is beaten by guards.

K.   Pardon?

JOEL   Omar Khadr. Detainee /

K.   Illegal enemy combatant.

JOEL   17379 is a Canadian citizen.

K.   Noted.

JOEL   His American lawyers have formally requested a Canadian addition to his legal team /

K.   Denied.

JOEL   I understood /

K.   Mistaken.

JOEL   What're you telling me?

K.   Access to 17379 is denied.

JOEL   By whom?

DOMINIC   This man /

K.   Your departure time is /

DOMINIC   is the kind that I know /

JOEL   The Canadian Constitution and American law /

K.   Clarification. This is a place beyond the law. In this place we are the law /

DOMINIC   He is one of the ones who come in the night /

K.   And point of fact: the detainee has had contact with Canadian government representatives.

JOEL   In 2003—four years ago, and all they had to say was, "I'm not here to help you. I'm not here to do anything for you. I'm here to get information from you."

K.   Your point being?

DOMINIC   Who pushes Papa down when we climb from the truck /

JOEL   They were not representing Khadr's interests, they were party to his interrogation!

DOMINIC   In Petawawa detention he beats Vito Deniro so his smile is still crooked /

K.   Departure at thirteen hundred hours /

DOMINIC   The one who sits in an office pushing the paper. He is the big one who opens his mouth, who says a few words, who is signing the paper. He is the one who stands on his porch when they come in the night, he stands there and watches /

JOEL   he watches /

DOMINIC   as they take us away. And when the truck pulls away, he returns to his bed, and his sleep. He is the one who knows, and /

JOEL   does nothing /

DOMINIC   does nothing /

JOEL   does nothing?

> *JOEL is looking out at the bay. He is unaware of SOLDIER #1 when he approaches.*

SOLDIER #1   Transportation's here, sir.

JOEL   ...Do something.

SOLDIER #1   Sir?... Yuh see somethin' out there, what do yuh see, sir?

JOEL   *(speaking more to himself)* Water.

SOLDIER #1   Yuh see somethin' in the water?... patrol maybe, is that what yuh see?

JOEL   Noo...

SOLDIER #1   ...Nah, there's nothin' out there, sir. Nothin' but water.

JOEL   Flying in it looked—it looked beautiful from the air. From a distance very pretty. *(at last acknowledging the SOLDIER)* The island you know. Cuba. The bay. The water.

SOLDIER #1   Sometimes things aren't what they seem.

JOEL   No they aren't…. And sometimes they are…. What's your name, soldier?

SOLDIER #1   No names, sir.

JOEL   Right. No names…. How long have you been here?

SOLDIER #1   Ever since I got here, sir.

JOEL   I see.

SOLDIER #1   That's… what they tell us to say—sir.

JOEL   What about your gut… what does your gut tell you to say?

SOLDIER #1   Nothin'. I should be sayin' nothin'. I'm just your transportation today, sir.

JOEL   Right… *(more to himself again)* Sunny day…. Sun on the water…. Sun /
   Faint sound of a dog barking.

DOMINIC   Son.

JOEL   and the water… today is… today…

SOLDIER #1   Today?

JOEL   Today. Five days till the end of a year.

SOLDIER #1   No, sir, that—that comes in December.

JOEL   *(back to the SOLDIER)* December?… Oh. Yes, December—for you.

SOLDIER #1   Well like, for all of us, sir. 'Cept maybe them. I don't know 'bout them.

JOEL   Them… have you—come "in contact" with detainee Omar Khadr? He's one of them.

SOLDIER #1   Can't answer that, sir.

JOEL   How about 17379?

SOLDIER #1   No, sir, can't /

JOEL   Right, can't answer that.

SOLDIER #1   No, sir. …Bu…

JOEL   Pardon?

SOLDIER #1   Nothin', sir.

JOEL   Right…. Nothing.

SOLDIER #1   …Skinny.

JOEL   Skinny.

SOLDIER #1 …Yeah. Skinny…. Was askin' for colourin' books from his legal team.

JOEL Was he.

SOLDIER #1 Yuh kinda remember somethin' like that.

JOEL A person would, yes.

SOLDIER #1 But…

JOEL But?

SOLDIER #1 But killed a guy… grenade they say.

JOEL Supposing he did, do you think that would justify his treatment?

SOLDIER #1 I wouldn't know, sir.

JOEL You wouldn't know? Or… or you don't know?

SOLDIER #1 I just… don't ask myself that question, sir.

JOEL Oh. How do you manage not to? *(Pause as JOEL and SOLDIER #1 look at each other as JOEL waits for an answer.)*

SOLDIER #1 …I just don't /

ERIN Talk to him.

SOLDIER #1 let myself /

SUZANNE You think he'll listen to me?

SOLDIER #1 go there.

JOEL It's just about time.

DOMINIC You thinkin' 'bout what, Joey?

JOEL Thinking about going there.

ERIN He has to listen to someone.

V

A flat map of the world comes up on the cyc. It is overlaid by the grid.

The soldiers return to guard duty, driving the detainees back into their cells.

JOEL, in his shirtsleeves, gets LELAND's package and unwraps a pile of documents. A lot of paper. JOEL starts reading them, going through them, discarding them on the floor and around him as he reads. He grows increasingly more agitated, he can't keep still, the papers increasingly litter the stage, cover the floor. He has to search among them to find the document, references, or particular statement he wants.

During the scene JOE's body language slowly and subtly changes. He may rub his wrists as if restoring circulation. His physicality and focus suggests potential action without being overt about it. Movement is minimal, doesn't draw attention. It is an expression of JOE's increasing internal readiness.

SUZANNE   Your sister phoned /

JOEL   Right /

SUZANNE   I told her you weren't at the house /

JOEL   Good /

SUZANNE ` She should call the Westin /

JOEL   Right /

SUZANNE   or maybe the office /

JOEL   Thanks /

SUZANNE   I told her you had a room at the Westin /

ERIN   What the hell's this? /

SUZANNE   She said you'd dropped in to see her /

JOEL   I did /

ERIN   What is all this?

SUZANNE   She said you were saying goodbye!

JOEL   That's right, I was saying goodbye.

SUZANNE   Goodbye?

JOEL   We'd lost touch. It felt good to see her.

ERIN   Joel /

JOEL   She looked older... and we talked... and I left. *(He continues with his papers, reading, discarding.)*

SUZANNE   Joel! /

JOEL   Not now, maybe later /

SUZANNE   Goodbye?

JOEL   Goodbye.

ERIN   What're you doing?

JOEL   What does it look like?

ERIN   Like you're running amuck and making a hell of a mess.

JOEL   I'm rushed and I'm reading /

K.   (*voice-over*) Advanced forms of biological warfare that can target specific genotypes may transform biological warfare from the realm of terror to a politically useful tool /

JOEL   (*thrusting documents on ERIN, which she rejects*) An American policy paper /

K.   (*voice-over*) American militarization and control of the globe and of cosmic and cyberspace is essential /

JOEL   Project for the twenty-first century /

K.   (*voice-over*) A revolutionary transformation that may require a long process absent some catastrophic and catalytic event like a new Pearl Harbor /

JOEL   And what do they call 9/11?

ERIN   I know what they call it.

JOEL   A "new Pearl Harbor," the catastrophic event they've been praying, planning, and waiting for, Erin!

ERIN   And this is all /

JOEL   Leland's package /

ERIN   Leland /

JOEL   He was just one among many.

ERIN   Many what?

> At some point SOLDIER #1's attention is caught by JOEL's words.

JOEL   Warnings! From foreign intelligence services, American intelligence, people like Leland and /

ERIN   Joel /

JOEL   Foreign intelligence! American intelligence! Leland and Glass and a hell of a lot higher up than either of those two /

ERIN   Come on /

JOEL   Timeline—July, August, into September 2001. Jordan tells them hijacked airplanes, high buildings /

ERIN   You're just /

JOEL   Putin tells them hijacked planes hitting American symbols /

ERIN   No /

JOEL   Iranians tell them week of September 9 imminent attacks /

ERIN   Joel! /

JOEL   Saudis tell them we're gonna be hit /

ERIN   Stop /

JOEL   It's here!

ERIN   Stop it!!!

JOEL   It's all here!

ERIN   It's just paper!

JOEL   It's documented! Look at it!

ERIN   Take a breath /

JOEL   They didn't make it happen.

ERIN   A big breath.

JOEL   They just *let* it happen!

ERIN   It's Gitmo, Joe.

JOEL   What?

ERIN   It's just Gitmo. It got to you, that's all.

JOEL   What?

ERIN   I said /

JOEL   I heard you…. Yeah… yeah you're right.

ERIN   Yeah, I'm right.

JOEL   In a way. In a way it was Gitmo.

ERIN   So we're just going to slow down now.

JOEL   Gitmo helped things come clear.

ERIN   Gonna take it easy.

JOEL   About Spencer, thinking of Spencer.

ERIN   Spencer?

JOEL   One year today, Erin.

ERIN   I know.

SUZANNE   I'm sorry.

JOEL   And I realized something. At Gitmo. Something important.

ERIN   About Spencer?

JOEL   About everything. He isn't gone, Erin. Spencer isn't gone. That's one thing. And then, and then, something else too. I realized we, we—are on the cusp.

ERIN   The cusp.

JOEL   Of tyranny, of Pax Americana, the new Rome— Don't look so worried. I haven't lost it, I've found it.

ERIN   It being?

JOEL   *(finding specific papers, discarding others as he searches)* Prior to the eleventh, four hijackers were identified and on watch lists, they had pictures of Mohammed Atta, CIA shut down further action. Here it is, read it.

ERIN   I'll do that. *(She discards the document.)*

JOEL   Pick it up! Read it!

ERIN   Okay, I'll read it. *(She doesn't but she picks it up.)*

JOEL   Attorney general, top Pentagon officials quit flying on commercial aircraft just prior to the eleventh. That's been reported. And here— Put options, betting airline stock will go down /

ERIN   I know what a put option is /

JOEL   Six hundred percent! Six hundred percent above average trading in put options for American and United Airlines September seventh and eighth, the institution handling the trading headed by a former executive director of the CIA. What do you think of that?

SOLDIER #2   What're yuh lookin' at, soldier?

SOLDIER #1   *(He's listening to JOEL.)* Nothin'—sir.

JOEL   Documented! President told of the first plane hitting prior to entering the elementary school, second plane hits and he sits reading a story about a goat for seven minutes after, and the Secret Service does nothing to remove him to safety? Why not?

ERIN   Maybe they /

JOEL   Maybe nothing, hell, he knew and they knew! Maybe they didn't know when, maybe they didn't know where, but they knew!

DOMINIC   These men.

JOEL   Goes back to the 1990s. Leland's got it all here. Hell, it goes further back than the '90s. I'm telling you, Erin, they just open their mouths /

DOMINIC   Today /

JOEL   they say a few words /

DOMINIC   citizen! /

JOEL   they close their mouths /

DOMINIC   tomorrow! /

JOEL   they sign the paper /

DOMINIC   enemy alien! /

JOEL   And we're screwed. Look at this *(whipping papers at her)* Enocal!—you know what Enocal is? A consortium of companies to bring oil from Turkmenistan through Afghanistan to Pakistan—

ERIN   Oh Jesus, Joel.

JOEL   Joe. Call me Joe. A pipeline was under negotiation with the Taliban who held out for recognition as the government of Afghanistan.

ERIN   You're losing me.

JOEL   Well try and keep up! July 15, 2001 American military option was put on the table at a meeting.

> *SOLDIER #1 has drawn closer to JOEL. JOEL passes him several of the documents as he reads them.*

Taliban given a choice, approval of the pipeline would result in—where is it—"a carpet of gold"—turn it down and it would be—"a carpet of bombs," an invasion.

SOLDIER #2   That's an order, soldier!

JOEL   American military outposts in present-day Afghanistan are strung along the original pipeline route and what will someday be the pipeline route, given American military success.

SUZANNE   What do you mean goodbye?

JOEL   I have to go, Suze.

SUZANNE   Go where?

JOEL   It's a year today.

SUZANNE   You wouldn't do anything stupid, would you?

JOEL   No, not stupid!

SUZANNE   Then what?

JOEL   What I'm doing, I'm doing for Spence.

SOLDIER #1   Afghan president Hamid Karzai /

JOEL   Worked for Enocal /

SOLDIER #1   Zalmay Khalilzad was the American ambassador to Iraq /

JOEL   Formerly under contract to Enocal—Bush administration peppered with Enocal /

ERIN   Stop and think, Joe /

JOEL And Iraq invasion plans on the table in 2001, prior to 9/11, and on hold waiting for a Pearl Harbor event, see the neo-cons twenty-first century paper.

ERIN You're not thinking clearly.

JOEL I've never been clearer.

> *SOLDIER #1 finds ED's slip of paper amongst the documents JOEL has passed to him to read.*

Enocal's consortium made up of Chevron for one—Condoleezza Rice on the board. Saudis' part of the consortium—9/11 hijackers primarily Saudi.

> *SOLDIER #1 passes the slip to JOEL.*

What? *(glances at the slip of paper)* Right. *(puts on his jacket, the note in his pocket)* That's it, it's all here, Erin, names, dates, document copies. Leland left it for me and I'm leaving it for you.

ERIN No you don't.

JOEL Look at it. Read it. You decide.

ERIN Decide what?

JOEL What to do, Erin. What to do.
I have to go.

ERIN Go where?

JOEL Wherever knowing this takes me—I'm not crazy, you know.

ERIN I've got to be honest, you're pushing the envelope, Joe.

JOEL Don't you get it? Spence isn't gone. Spencie is here right now. And I'm going for Spencie, and I'm going with Spencie. Now you may not understand that—but—Spencie does.

All the Spencers, all over the world, they understand. I'm taking action for them.
I won't stand by and watch.

I'm not going to do that. *(He exits.)*

ERIN Joe!

SUZANNE Joe!... He's gone...

VI

SOLDIER #1 passes a pile of papers he's accumulated to ERIN. He puts his gun down, kneels, and continues to read through documents. ERIN begins by picking up paper but is caught by information on one and starts to read. SUZANNE draws closer. She too starts to pick up and read documents. All three are down on the floor, kneeling or bending down to read.

K. appears. Perhaps he is backlit, so first is seen as a large and growing shadow on the floor, or a full figure in silhouette, features in shadow. JOE watches K. SOLDIER #1, SUZANNE, ERIN (similarly DOMINIC and ED) become aware of K.'s presence as K. stands, a figure of authority observing them.

SOLDIER #1, SUZANNE, ERIN, from their kneeling positions, look up at the figure of K.

JOE takes in this tableau, the three kneeling on the floor with documents in their hands, their focus on K. JOE's attention returns to K.

During the following JOE will stand at some point and put on his pants, his suit jacket (both identical to JOEL's pants and jacket except they are dusty, dirty, torn, and well worn), and his boots.

JOE   I remember, when Spence was born… I remember… I took him in my arms, and he opened his eyes, and he looked at me.

They say they can't really see then, but he could. And it was a… a strange look. For a long time, I don't know, until he was almost a year old maybe, he would look at me, and his mother, he'd look around and I could, I could feel him thinking.

I started to believe in reincarnation. That's funny isn't it. I started to believe in reincarnation because I thought it explained that look. His look. He knew something. Something I didn't know. Or maybe forgotten. And maybe one day, he'd forget too.

Spence… Spencie had a big vocabulary, lots of words. And he noticed things. He was maybe two and a half, I took him down to the office on a Saturday and we passed a homeless man on the street and Spencie said, he said, "He's cold, Daddy. That man is cold." …He noticed things like that.

He'd see a child and say, "She's not very happy" or "I think she's hungry, Daddy… what should we do?" …That's what he'd ask. "What Should We Do?" …He was… he was almost three then. Almost three.

On the back of JOE's chair is a kaffiyeh-style scarf. He picks it up and puts it on, traditionally, round his neck, over his head. As he exits he will pass by the kneeling figures of SOLDIER #1, SUZANNE, ERIN, their focus still on K.

JOE stops and turns to look at K. When he does so, SOLDIER #1, SUZANNE, ERIN rise from their kneeling position, DOMINIC and ED move closer, the group of three, plus JOE and, a little further away, DOMINIC and ED, stand motionless in opposition to K.

JOE picks up the gun SOLDIER #1 had put down. With his focus on K., JOE shoulders the gun—a brief pause, and JOE turns and exits.

Blackout.

The end.

Bibliography

This bibliography includes works cited in the introduction and a selection of works for further reading.

A Brush with War: Military Art from Korea to Afghanistan. A Canadian War Museum Exhibition Guide. Ottawa: Canadian War Museum, 2009.

Abella, Irving and Harold Troper. *None Is Too Many: Canada and the Jews of Europe, 1933–1948.* Toronto: Lester and Orpen Dennys, 1982.

Adorno, Theodor W. "Kulturkritik und Gesellschaft." In *Kulturkritik und Gesellschaft I.* Vol. 10.1 of *Gesammelte Schriften.* Frankfurt: Suhrkamp, 1977. 1–30.

Agamben, Giorgio. *State of Exception.* Trans. Kevin Attell. Chicago: University of Chicago Press, 2005.

Arseneault, Michel. "Solidarity of the Shaken: Wajdi Mouawad's Theatre of War." *The Walrus* (Dec./Jan. 2007): 89–93.

Bartley, Jim. *Drina Bridge.* Vancouver: Raincoast, 2006.

Bradshaw, James. "United By the Theatre of War." *The Globe and Mail,* Apr. 18, 2009, R 5, 7.

Carlson, Tim. *Diplomacy.* Vancouver: Talonbooks, 2009.

Clark, Bob. "Judith Thompson Is Still Breaking the Rules." *Calgary Herald,* Oct. 25, 2008, C 4.

Clements, Marie. *Burning Vision.* In *Canada and the Theatre of War,* Vol. 1, edited by Coates and Grace. Toronto: Playwrights Canada Press, 2008. 423–84.

Coates, Donna and Sherrill Grace, ed. *Canada and the Theatre of War,* Vol. 1. Toronto: Playwrights Canada Press, 2008.

Cook, Kathy. *Stolen Angels: The Kidnapped Girls of Uganda.* Toronto: Penguin, 2007.

Courtemache, Gil. *A Sunday at the Pool in Kigali.* 2000. Trans. Patricia Claxton. Montreal: Alfred A. Knopf, 2003.

The Reader. Dir. Stephen Daldry; screenplay by David Hare. Weinstein Co., 2008.

Echlin, Kim. *The Disappeared.* Toronto: Penguin, 2009.

Egan, Susanna and Gabriele Helms. "Generations of the Holocaust in Canadian Autobiography." In *Auto/biography in Canada: Critical Directions,* edited by Julie Rak. Waterloo, ON: Wilfrid Laurier UP, 2005. 31–51.

Forsyth, Louise. "Resistance to Exile by Girls and Women: Two Plays by Abla Farhoud." *Modern Drama* 48.4 (Winter 2005): 800–18.

Fréchette, Carole. *Helen's Necklace.* In *Carole Fréchette: Two Plays,* trans. by John Murrell. Toronto: Playwrights Canada Press, 2007.

Grace, Sherrill. *Making Theatre: A Life of Sharon Pollock.* Vancouver: Talonbooks, 2008.

Grass, Günter. "To be continued… Nobel Prize Lecture." Nov. 7, 1999, http://www.nobel.se/literature/laureates/1999/lecture-e.html (accessed August 12, 2009).

Passchendaele. Dir. Paul Gross. Alliance Films, 2008.

Hage, Rawi. *De Niro's Game.* Toronto: House of Anansi, 2008.

The Lives of Others (*Das Leben der Anderen*). Dir. Florian Henckel von Donnersmarck. Sony, 2006.

Holloway, Ann. "Hedda and Lynndie and Jabbie and Ciel: An Interview with Judith Thompson." In *The Masks of Judith Thompson*, edited by Ric Knowles. Toronto: Playwrights Canada Press, 2006. 138–44.

Jenkins, Karl. *The Armed Man: A Mass for Peace.* The Platinum Collection. EMI Classics, 2007.

Kubick, Jeff. "Confronting Injustice through History: Downstage Debuts New Sharon Pollock Play, *Man Out of Joint.*" http://www.ffwdweekly.com/Issues/2007/0503/the2htm (accessed August 12, 2009).

La Capra, Dominick. *Writing History, Writing Trauma.* Baltimore: Johns Hopkins University Press, 2001.

Morrow, Martin. "Hot Topic: Wajdi Mouawad Discusses *Scorched*, His Searing Play About the Lebanese War." CBCNews.ca, Sept. 22, 2008, http://www.cbc.ca/arts/theatre/story/2008/09/19/f-wajdi-mouawad-scorched.html (accessed August 12, 2009).

———. "From Hell: Judith Thompson's New Play Finds Scapegoats and Heroes in Iraq." CBCNews.ca Jan. 16, 2008, http://www.cbc.ca/arts/theatre/thompson.html (accessed August 12, 2009).

Moscovitch, Hannah, *East of Berlin.* Toronto: Playwrights Canada Press, 2009.

Moss, Jane. "The Drama of Survival: Staging Posttraumatic Memory in Plays by Lebanese-Quebecois Dramatists." *Theatre Research in Canada.* 22.2 (Fall 2001): 172–89.

Murrell, John. *Waiting for the Parade.* Vancouver: Talonbooks, 1980.

Nestruck, J. Kelly. "'Art Person of the Year': #2 Wajdi Mouawad." *The Globe and Mail*, Dec. 27, 2008, R 5.

———. "Where's Our War On Our Stages?" *The Globe and Mail*, April 17, 2008, R 3.

Paris, Erna. *Long Shadows: Truth, Lies, and History.* Toronto: Alfred A. Knopf, 2000.

Pollock, Sharon. *Sweet Land of Liberty*. In *Sharon Pollock: Collected Works*, Vol. 1., edited by Cynthia Zimmerman. Toronto: Playwrights Canada Press, 2005. 177–212.

Redhill, Michael. *Goodness*. Toronto: Coach House Books, 2005.

Sanger, Richard. *Not Spain*. Toronto: Playwrights Canada Press, 1994.

Sherman, Jason. *None Is Too Many*. In *Canada and the Theatre of War*, Vol 1., edited by Coates and Grace. 375–422.

———. *Three in the Back, Two in the Head*. Toronto: Playwrights Canada Press, 1994.

———. *Reading Hebron*. Toronto: Playwrights Canada Press, 1995.

Sherriff, R.C. *Journey's End*. London: V. Gollancz, 1929.

Skvorecky, Josef. *Ordinary Lives*. Trans. Paul Wilson. Toronto: Key Porter, 2008.

Taylor, Kate. "Breaking the Silence." *The Globe and Mail*, Nov. 6, 2002, R 3.

Todorovic, Dragan. *Diary of Interrupted Days*. Toronto: Random House, 2009.

Tompkins, Joanne. "The Shape of a Life: Constructing the 'Self' and 'Other' in Joan MacLeod's *The Shape of a Girl* and Guillermo Verdecchia and Marcus Youssef's *A Line in the Sand*." In *Theatre and Autobiography: Writing and Performing Lives in Theory and Practice*, edited by Sherrill Grace and Jerry Wasserman. Vancouver: Talonbooks, 2006. 124–36.

Youssef, Marcus, Guillermo Verdecchia, and Camyar Chai. *The Adventures of Ali & Ali and the aXes of Evil*. Vancouver: Talonbooks, 2005.

Zimmerman, Cynthia, ed. *Sharon Pollock: Collected Works, Volume Three*. Toronto: Playwrights Canada Press, 2008.

About the Editors

Donna Coates is Associate Professor of English at the University of Calgary. She has published numerous articles and book chapters on Canadian, Australian, New Zealand, and American women's literary responses (fiction and drama) to the First and Second World Wars, and to the Vietnam War. She has co-edited with George Melnyk *Wild Words: Essays on Alberta Writing* (2009).

Sherrill Grace is Professor of English and Distinguished University Scholar at The University of British Columbia. She specializes in Canadian literature and culture and her most recent books include *Canada and the Idea of North* (2001; 2007), *Inventing Tom Thomson* (2004), *Theatre & AutoBiography* (2006), co-edited with Jerry Wasserman, and *On the Art of Being Canadian* (2009). She published the biography *Making Theatre: A Life of Sharon Pollock* in 2008 and is currently doing research for a book on Canadian representations of war. She is the winner of the 2008 Canada Council Killam Prize in Humanities.